College Admissions Trade Secrets

A top private college counselor reveals
the secrets, lies, and tricks of
the college admissions process.

Second Edition

Andrew Allen

Writers Club Press
New York   Lincoln   Shanghai

College Admissions Trade Secrets
A top private college counselor reveals the secrets,
lies, and tricks of the college admissions process.

Writers Club Press
an imprint of iUniverse, Inc.

For information address:
iUniverse
2021 Pine Lake Road, Suite 100
Lincoln, NE 68512
www.iuniverse.com

ISBN: 0-595-19897-X

Printed in the United States of America

College Admissions Trade Secrets

Contents

Chapter 1

Welcome to the Circus: An Introduction

> "Applying to college sounds complicated and painful,
> but it's the only way to get out of my parents' house."

Perhaps you've heard that Princeton's Director of Admissions hacked into Yale's secured admissions website to find out who Yale had accepted and rejected. Perhaps you've heard that Boston College's average SAT score is up to 1370 and Boston University's average SAT score is up to 1320. Perhaps you've heard that Carnegie Mellon offers spots on a priority wait-list to students who send in cash—and most of those students get admitted.

Well, it's all true. The Princeton Director of Admissions is Stephen LeMenager, and a FBI investigation traced Yale's problems with its hacked website back to LeMenager's computer in Princeton's admissions office. And BC's average SAT score is the same as Cornell's and close to Penn's (both Ivies). And Carnegie Mellon does have a "priority" wait list—it costs $400 to be on it and the admissions rate is 95%. Welcome to the circus.

It's daunting. You see the college list published by your high school's guidance department. On it is listed every acceptance and rejection from the prior year. Next to each entry you find a GPA, a SAT score, and the number of AP classes taken. The list is usually ordered from highest to lowest GPA. The first entry: 4.19 (unweighted), 1430 SAT, 7 AP classes, Princeton-rejected, Yale-rejected, Harvard-rejected, Stanford-rejected, Columbia-rejected, Vassar-accepted.

Ouch. You scan down the list looking for Yale. *Did anyone get into Yale last year?* You go down to the ninth entry: 3.93, 1450 SAT, 6 AP classes, Brown-accepted, Yale-accepted, Georgetown-accepted.

Okay, anyone else? You scan down to the twenty-second entry: 3.88, 1560 SAT, 7 AP classes, Yale-accepted, Duke-accepted, William and Mary-rejected.

This doesn't make any sense, you think. *Many of the students with the best grades didn't get into any top colleges and still others were rejected at colleges that are ranked lower than some of the colleges to which they were accepted. This doesn't make any sense.*

Welcome to the world of college admissions. This book will help you make sense of those entries mentioned above.

I wrote this book because most college admissions books either contain useless information or interesting information that isn't presented in a helpful format. I'm going to give you information that will upset high school counselors and college admissions officers. In the past, counselors and officers controlled the information and kept secret much of the admissions process. Information is power, and now you have the information. Do you want to know the truth about admissions rates, indices and formulae, and what colleges really think of your transcript? Before this book, you had to wade through a dozen college admissions books just to get a few bits of useful advice. One book tells you there's a precise formula used to admit applicants, another tells you there's no formula. One tells you that grades are most important; another tells you that test scores are most important. Finally, the truth is right in your hands.

A warning: do not bring this book to your high school or on a college visit. All the dirty little secrets of the college admission world are revealed in this book, and many counselors and admissions officers are not happy about it. Recently, one dean of admissions said to me, "I can't believe you're going to print that information about student-to-faculty ratios!" I said, "But the claims you make to students and parents aren't true." He replied, "That's not the point."

The point is that colleges have long been able to say whatever they wanted to say; few people investigated, and no one regulated. This book changes all that. In most cases, whenever I reveal a secret or make a point, I'll give you a specific example too. When I claim that colleges make outrageous assertions when discussing the cost of private college education, I'll give you an example from the University of Pennsylvania. When I discuss how course catalogues can be misleading, I'll take you through Harvard's catalogue.

The admissions labyrinth. The college admissions process is ludicrously arcane. It's almost impossible to find out useful information from colleges (most of the information you get from colleges is useless, inaccurate, or both-I'll tell you why later). To prove my point, I'll ask you one very simple question: what's the substantive difference between a Columbia and Harvard education? (By substantive, I'm excluding considerations such as the location, size of the student body, et al.) What about Columbia and Yale? The education you are likely to get from those colleges varies widely, and yet few parents and students know the difference. In fact, most high school counselors don't know why Yale is a far better college than Harvard, and why one can be absolutely assured of getting a better education at Columbia than at Harvard. Unless you are an insider in the world of higher education, this sort of information is not available to you.

Most colleges are eager to tell you about the new gymnasium (complete with coed sauna) but don't wish to discuss important information, such as crime statistics. They won't discuss average teacher salary or the number of professors who actually teach. Most top colleges aren't likely to tell you that your chance of being admitted as a regular applicant is less that 5%. (Yes, that's less than 5%.) Most top colleges won't tell you why three different applicants to the same top college with the same SAT scores, grades, courses, and teacher recommendations have admission rates varying from 90% to 40% to 2%. This book will help you navigate through this morass.

Colleges try to be helpful, but only insofar as they help themselves. Very few colleges are honest-there is some potentially helpful information colleges simply refuse to publish. In many cases, I've caught competitive colleges actually lying to potential applicants. This may seem surprising, but what do you expect in a multibillion-dollar, largely unregulated business? The more you know, the better your decisions will be.

In most cases, colleges cannot be broadly defined as "good" or "bad." The best one can do is to say that Duke's English department is an ideological bog and Yale's history department is wonderful. Similarly, there is no singular "right" way to apply to a top college. With that caveat, I'm going to present you with, in essence, formulae for applying to top colleges. I recognize that you need applicable information, not broad generalizations interspersed with cute stories. So while I'm going to tell you exactly what a top applicant looks like and give you specific prescriptive advice, keep in mind that the qualities of successful applications vary widely. It should be noted up front that I am a strong advocate of cultivating a seriously educated and cultured self, so I'm not going to advise you to get involved in some enormously time-consuming activity that has no relevance outside of the admissions process.

This book assumes that you are applying to a competitive college. There are more than 3000 colleges in this country: fewer than 200 are competitive. "Competitive" means that the college actually rejects qualified applicants. Many of the colleges listed in college guides, including guides that claim to include only the "top" or "best" colleges, are actually not competitive. Yes, they reject applicants, but those rejects weren't qualified in the first place. (Trade secret: sometimes as many as 15% of a college's applicants aren't fundamentally qualified to apply to college, yet the college counts them as "rejects.")

This book will help you regardless of how serious you are: maybe you have everything in place and want to apply to Yale, or maybe you have C grades and want to know what to do in two months to greatly improve your chances of being admitted to a top college. The chapters in this book are short and direct; while it's advisable that you read the entire book, you may skip around and read only a few chapters. Some information and advice is repeated to facilitate skipping around-but don't worry, I only repeat the most important advice.

Throughout the book, I give many specific details (Harvard does this, and Princeton does that). Please keep in mind that a college may change their requirements or processes at any time. One year, a college may require two recommendations and the next year that college may require no recommendations. There are no general rules or guidelines, and colleges are free to change anything they like at any time. So regardless of what you read here, be sure to check with each college. Who knows...perhaps after reading this book, colleges will change the way they process their applications.

If you have a comment or inside information, feel free to send it to me at collegeadmissions@mail.com. Due to the high volume of e-mail, I can't reply to everyone, but I'll take your thoughts under advisement.

Good luck and one final bit of advice: whatever you do, start today! The first and greatest obstacle you have in applying to college is limited time. The sooner you start, the better.

Andrew Allen
NYC, 2003

Chapter 2

Why You Need This Book

"You've got to be joking. My mom gave me
a college guide that looked like a telephone book.
I'm supposed to read that? I went back to playing Nintendo."

The process is nebulous. Harvard once said that they are looking for applicants who exhibit honesty, fairness, compassion, altruism, leadership, and initiative. What? Where are great grades and high AP scores? And how are you supposed to show fairness and altruism? That's what this book is for.

The process is not fair. Three applicants to Princeton have the same high SAT scores, the same high SAT II scores, the same great grades in the same difficult courses, and the same wonderful teacher recommendations, and yet one will be admitted, on average, at a 90% rate, one at a 40% rate, and one at a 2% rate. How can three applicants with the same numbers (grades, test scores) be admitted at such different rates? And how can you make sure you're not in the 2% group of students (98% of whom are rejected)? Almost everyone can be (at the very least) in a group that's admitted at a 40% rate. I'll tell you how.

Education is big business. Colleges paint a lovely picture of themselves: they are caring institutions, keepers of Civilization, promulgators of the Enlightenment, and seekers of Justice and Truth in a troubled world. Then you discover that the University of Tennessee markets its own brand of paint: Tennessee Orange Interior Semi-Gloss is available at Home Depot for $25 per gallon. The University even sent its mascot ("Smokey") to Home Depot to make sure the paint sells. Sometimes it's hard to figure out if it's truth or money that drives most university decisions.

In many cases, the top colleges are even more culpable. Columbia, like all top private colleges, is largely funded by public moneys (loans, student grants, research grants, tax-exemption, and so forth). And, of course, Columbia's research efforts are largely funded by public money and correspondingly produce a great many discoveries that benefit the public. This financial arrangement seems to fit our conception of the publicly-funded, private college working for the public good. Then you discover that Columbia patents and licenses those discoveries-and those patents earn Columbia about $90 million per year. You would think that since public money paid for the research, the patent revenue ($90 million per year!) should be repaid to the government or that the discoveries should be licensed for free. But like a good (if not greedy) businessman, Columbia has discovered a way to get someone else to pay for its research and development, and it's not about to let a moral quandary inhibit $90 million in annual revenue. Similarly, Columbia's downtown rival, NYU, recently announced that they would tear down Edgar Allan Poe's historic Greenwich Village row house. Despite the vociferous objections of historic, literary and preservation societies, NYU decided that its growing law school needed a bit more space, and history would simply need to step aside. NYU's successful year-long bout with district councils to raze the four-story building made it clear that NYU's primary objective was growth, not maintaining the things that comprise our history and heritage.

Education is the second biggest business in the United States (health care is first), and yet, colleges and universities are largely unregulated. Higher education is certainly the least regulated major business in this country. Colleges hire lobbyists to lobby Congress (Boston U. spent almost $800,000 last year lobbying Congress) and employ expensive marketing companies to produce marketing materials. A college can make assertions that your stockbroker or car dealer can't. A college can say things that would land a pharmaceutical company in hot water with regulators. The fact is that colleges can say and do almost anything when it comes to the general regulation of their business and the recruitment of students. A few academics have suggested that colleges regulate themselves, but this "self-regulation" is happening now, and it is not working. Most substantive information that prospective students can get on a college comes from the college, not from independent sources. And colleges show themselves willing and able to spin information in order to promote their own interests.

The college admissions process has become more competitive for students and colleges; it is more difficult to get admitted to a top college, and it is more difficult for colleges to attract top students. Different colleges use different methods for attracting students. For example, Princeton simply gives away money to lure students, while other colleges spend millions on advertising. If Ford Motor Company mailed you a car brochure that contained photos that were airbrushed to make the car look better, Ford would be in trouble with the law. If a Wall Street firm made promises in writing and then didn't follow through, they would probably be shut down. And yet colleges do this all the time. Every college from the best to the worst spends thousands of dollars on professional photographers to take beautiful pictures of the campus, even if that means trucking in snow from hundreds of miles away to make the campus look better, even if that means super-imposing lakes or a city in the background, even if that means flying in fancy ducks for the pond or stringing up ivy for the walls. Despite claims to the contrary, a college admissions office's primary objective is to get the best students to apply by making the college appear as pleasing as possible. And without any objective source, any regulation, any oversight, parents and prospective students have no choice but to accept the college's claims. (See "Worthless Information" for more on this.)

What's the difference? When you do get your hands on one of those big college guides, they don't tell you much. So what is the difference between Princeton and Yale? I know one is in New Jersey, and the other is in New Haven. I know Yale has a law school, and Princeton doesn't. But really, what's the substantive difference between Princeton and Yale? What are their philosophies? How does it affect students and professors? What are the topics on campus that would affect your education? Pick up any best-selling college guide, and try to answer those questions. It's very difficult (if not impossible). Most college guides read like telephone directories, and what does a telephone directory tell you about the people listed? Their names, addresses, and phone numbers. That's it. You wouldn't give someone in a telephone directory a check for $150,000, would you? Well, that's what you're doing with colleges.

Chapter 3

How to Think About a College Education

"I'm applying to college because my father will kill me if I don't.
Or he might make me get a job, which would be worse."

I've been on the inside of the college admissions and testing business for over a decade. I've worked with thousands of students and hundreds of colleges. And in researching and analyzing colleges, I have a few guiding principles.

Colleges cost a lot of money. An in-state education will cost you about $40,000 and that's as cheap as it gets. A private education can cost you over $160,000. Colleges have raised their tuition far above inflation annually for decades. In fact, all but one private college have raised their tuition fees every year for the past four decades. I think that $100,000 is a lot to ask a middle-class family to spend on something that has no guarantees. Some colleges take this responsibility seriously, but many do not. There are colleges that continue to increase tuition and then spend $50,000 buying teak trashcans at $4,000 each. (No, I am not making this up.) Many colleges continue to raise tuition despite the fact that they do not need the money; they know, however, that students can borrow the money via government programs. Colleges are alone in this country in being able to ignore cost; not even health care providers can escape the pressures of cost versus benefit. So one of the questions I ask is: what does the student get for the money? Does the student get more at a college that charges $100,000 for a bachelor degree than from one that charges $50,000?

To make the problem worse, colleges are increasingly offering loans instead of grants to students. In 1980, loans comprised about 40% of all financial aid; now, loans comprise about 60% of all financial aid. Recently, a few elite colleges, such as Princeton, have decreased or eliminated loans; most or all financial need will be met with grants instead of loans. But this trend is limited to a few very wealthy colleges. More than ever, most colleges expect students to borrow money and bear the brunt of these excessive, continuous tuition increases.

For example, Amherst raised its tuition 3.6% this past year despite its booming endowment (which is approaching $700 million). Amherst's response to the criticism that tuition has far outpaced inflation for many decades is that the 3.6% increase is the lowest in 35 years! (To summarize: you're not being ripped off as badly now as you were in the past, so stop complaining.) Amherst says that it is increasing its financial aid (I suppose it would need to increase financial aid given the rapid rise in tuition), and it hopes to "moderate" tuition increases in the future. Given that they haven't "moderated" tuition increases in the past 35 years, I wouldn't assume they will start now.

In the decade of the 90s, the average cost of a private college education increased by 74%. For 2001, the average annual tuition for private colleges is $16,332; a year at a public college will cost you, on average, $3,510 ($9,020 if you're out-of-state). While $16,000 doesn't sound too bad for a year at a private college, keep in mind that this number is an average of all private colleges, including over a hundred low-cost, church-supported, rural religious colleges. The tuition fees of the most expensive private colleges are mind-boggling: Columbia $27,190; Sarah Lawrence $28,680; Brown $27,856; Tulane $28,310; Wesleyan $29,784; Princeton $28,540; MIT $28,030; and NYU is a bargain at $26,646. Keep in mind that room, board and fees usually add another $12,000.

To better understand the cost of college, you should think of college tuition as the aggregate cost of a four-year education. There is no point in thinking of the cost of college in annual terms since one year of college doesn't do you any good. You need to earn a bachelor degree, which in most cases consists of four years. If a college charges an annual tuition of $25,000+(as most good private colleges do), and $9,000 for room and board, and another $2,000 in fees, the total cost of a bachelor degree is $144,000. This number excludes books (which you will probably need), incidentals (like shampoo), and inevitable tuition increases. In the end, you will probably spend about $150,000 for the bachelor degree. It is remarkable how many people will commit to spending that much money on an education without knowing very much about the college, with little or no independent research, and with no guarantees. (Imagine if you bought $150,000 worth of stock from a company without any independent analyses, without any SEC regulation, and without any recourse if you later discover that the company did not tell the whole truth in its prospectus. That would be crazy, wouldn't it?)

Currently, there are 35 colleges that charge 4-year tuition of $100,000 or more. Those 35 colleges include all the Ivies (except Cornell) and nearly every desirable private college in the country (Duke, U. Chicago, Johns Hopkins, Swarthmore). When you add room and board ($6,000-$10,000 per year), student fees ($1,000-$4,000 per year), and books ($500-$1,200 per year) to the cost of tuition, then you can reasonably conclude that there are 35 colleges that charge $150,000 or more for a bachelor degree (that's about the median cost of a home). Colleges expect you to pay a lot, and they will expect you to graduate with $20,000 (or more) in debt; you should keep these numbers in mind as you investigate colleges. Be aggressive and thorough in your research.

College research is very difficult. Some people say that they do research colleges. The question is: where does your information come from? A college's view book and web site are almost entirely useless. We will discuss a few pieces of useful information later, but you should understand that most college view books (and other marketing pieces) are designed by outside marketing firms whose job is to sell the college. Typically, the marketing firm knows little about a college. View books often provide the most useless information (Maya Angelou and Tom Brokow spoke on campus last week) while withholding relevant data (crime statistics, teacher salaries). Until college marketing is regulated, it simply cannot be trusted.

For example, Marlboro College's recent view book contains pictures of and facts on Langston Hughes, Eleanor Roosevelt, Jack Kerouac, and Janis Joplin. Are they alumni of Marlboro College? No. In fact, only Hughes even graduated from college. But that didn't stop Marlboro from co-opting these famous names (or infamous, since Kerouac and Joplin died young from boozing and drugs). The view book was created by Mindpower Inc., a college marketing company in Atlanta (Marlboro College is in Vermont). Most Marlboro students felt the view book did not represent the college; one Marlboro student called the view book "grossly inaccurate." Once again, view books are marketing tools created by distant companies, typically without the input of students or faculty, designed to sell the college.

In 1998, Wesleyan dubbed itself "The Independent Ivy" even though Wesleyan is not a member of the Ivy Group (which regulates the "Ivy League"). Wesleyan has subsequently dropped the slogan. Open Union College's view book and you'll find a list of famous speakers; of course, anyone can get famous speakers if one has enough money to pay them. The Washington and Lee view book boasts the names of its famous past presidents: President George Washington and R. E. Lee. R. E. Lee? They try to conceal that fact that R. E. stands for Robert E., General of the Confederate Army. Siena College will enter you in a contest to win a Palm Pilot if you request a view book. The University of Miami will send you a letter from Gloria Estefan. Princeton will gladly associate its name with F. Scott Fitzgerald (who isn't a graduate of Princeton).

Recently, the University of Wisconsin at Madison was creating a view book for prospective students; the cover photo was to be of spectators at a raucous

Wisconsin football game. The only problem was that all of the spectators, like most of the inhabitants of the University and state, were white. So the marketing department got busy and spliced in a requisite black student, and now the crowd appears more diverse and less like the real University of Wisconsin. Is this a blatant distortion of the truth? Sure. But Wisconsin isn't so much interested in the truth as they are in appealing to the demagogic fancies of the academy and their own delusions of what sells to teenagers. Like any business, colleges are trying to develop and sell a brand. Princeton has an easier time selling its brand, so the misrepresentations in its view book are more subtle, while schools like Marlboro must be more hard-selling.

One of my favorites is the recent University of Pennsylvania view book. The first four words (emblazoned in black ink on a red background) on the outside cover are "THE NATION'S FIRST UNIVERSITY." I suppose if using the word "university" makes you a university, then this might be true. (In this case, I will start referring to myself as a "billionaire.") But this statement is disingenuous at best. Yale was the first college to offer a Ph.D. (in 1860), and Harvard, U. Michigan, and U. Chicago were far more university-oriented than Penn. In fact, in the "THIRTY-SIX YEARS" before the American Revolution to which the Penn view book so fondly refers, Penn was an anemic, languishing college largely ignored by serious students and scholars.

Near the center of the same view book is a two-page, full-color overhead photograph (presumably) of a class being conducted. The room is an impressive, imposing oak-and-brass library of the private 18th century sort (e.g. books behind glass, statuary of famous dead Greeks and Romans, big white-faced clock with roman numerals, grand round oak-looking table). The accompanying caption informs the reader that "Nearly 75 percent of all classes in the college at Penn have fewer than 20 [students]." The message Penn is trying to convey to you is clear: we have fancy classrooms, and almost all our classes have fewer than 20 students. What's so funny about this? There are at least 25 students in the picture (the back of the classroom is cut off, so there may be more). You would think that if nearly all Penn classes have fewer than 20 students (as claimed), they could have found one of these small classes for the view book. Penn must assume that applicants won't (or can't) count. Also of note is that of the 25 students and one teacher in the picture, only twelve are actually at a table; the others are crammed into fold-away chairs, and at least one student is relegated to sitting on the floor. For the $32,140 Penn charges students each year (listed under "Costs" in the same view book), you'd think they would at least give every student a chair to sit in!

On a side-note to Penn's small-class claim: one Penn language professor recently wrote gleefully about how he increased the size of his *Faust* class from 12 students to 86 in just three years. Why did enrollment stop at 86 students? Was his concern about effective teaching? Was it an obtuse teaching rule that each class must have no more than 86 students? No. The class was capped at 86 students because the classroom could hold only 86 chairs. It seems that class size at Penn is determined more by room capacity than anything else.

The second major sources of information are college guides and special "college editions" of magazines. Here you will find average SAT scores, acceptance rates, the number of applicants, the number of minority applicants, the student/faculty ratio, and many other seemingly objective facts. The problem is that the majority of these "facts" are self-reported: colleges report any number they wish. While most of these numbers are inevitably based on truth, colleges massage the numbers to make them look better. For example, a college may exclude "special admits" when calculating its average SAT score, and for this college, a "special admit" may be anyone whose SAT score is low! So while the college reports an average SAT score of 1200, this excludes nearly everyone who scored lower than an 1150. The college's actual average SAT score may be closer to 1100. Some colleges count international students as both "international" and "minority" students, so when they report that they have 400 minority students, half of them may actually be international students. Colleges massage numbers all the time, and they occasionally get in trouble, but because there are no regulations regarding methodology, colleges continue to report whatever numbers they choose. So even the college guidebooks are misleading because most of the information comes from the college marketing departments.

Several guidebooks contain the results of student surveys. While these can be useful, they are more often entertaining than informative. A student may say that the college's registrar is awful or the library is great, but such conclusions are naïve unless the student has compared his college's registrar and library to other colleges' registrars and libraries. Since most college students have only attended one college, they have no comparative basis to conclude whether or not their college is better or worse than any other college. Therefore, student surveys are of limited value. In addition, most student surveys are highly unscientific, and the student sample size is too small to be statistically relevant. I know of no college guidebook that publishes student surveys that are actually statistically valid.

College admissions can be very emotional. College is a very expensive choice, and it should not be an emotional choice. It's very easy for a younger person, particularly one who is sick of high school or bored of the suburbs, to get attached to a college. Perhaps you've fallen in love with Princeton or Harvard. It's unfortunate that colleges promote emotional attachments—once you're emotionally attached, you can no longer make critical judgments. Once you fall in love with Harvard, you won't care when you're crammed into a lecture hall with 500 other students. Look at a college's view book: does it remind you of critical inquiry or a pep rally?

Look at a college's bookstore; many of them sell more logo T-shirts and hats than books. Harvard's licensed clothing is as prevalent in Boston as Disney's is in Orlando, and both have the same goal: to get you emotionally attached (so they can make more money). Emotional attachment is the most powerful of marketing schemes, and it's incredible that colleges—from Harvard to Howard—try to take advantage of the naiveté of teenagers in this way. If you're thinking about the University of Miami, you may receive a letter from Gloria Estefan (class of '78) complete with picture and autograph. Ms. Estefan has nothing substantive to add, but U. Miami hopes you'll be impressed. Some colleges actually offer prizes, such as Palm Pilots, to randomly selected students who request applications. Other colleges mail letters from their local pro sports team (using the team's stationery!). None of this is done to help you make an intelligent, informed decision. It's all done to get you to think things such as "I'm going to U.M. because Gloria Estefan went there!" Of course, if you wanted to see Gloria Estefan, you could probably do it for less than the $130,000 you will spend at U.M. (not to mention that you probably won't see her there—she doesn't work there).

I've witnessed the emotional entanglement of the college admissions process hurt many people. Parents have yelled at me, at their high school counselor, at the college admissions officer, at each other, and at their children. Mothers have become highly irrational; fathers have grown domineering; college counselors become haughty. Many families who are under the normal strain of rearing a teenager can barely survive the additional stress of college admissions. While no single prescription will cure every ailment, there is something that always helps: good information.

Why attend college? Some college admissions books assert that everyone should attend college without explanation or goals. Other admissions books claim that only those who want specific pre-professional training or have a love for learning should attend college. Both answers are inadequate.

Before discussing the merits of college, I will discuss the basic structure of American colleges. Colleges are divided into two broad categories: liberal arts schools and pre-professional schools. The objective of "Liberal Arts" colleges is a broad-based education that develops your mind, your character, your ability for critical thinking, and your appreciation of the achievements of civilization. (The "liberal" in "liberal arts" has nothing to do with the political label. In fact, it's usually conservatives, traditionalists, and Republicans who favor the liberal arts education.) A liberal arts college believes its duty is to generally prepare you for a career or graduate school, not for a particular career or specific graduate school. Your high school education is most likely what one would refer to as scholastically "liberal."

Most small rural colleges are liberal arts schools. All of the Ivies except Cornell and the University of Pennsylvania (and Harvard to some extent) are liberal arts colleges. A liberal arts college focuses on traditional subjects of study such as English Literature, History, Economics, and Biology. Many liberal arts colleges do not have "pre-med" or "pre-law" majors because these liberal arts colleges wish to discourage students from focusing too narrowly. A liberal arts college is what one would refer to as "traditional."

Pre-professional colleges, on the other hand, encourage students to focus narrowly on pre-professional studies, usually have very specific pre-professional majors (like nursing or hotel management), and often focus on technical, vocational, or business training. Pre-professional colleges range from Stanford and the Massachusetts Institute of Technology to open-admissions two- and four-year commuter schools. Because many pre-professional colleges concentrate on science and technology, they typically have extensive research programs (usually operated via their graduate school or through institutes). Pre-professional colleges also typically have graduate business schools and medical schools.

Liberal arts and pre-professional schools overlap in many areas. For example, Harvard is a combination of the two types of college: it has the attitude of a liberal arts school with many of the options of a pre-professional school (law, business, and medical schools, massive research and graduate programs, and a bevy of institutes).

Most undergraduate programs that are not outwardly "pre-professional" are labeled as the "College of Arts and Sciences." This does not mean that the college adheres to the "Liberal Arts" philosophy. Most public colleges contain an undergraduate college of arts and sciences, and yet public colleges overwhelmingly tend to be pre-professional.

Later, I will discuss the pros and cons of these types of colleges but for now must answer the question: what is college good for? I don't believe that college is only for those who either want pre-professional training or have a love of learning. I don't expect teenagers to have made "pre-professional" decisions before entering college and strongly discourage all teenagers from making such decisions so early. It is naïve to decide what you want to do with your life when you are seventeen years old. There is still a world of things—experiences, ideas, professions—that you have yet to experience, and many of them you will experience at college. Keep your mind open and your future free of career decisions until (at least) your second year of college. People who make career decisions at seventeen too often find themselves in a life they don't want at forty. It's fine if you love engineering and think you want to be an engineer, but don't choose your college and your freshman and sophomore courses based on such a specific goal.

The other assertion—that college is for those who love learning—seems absurd. I have known very few seventeen-year-olds who "love learning." Most of them tolerate it to an extent, some enjoy it, but very few love it. If college were meant only for those who loved learning, I suspect that most public universities would close due to lack of enrollment.

College is intended for three reasons, all more vague and noble than any mentioned above. First, college is needed to educate the public, and an educated public is needed to maintain a healthy, modern democracy. It is good for our nation and civilization that so many people take time to study the achievements, questions, and solutions of the ages. Education is a luxury, but our country is (comparatively) very wealthy, and our continued success depends on an increasingly educated populace. And by "educated" I do not mean that they can program COBOL or can solve a differential equation. By "educated," I mean people informed of history, aware of culture, and capable of critical inquiry. College is probably the last time you will study European history or read Dante; it is probably the last time you will discuss the causes of the Civil War and debate the merits of bicameral legislature. These studies will (or should) make you a better citizen and (hopefully) a better human. This educational process is the primary reasons you should attend college.

The second reason that college exists is so you can develop your skills and discover what you may be good at and what profession you may wish to pursue. There is a process of mental maturation at college. A good college experience should make you aware of your mental and professional strengths and weaknesses and provide you with direction for your professional life. (As we shall see later, many colleges fail to provide any direction, leaving graduates more confused upon graduating than they were when they applied for admission.)

Finally, there is a significant non-academic side to college; your four years at college should help you mature socially. Unfortunately, many aspects of collegiate life are more likely to socially retard you than to help you grow, but one cannot ignore the very important (albeit potentially detrimental) social aspect of college. This aspect becomes particularly clear when you consider that some colleges spend more money on developing the college's "social" side than on its academic side. You should aggressively take advantage of a college's social activities—after all, that's largely what you're paying for.

However, not everyone should go to college and not everyone should attend college directly out of high school. The standard American four-year college has evolved into a peculiar kind of institution whose values are often not mainstream. (For example, Cornell's Health Center sells vibrators and UC Berkeley funds an online message board so that gay students can discuss good campus locations for sex.) The world needs many kinds of people, from car mechanics to zoologists, and one can find successful people throughout the spectrum of society who did not attend or complete college.

Perhaps more importantly, many high school students are not ready for college immediately upon graduation. Post-graduate years ("PG years") are popular, particularly in the Northeast. (A PG year is an extra year spent in high school, usually at a private school from which you did not graduate. Usually students spend their PG year playing sports and improving their grades.) If you are not sure college is right for you upon graduating high school, then consider a PG year or taking a year or two off. One word of warning: if you take a year or two off before attending college, then you should spend your time engaging in a substantive activity (traveling, writing, art classes, sports, music lessons, building churches in the Caribbean). Getting a job during your PG year is not good enough unless the job is unusual (like being a research assistant at an important lab). Simply goofing off—working at McDonalds and playing Nintendo—will not improve your chances of being admitted to a good college.

Why are these breaks important considerations? Because tens-of-thousands of students transfer from one college to another each year. Tens-of-thousands more drop out of college. Probably half of these students chose the wrong college and many others simply started college too early. If you start college too early, you may waste your money and time. The result will be not learning very much and resenting the college experience. If the thought of more high school makes you sick, then perhaps you should consider getting a job and taking sailing lessons for two years. While college is in many ways different from high school, the academic side is remarkably similar: you go to classes, read books, take tests, and write papers. However, college is more demanding, and your parents will not be there to make sure you complete your homework. You must be ready, willing and able to make a success of it.

The goal of this book is to make the process less nebulous and more fair. I hope to give you the tools you need to better compare colleges and to be able to truly gauge what a college can offer you. Hopefully, you will better understand colleges, the admissions process, and your reasons for choosing a college. If you use this book, the entire process should be less emotional and more rewarding.

Chapter 4

A Note to Parents

"My mother is going crazy. All the papers. The forms.
The questions. She thinks I'll be lucky to get into beauty school."

Relax. This is the single most important piece of advice I can give to parents. I've seen too many families implode while going through the admissions process. I know you want to be encouraging and organized and many other things, but nothing is worth ruining your relationship with your son or daughter. Chances are that your child is already under incredible stress from many different sides: parents, teachers, friends, girlfriends, boyfriends, coaches, piano teacher, SAT tutor, high school newspaper editor, and his boss at the GAP. Add all that to the daily struggle to look cool, act hip, and fit in, and you've got an explosive package. Added pressure from you could be the match to set it off. Try to be informed and involved, but tread carefully. Take my word for it: you probably think you're only being helpful, but you may be causing deep anxiety and resentment.

So relax. No one has ever died because of the college admissions process. No one has ever had his or her life ruined because of a missed deadline. You may think that all your responsibilities as a parent culminate in this one 6-month process, but this is far from the truth. Your responsibilities as a parent culminate in developing a good person, and whether or not your child is a good person is in no way related to which college he or she attends. Good people go to Princeton. Good people go to Pace University. And many good people never go to college. Stay focused on the big picture.

Relax. It will help your child make good decisions. And it's important—crucial—that your child makes the decision, not you. Tens of thousands of students drop out of and transfer out of colleges every year—they drop out of Ivy League colleges, Stanford, MIT, Duke, and everywhere else. A large number of these students never wanted to attend the college in the first place; they were pushed/pulled/aided by their parents into a decision they would not have made

17

on their own. Let them make their own decisions, and let them be happy with the college they are attending. Happy students produce good grades. Unhappy students produce poor grades, fail courses, drop out of college and worse.

Keep college in perspective. Over 2,000 studies have been done over the past three decades on the relationship between the college one attends and one's future happiness, wealth, and/or station in life. No study has ever shown a statistically significant correlation between the college one attends and anything that occurs in one's life—not one's health, wealth, or happiness. The bulk of the college experience is contained within four years, and the residual effect of college is a more ineffable quality than cannot be measured from a survey. Do not think your child's destiny is written by which college he or she attends; it is not. Do not assume that a college's name determines one's future; it does not. Many top private colleges have sought to prove that their $100,000+price tag pays dividends in the future, but not one has been able to offer such evidence. The fact is this: when your child is 40 years old, it simply will not matter where he went to college. What will matter is the quality of the work he did while at college, and the quality of his work will be determined by his efforts and happiness in doing the work, not by the name of the school.

Don't listen to rumors. You will hear that one student with a 1500 on the SAT was rejected by NYU while another with a 1200 was offered a scholarship to Stanford. Such rumors may or may not be true, but the fact is that you have no idea how or why someone was accepted or rejected unless you can review their entire application. Top colleges simply do not make decisions based on academic numbers, so the grades and SAT score information you have on students is grossly inadequate. Top colleges accept students with sub-1300 SAT scores all the time, just as they reject valedictorians all the time. You cannot possibly know if a student will be accepted or rejected to a college based on grades and test scores. Your neighbor's son was accepted or rejected to a college, and you're mystified? Perhaps his essay was awesome, or perhaps it was awful. Perhaps one of his teacher recommendations was particularly bad. Perhaps he forgot to mail in SAT II scores, so he was rejected because his application was incomplete. Perhaps he was accepted despite low test scores because he is a great tuba player (and maybe you didn't even know that your neighbor's son played the tuba). I know it's difficult, but please do not listen to rumors or stories. If you get a story in your head, take it to your counselor. The counselor will be able to straighten it out for you.

College admissions is not a lottery. The more you listen to rumors, the more you will think that college admissions is simply a lottery. It is not. It is foolish to apply to twenty colleges on the theory that the more "tickets" you buy, the better your chance of winning. Colleges tend to have very predictable standards and follow very stable patterns. If you send the same application to Swarthmore,

Dartmouth, Amherst, and Brown, chances are you will be accepted or rejected by all four colleges. If you are a non-recruited student relying on your academics, then colleges of the same caliber will typically respond to your application the same way.

Your child is not the best child. I know you love your child, and I know you may feel that everything you've done up to now culminates in a college acceptance. However, you need to understand that your child will be competing against others who are smarter, better athletes, more talented musicians, and/or more interesting. In fact, if you're applying to a top college, then your child is—if he or she did everything right—average. Your son is special, but I can assure you that his transcript isn't; Penn will receive 1,000 other applicants whose transcripts look exactly like his; Princeton will receive 100 other activities lists that look almost the same; Columbia will receive 1,000 other essays that are so alike as to be totally unmemorable. If you understand this, then you will be able to respond to an acceptance with calm reassurance and a rejection with informed sympathy. An acceptance is not a sign that your child is singularly extraordinary; your child is outstanding, but probably in the exact same way that 1,000 other students who were accepted by that college are outstanding. On the other hand, a rejection should not engender anger in you; some parents cannot understand how a college could reject their extraordinary child. The harsh reality is that your child is extraordinary to you, but your child's A average and 1410 SAT scores are average to Princeton. At most top colleges, average students are rejected.

Do not get hung up on one college. Colleges encourage emotional connections. They encourage you to become emotionally attached: the view books preach this sort of attachment; the bookstores solidify this emotional attachment with T-shirts, hats, coffee mugs and bumper stickers. This stuff is okay for college students, but it's dangerous for applicants. If you or your child becomes emotionally committed to a college while still in the application process, then you will be unable to make objective decisions and unlikely to handle rejection well. Keep a cool distance until your child is accepted. Don't say, "I think Penn is best" without adding "but Haverford is also great." The popularity of early decision has made it necessary for an applicant to single out one college as "most desirable." While your child's early decision choice may be "most desirable," he should also have two or three other choices that are "as desirable."

The admissions process is unfair to everyone. Regardless of what happens to your child, an admission department has not singled him out. The recruited athlete will have a 70% chance of being admitted to Princeton. The wealthy white suburban student will have the money to pay for tutors and attend a high school that offers twenty AP courses. The Hispanic student who doesn't even speak Spanish will be very competitive with a 1250 on the SAT. The great flutist is accepted despite her low test scores and grades simply because the college orchestra desperately needs a flutist. In some way, the process is unfair to everyone. What about those wealthy white suburban students who attend great prep schools? Colleges will hold them to almost unattainably high standards. If your child is rejected, do not consider suing. Do not write an angry letter or make an angry phone call. Do not swear that Princeton is now your mortal enemy. The process is unfair; accept that now and everything else will be a little easier.

Kill your television. Get them off the Internet. Encourage your child to read and to talk. The dean of admissions for Princeton once said that the best advice he could give to parents is to encourage their children to read. It's that easy and that complex. Most top colleges are more interested in good readers than anything else. A student with an 800-math and a 620-verbal is much more likely to be rejected from a top college than one with an 800-verbal, 620-math. If your children aren't readers in middle school, then the chances aren't good that they will be readers in high school, but your encouragement can be the catalyst. And, as always, lead by example. If you sit in front of the television for four hours every night, then your children will too. You should read, and hopefully they will follow.

Teach your child. Home schooling does not only describe those who do not attend formal school. Home schooling is an attitude: your child's schooling does not end when they leave school. Home is also a school. You are your child's teacher from 3pm to 8am. You are the weekend teacher and the holiday teacher. When your child does homework, work with him. Read his essays, discuss what he's reading, and ask him to teach you the math he learned in school. During weekends or holidays, compose little quizzes for your child. Require him to write essays on various topics. There is no law that states that only a schoolteacher can assign homework. You can assign homework too. Ask your child to cook dinner and give a nutritional report on that dinner. Ask your child to write a 200-word essay on the sit-com he watched last night. Enroll your child in community school classes: pottery, painting, video production. Ask him to make you something. Support him in his wildest dreams. These little things will add up over the course of years. None of this means you should be overbearing; the point is that home should not be a refuge from learning, but a continuation of it.

Your child should always take the hardest courses possible. It is much better to gets B's in hard courses than A's in easy courses. All top colleges agree: a student who consistently shies away from the hardest courses will probably not survive in the rigorous environment of a top college. Obviously there's no point in taking hard courses and failing out of school, but if that's the only option, then a top college isn't in your future (unless you are recruited). Top colleges simply do not accept non-recruited students who have not taken hard classes in high school.

Public vs. Private? A number of people will claim that it makes no difference if you attend a public or private school and will buttress the claim with statistics that show that top colleges admit public and private school students at the same (or similar) rates. For example, Dartmouth accepts 33% of the applicants from New York's Stuyvesant High School (a public inner-city magnet school) and only 25% of students from Horace Mann (a swanky prep school also in New York City.) This comparison supposedly proves that it doesn't matter where applicants attended high school. But as you will see, the do-gooders at colleges give significant leeway to minorities, poor applicants, applicants whose parents didn't attend college, and so forth, but wealthy white urban students are held to the highest standards. So a minority inner-city student may be accepted with an 1100 on the SAT whereas the wealthy white student will need a 1400 or higher. Most wealthy New Yorkers would not send their children to Stuyvesant; they would send their children to Horace Mann. So it's not fair to compare these two high schools because the students are held to two different—often widely differing—standards.

If you look closely at these statistics, you will find that many of the private school students who are rejected would have been accepted had they had the same scores and grades at a public school. As you will learn, admissions offices hold private school students to a higher standard than they do public school students. In addition, because class rank is so much more important than grades, it's much more difficult to be in the top 10% of the graduating class at a top private school (where 100% of the graduates attend college) than at an average public school (where perhaps 60% of the graduates attend college). This becomes obvious when one considers that most top private high schools accept only 25% of those who apply, so students at those schools are competing with other top students for good grades and a high rank. (As an aside, most top private high schools do not actually rank, so I'm using the word "rank" rather loosely. More on this in later chapters.)

Given that, it may seem that you would have a better chance of being admitted to a top college if you attend a public school. At first glance, this is true since colleges hold private school applicants to a higher standard, but this assumes you would get the same grades and test scores at the public school. In fact, the primary benefit of a private school isn't, purely speaking, a high probability of being accepted to a top college but rather an environment in which students excel. Studying, learning and academic success are more likely for students at a private school than at a public school simply because a private school provides an environment in which academic success is supported and expected. You will find students at a top private school willingly studying Virgil (in Latin, of course) for years; at a public school, such a student is likely to be viewed as a geek. I have considerable experience with both private and public school students, and I can assure you that from an educational point of view, private school students have a significant advantage. These students may or may not be more intelligent; the teachers may or may not be better; often, the college counselors are not better than their public school associates (though they act as if they are). But almost without fail, the environment for learning and the expectations for success will be significantly better. And because so much in the teenage world is a result of expectations and peer pressure, one can ask for no more than the pressure to succeed academically. This is not to say that private high schools are "high pressure"—most are not. But they do have certain academic expectations; in fact, they have the same expectations that top colleges have, which is why most private school students are better prepared for college than public school students. What a private school offers and what most public schools cannot compete with is an environment that enables and encourages students to succeed.

A final digressive observation: private school students are far more likely to develop lifelong habits of learning and scholarship. The habits of a scholar are instituted in private schools: owning books, making notes in books, keeping books for years, referring back to them, developing one's own dialogue with differing books and authors from different classes, assembling an appreciation for bigger pictures and broader ideas. These habits are not encouraged in public schools (where books are treated more like untouchable artifacts than like ideas to be digested).

After you have encouraged and supported, taught and shown, you must get out of the way. Your child should manage the application process. Your child should do most of the work. If your child isn't doing much of the application work, and you find it necessary to step in, then perhaps your child isn't ready for college. So get out of the way, and let him take over.

Chapter 5

A Note to Students

> "Why would Princeton want me? I don't have
> the time to rebuild churches in Guatemala and
> discover a vaccine for Ebola. I just play the flute."

Here are a few notes for you; keep these in mind, and you'll be fine.

This book is for you. You need to read it (yes, all of it) and understand it. Don't let your parents read it and tell you what's in it—find out for yourself. Ultimately, only you are responsible for your future. The college admissions process depends on your grades, your test scores, your essays, and your activities. It's all about you, so take control.

What Colleges Want: the Big Picture. Most students think that top colleges are looking for the overall "well-rounded" student, the student that's pretty good at everything. Wrong. Top colleges are looking for two things: first, you must be able to do the work; second, you must add something significant to the college community. Colleges usually assume the first; Princeton assumes that 75% of those who apply can do the work. Will a college reject you if it's clear you cannot do the work? Yes, if you show no other signs of extraordinary achievement. However, even top colleges will overlook academic weaknesses if a candidate exhibits some extraordinary ability. Many great athletes who are admitted to top colleges, including Ivy League colleges, would never have been admitted based solely on their academic records. A great artist, musician, or actor can get admitted to top colleges despite a poor academic record, which is how a student with an 1150 on the SAT gets admitted to a top college. If you hear that a famous person was admitted to a top college, do not assume that she was academically qualified to be admitted. Extracurricular achievement may be what earned her admission.

So top colleges are not looking for "well-rounded" students; they are looking for students with unique talents and extraordinary skills. Obviously, most students need to support their application with evidence of academic achievement and the ability to perform well at college, but the average top student usually doesn't get admitted to a top college. After all, most top colleges reject over 50% of all valedictorians who apply (a valedictorian is the top student in a graduating class). And often, the #10 ranked student in a class will be admitted over the #1 ranked student. The academically superior student did not offer anything unique to the college, while the #10 ranked student had something special.

The "Unique Factor" has one serious consequence. You probably have heard of the student who had a 1500 on his SATs, seven perfect AP scores, was ranked #1 in his class, and was a nice guy, but was rejected from Yale. You know of another student with a 1350 on the SAT, a few good APs scores, and who was ranked #10 in his class but was admitted to Yale; this makes you think that the entire college admissions process is a little crazy. Why does this happen? Top colleges are not simply looking for the "best" students—those would be easy to find (colleges would just admit everyone by using high school grades). Colleges are looking for students who will contribute to their community.

Recently, 1,534 valedictorians applied to Princeton. Only about 32% were accepted. Princeton also received 2,669 applications with scores between a 750 and an 800 on the math SAT. Princeton accepted only 24% of them. In part, this is the "Unique Factor" at work. There are also many other factors that I will discuss later.

Imagine you are charged with the task of building your own 8,000-person city. Who would you pick? You would want some very smart people. You would want people who were honest. Perhaps most importantly, you would want people who were interesting, exciting, and unique, right? The last thing you would want is a boring city! The admissions office of a college is charged with this process of "city-building."

Consider Cornell: it is way out there in the middle of New York, surrounded by nothing. Cornell is its own town, whose largest sub-population is 8,000+undergraduates. Cornell is a largely self-operating, self-policing, self-regulating town. Not only is the admissions office building their own little city, but they are also populating this city with a bunch of teenagers! Who do they want? Obviously, they want smart students, but they don't want a bunch of boring eggheads. Of course, they want students who will work well together, be honest with each other, and behave maturely. They also want students who are interested in participating in the community, starting clubs and managing organizations. (Students operate most of the activities that go on outside of the college classroom.) Academic achievement is really only one factor in admissions; the college is also looking for integrity, maturity, initiative and, above all, creativity. No college wants to be boring!

Your application is a sales package, and your "hook" is your uniqueness. What makes you a superstar? Something does, I guarantee it. A good college counselor can find it. Your parents may know what it is. But something unique is within you, waiting to be brought out, developed, and packaged for colleges to consider. Don't try to tell a college that you're good at everything; tell them you're great at something.

The Smoke-filled Room. The college admissions process is certainly crazy. There's simply no other way to describe it. Students far less academically qualified than you will be admitted ahead of you—I can almost guarantee that. Some will be admitted ahead of you because of the accident of where they were born or what language their parents speak at home or where their parents went to college. A few will be admitted ahead of you because they attended much better high schools, and still others will be admitted because they attended much poorer high schools. This selection process is done in a building far away by a bunch of people you don't know. You will be carefully compared to other students you don't know, and the comparisons will have serious consequences.

You may think this is the first time you've been compared by a bunch of strangers to a bunch of strangers, but it's not. The SAT is another screwy process in which you're judged in a building far away by a bunch of people you don't know. The result (your SAT score) is the product of a comparison with many other students, most of whom you will never meet. The core of the admissions process is a beauty pageant: the admissions officers are the judges, and the other applicants are the contestants. It's important to keep this in mind because it will give you perspective; in your own family, you probably win the beauty pageant (or maybe come in second); your parents probably think you're reasonably intelligent. Your mom thinks you're a "good kid." Your teachers like you. That's nice, but the college admissions process plays by a different set of rules. What your mom thinks is irrelevant. All that counts is how you compare to the thousands of other students applying to the college. How desirable are you? And like a beauty pageant, there are some things over which you have no control. However, you have enough control so you can get admitted to almost any college in the country. All it takes is starting early enough (10th grade at the latest), careful planning, and, of course reading this entire book.

Chapter 6

College Rankings

"Dude, I can't go to Michigan. It's not top-ten. I'll be an
embarrassment to my Yale-loving family."

First, I've decided to start with a little background on how I rank colleges. These
rankings are used throughout this book and are often the cause of confusion. An
initial warning: acceptance rates do not indicate quality. A college that accepts
only 30% of those who apply is not necessarily "better" than one that accepts
50%. There is no direct correlation between an acceptance rate and the quality of
education; a college may be popular for all the wrong reasons. For example,
although Harvard has one of the lowest acceptance rates in the country (usually
10%-14%), I don't think it provides one of the best educations (in fact, I would-
n't put Harvard in the top 20). Similarly, New York's DeVry Institute of
Technology, a for-profit vo-tech school, has a reported acceptance rate of 47%
(lower than Smith, Wellesley and U. Michigan!). Obviously this number is bogus
and meaningless. So don't conflate acceptance rates with the quality of education.

In theory, you could get the same education from almost any college. Most
colleges offer the same courses, use the same books, and have the same general
requirements for graduation. Intelligent, motivated students can learn the same
things at a non-competitive public college as at Princeton. It's Princeton's low
acceptance rate that makes it a "top" college. And it's the environment at
Princeton, as well as the reputation, that differentiates it from your local non-
competitive public university. In fact, the few studies that have been conducted
on top colleges show that future earnings aren't significantly affected by which
college you attend, so you're just as likely to become a millionaire if you graduate
from Eastern Michigan State or from Penn.

And finally, I'll mention here something I mention a few times in this book:
the importance of attending a top college is often over-rated and certainly misleading. Thousands of studies have been conducted from the 1970s to the 1990s,

and they typically show that the degree to which one is "educated" and the amount that one earns after graduation has very little to do with the college one attends. What, then, are the primary influences on education and future earnings? The qualities of one's character. This doesn't mean you should attend SUNY Albany over Yale (God forbid) as much as it means you shouldn't be discouraged with your lot in life if you must attend SUNY Albany (for whatever reason). Your life is what you make of it, not what college you attend.

Top College. Caveats aside, we must agree on a criterion for ranking colleges for the sake of discussion. It would be fruitless to discuss all types of colleges because colleges vary widely—there are over 2000 colleges in this country and many of them have nothing in common with each other. The most commonly used criterion for ranking colleges and the most conspicuous distinction among colleges is admission rates. As noted previously, comparing admissions rates is a fairly useless way to distinguish among colleges, but this is the way most people do it. So whenever I write about a "top college," I am referring to colleges that admit less than 30% of those who apply. These colleges are the most competitive colleges in the country. Many students are surprised to learn that there are only about thirty of these top colleges in this country. Traditionally, the top colleges include six of the eight Ivies: Yale, Columbia, Harvard, Princeton, Dartmouth, and Brown; all the service academies: USMA (West Point), Air Force (USAFA), and Navy (Annapolis); the three Tech Giants: MIT, Cal Tech and Stanford; the Li'l Ivies: Amherst, Williams and Swarthmore (not actually Ivies, though); the New Kids on the Block: Georgetown, Rice, Northwestern, Cooper Union, and Duke.

Those colleges are firmly entrenched in "top college" status. Every year, several other colleges may slip below the 30% level and achieve top college status. On a good year, Cornell and the University of Pennsylvania (Penn) slip below 30% and are "top colleges." Some other colleges that are usually close to the 30% range and occasionally fall below are: Pomona, NYU, Washington & Lee, University of Virginia, UNC-Chapel Hill, Davidson, Wesleyan, Bates, Bowdoin, Colby, and Tufts. There are about 21 firm top colleges and five to ten floaters each year. (It's interesting that despite what one may assume, both Maine and Virginia/North Carolina have many very good colleges.)

It should be noted that many colleges that have a 26%-29% acceptance rate might actually be over 30% because most colleges count as "rejected" any student who applies and is not accepted. This may seem to make sense but that includes thousands of applicants who send incomplete applications (and do not choose to complete them even after being notified). These people are not qualified applicants because they never completed their application, and yet most colleges will count an incomplete application as "rejected" to help lower their acceptance rate.

This may surprise you, but as many as 4% of all applicants to top colleges never complete their application. This means that a college that has an acceptance rate of 28% may actually have an acceptance rate of 31% once the incomplete applications are excluded. In short, don't make a big deal if a college drops from a 31% acceptance rate to a 27% acceptance rate; the college may have become more competitive, or it may have changed its application accounting practices. (By the way, almost any college could, if it wanted, "magically" increase its rejection rate by 1-2% simply by changing its accounting and statistical procedures.)

The other fact that may surprise you is that the most competitive colleges do not necessarily have the most difficult course work. You can sail through almost every college, and many top colleges are very forgiving when it comes to slacking students. For example, if your grades are horrible, and you need to take a semester off to regroup, most top colleges, such as Swarthmore, will gladly accommodate you. Another example: U.S. Senator and former presidential candidate Bill Bradley was admitted to Princeton with a verbal SAT score of 460; he was a heavily recruited high school basketball star. Even though Bradley would never have been admitted to Princeton based on his academic credentials, he did well there. Is it because Bradley was a hidden genius who blossomed in college? Or is it because getting out of Princeton is so much easier than getting in? (The answer is the latter.)

Top colleges are eager to keep their dropout rates low, so they are loath to expel failing students. You are more likely to be expelled from a public university than from a top private college for poor academic performance. Some top colleges, such as Princeton, are known for being less than rigorous; in this case, the rumor that the hardest part is getting in is usually true. In nearly every case, if you can get admitted to a top college, then you can do the work. (The only question is whether you will want to do the work. After years of slaving away in high school, many students wish to relax a little in college.) And given the incredible grade inflation at most top colleges, it's very difficult to get bad grades even if you are lazy. It's common at colleges such as Princeton and Stanford for 75%+of the undergraduates to earn all A's and B's, and at many top colleges, over half the students graduate with honors. At Harvard, over half of all undergraduates earn an A- or higher, a fact that Harvard professor Harvey Mansfield calls "scandalous." He gives two grades to students in his political science courses: a "real" grade that reflects how they actually performed in his class and an inflated grade for their transcript. Mansfield says that he's trying to "undermine the Harvard system of grade inflation by exposing it as the laughable mistake it is." As noted, it's almost impossible to fail out of a top college, and many do not even have failing grades (either the grade of "F" doesn't exist or isn't recorded by the registrar). And at many top colleges such as Harvard, it's almost impossible to receive any grade below a B.

Rampant grade inflation exists at many top colleges and can be explained by two reasons. First, grade inflation started in some cases during the 1960s so that activist students (who rarely attended class) could remain in college, thereby being ineligible for the draft. Even though many of these students should have earned F's and should have been academically expelled from college, sympathetic professors gave them better (passing) grades. The second reason grade inflation exists is so professors and departments can attract students. Smaller departments or new "studies" (such as Women's Studies) often offer easy classes so that more students will enroll. Colleges allot money and power according to the number of students enrolled or majoring in a department's or studies' courses. Departments with decreasing enrollment get downsized or dismantled. Departments with increasing enrollment get more money and more power to hire professors, determine requirements, and plan for the future. "Studies," such as African-American Studies, Women's Studies, Gender Studies, and Gay/Lesbian Studies, are usually sub-departments; they are not actual departments and usually do not have the power to spend money (meaning they cannot hire their own professors). "Studies" are often very easy majors (or minors) because if a "studies" can attract enough students, it will be promoted to a full-blown department and therefore have the ability to spend money without accountability.

Competitive College. There are about 3,000 colleges in the United States; however, very few of them are actually competitive. By "competitive," I mean that the college actually rejects qualified applicants. By "qualified" I mean students who meet all the qualifications and successfully complete and submit their applications by the deadlines. There are many college guides that list 300-350 colleges, but there are only about 200 colleges in this country that are actually competitive, and only about 130 accept fewer than 50% of those who apply. Many of the colleges in those guides with admissions rates of 75% or higher finagle their numbers in order to appear more competitive when, in fact, they are probably not competitive at all; they accept every qualified applicant on a first-come, first-serve basis. You can usually assume that any college that admits 80% or more of those who apply is not a competitive college. In many cases, colleges that report acceptance rates below 80% are not competitive. There are several locations of the for-profit DeVry chain of vo-tech schools that report acceptance rates of 40%-60%. These rates are meaningless. DeVry will admit anyone who is able to pay (or secure financial aid) and meets its minimal requirements (for example, they must have legally entered this country and speak some English).

Most public colleges and universities and over half of all private colleges are not actually competitive; they will admit almost everyone who meets their basic requirements (a high school diploma or GED, speak some English, and so forth). Competitive colleges range from Cornell, Boston College and NYU to U.

Michigan, U. Florida, and New College. Nearly everyone applies at least to a few competitive colleges.

Open Admission College. Most colleges are "open admission," meaning you are admitted if your check doesn't bounce, and you have all the required vaccinations. All junior, community, and vo-tech colleges are open admission, as are most public colleges. Any proprietary college is open admission; "proprietary" means "for-profit." Most proprietary colleges teach vocational skills such as surveying, air-conditioning repair, mechanics (auto, truck, airplane), technical/computer repair, and computer network administration. These for-profit colleges are only interested in your money (in many cases, they are publicly owned and listed on major stock-exchanges). Many private colleges, such as Iona (New Rochelle, NY), Pace (NYC), and Hofstra (Hempstead, NY) are virtually open admission. Chances are if you hear advertisements on the radio or on television for a college, it's open admission.

This book does not address open admission colleges for the obvious reason that if you're minimally qualified, you will be accepted. However, I will quickly address the pros and cons of these types of colleges.

Colleges listed as "proprietary" are colleges that are owned, privately or publicly, in order to make a profit. They are businesses like any other business; they are primarily concerned with profit/loss statements, not with the quality of education. Many proprietary colleges are publicly traded and attract many outside investors. One college company, The Apollo Group, has attracted such investors as Kaplan (the test prep company) and Chase bank (via its venture capital subsidiary). Kaplan, which is known for SAT prep, recently bought its own chain of for-profit colleges for $165 million. It's rare for a proprietary college to hire stellar professors because for-profit colleges do not spend much money on teaching. (Most teachers at for-profit colleges do not have PhDs and are hired on a part-time basis which pays $800-$2500 per class.) Although these colleges have "admissions" offices, they are, in reality, simply sales offices. Many admissions officers at these colleges earn commissions or bonuses the same way a car salesman does. Sometimes for-profit colleges are franchised, while other times they are owned by a conglomerate. For-profit colleges usually award certificates (e.g. for computer network administration), associate degrees, and, in many cases, bachelor, master and (believe it or not) doctorates. (It should be noted that no reputable college or university would hire a professor who earned his degree from a for-profit college.)

For-profit colleges do one thing remarkably well: unlike non-profit colleges, these for-profit colleges are committed to making sure their graduates are employed (or, at least, employable). These for-profit colleges are called "trade schools" (which means they teach a skill). In order for these trade schools to be certified, they must prove that their graduates are employed and/or employable. It's interesting to note that trade schools must prove that their students are learning marketable skills, whereas top colleges need not prove this and, in fact, are usually not even concerned with it.

Most for-profit colleges take their mission of fully-employed graduates very seriously and achieve employment rates of 90%+(meaning that 90%+of their graduates are employed within six months of graduation). This rate is much higher than most top colleges. Very few competitive or top colleges believe that the employability of their graduates is a serious concern. Yes, they have career centers, but if colleges were seriously interested in the ability of their students to be employed, they wouldn't permit their students to major in fatuous subjects such as Environmental Justice (if trees could sue in court, how much would they sue for?) or Gender Studies. Students who major in these areas and who have a weak academic foundation (i.e. they take few courses outside their area of concentration) often find it difficult to find a job in the "real world." Although for-profit colleges neglect actually educating students—for-profit colleges do not educate, they train—they do believe that a measure of their success is the employability of their graduates. For-profit colleges include the chains DeVry, Phoenix and ITT (all of which serve up training like McDonald's serves up hamburgers) and smaller colleges such as Berkeley College (NJ & NY) and Westwood (CO). The Apollo Group, which owns The University of Phoenix and other for-profit schools, enrolls about 95,000 students, making it the largest private college in the country. Many large college guides, such as Peterson's bloated directory, actually list these for-profit colleges next to Harvard and Columbia. If you look through Peterson's guide at the colleges listed in Colorado, you will find that twelve out of the thirty-three colleges (36%) listed are actually for-profit education companies.

I do not mean to imply that for-profit colleges are the only ones interested in money. Most public and private colleges are acutely aware of their revenue numbers and manage their college in the same business-like manner that for-profit colleges do. Harvard, for example, once pondered abolishing their undergraduate program, but decided against it, because, in part, of the revenue that undergraduate tuition brought the university. Most colleges have a more complex system in place to monitor cash-flow than they do to monitor quality. (Ask a college how they monitor the quality of their teaching and most cannot give you an answer. Most colleges have students complete course evaluations, but such evaluations are rarely given any weight. Tenured professors, of course, who have guaranteed lifetime employment, are completely sheltered from efforts to monitor the quality of their teaching.)

What place do for-profit colleges have? Well, for-profit colleges do serve a few very useful purposes. Most academics at competitive colleges deride the for-profit college sector; their derision springs from arrogance and ignorance. For-profit colleges are good for non-traditional students, particularly those who do not have the qualifications to be admitted to regular colleges or who have the tendency to drop out of college (for example, those students who have tried community college three or four times and keep dropping out should try a for-profit college). For-profit colleges are also good for those students who are seeking to be trained in specific skills and then be employed using those skills. If you're unfocused and lack direction, a for-profit college will guide you from the learning phase to employment. Remember, the primary mission of a for-profit college is to make sure you are employable and employed, so if you lack skills and direction, a for-profit college is for you.

Why do I recommend for-profit schools for those who lack direction? Because for-profit colleges want your money, so they won't let you drop out. If you don't register for classes for the following semester, they will call and write you. If you need a little nagging to stay motivated, then the for-profit college may be for you. Their competition is the community college; in most cases, you can get as good or better training for much less at a community college, but you will need to navigate through the morass of courses in order to achieve some semblance of training. Community colleges do not provide direction, are often incompetent and impersonal, and usually do not care if you drop out. Once again, you can take the same courses for much less at a public community college, but you won't get much guidance, and community colleges are not as concerned with employability. Think of this difference: many community colleges have 40,000+students, whereas most for-profit colleges have fewer than 4,000 students. Which one do you think will give you more personal attention?

The one caveat is this: you would be crazy to attend a for-profit college for anything other than vocational training (training for a specific job). Do not attend a for-profit school to earn a humanities degree; you will receive a poor education and pay far too much for it. Most for-profit colleges are quite expensive, but they are usually very good about securing financial aid for their students. You should remember that most (if not all) of the financial aid a for-profit college secures for you will be a loan, which you will be required to pay back upon graduation.

Chapter 7

The Players

"Sometimes I feel as though I'm running a circus.
My parents in one ring, my counselor in another, Penn in another."

Here is a summary of the people or offices that you will come into contact with during the admissions process. I put this up front so you have a good idea of everyone's role.

Your Counselor. There are a few different counselors who may be involved in your college admissions process. The first is a guidance counselor, who is the person who schedules your classes and arranges for excused absences and that sort of thing. The second is a college counselor, who focuses exclusively on students who are college-bound and assists them in applying to college. A few high schools do not differentiate between guidance and college counselors; if you attend a public school, you may be assigned one counselor or two. At a few small private schools, the college counselor and the vice-principal (or assistant dean) are the same person. In either case, when I refer to a high school counselor, I am referring to the counselor who assists you in applying to college. Third is a private admissions counselor or consultant; this person is an independent counselor you hire to assist you.

The college counselor at your high school may be very good or may be quite useless; counselors vary widely in quality, and the quality of your counselor may have nothing to do with the overall quality of your high school. I've worked with prestigious prep schools whose college counselors are surprisingly inept, and I've worked at large urban public schools whose college counselors are capable and caring. You can never tell until you start to work with them.

Before I begin discussing counselors, I would like to say up front that most college counselors working in high schools are overburdened; regardless of how competent they may be, they can never do everything for every student simply because they have too many students. I find that I can typically only work with about 25 students at a time, and I require much of students and parents. So even the most caring and expert high school counselor will not be able to do everything he or she wants to do for you. I also believe that most high school counselors are caring and interested in helping you. So if you have troubles with your counselor, it may be that your counselor is apathetic or uninformed, or it may be that your counselor is overworked—which isn't your counselor's fault at all, it's the fault of the principal, the superintendent, and the Board of Education.

Your high school counselor has many priorities. If you attend an average or below-average high school at which less than 50% of each graduating class attends a four-year college, then it's likely your counselor spends more time dealing with bureaucratic issues than with college admissions issues. In this case, your counselor probably focuses on class schedules, attendance and tardiness rates, bilingual issues, detentions, and other assorted administrative problems (counselors, like vice principals, are often the high school's all-around problem-solvers). If your counselor is primarily focused on issues other than college admissions, then you must be acutely aware of every detail of the admissions process, because college admissions is not a high priority for your counselor and details may slip through. A tell-tale sign that college admissions is not a high priority to your counselor is whether his office is plastered with posters for the Army ROTC, local colleges, and proprietary (for-profit) colleges. This evidence is usually a sign that the counselor permits these kinds of colleges to manage the admissions process at the high school because the counselor has no time to do it himself.

Chances are that you attend a high school that has a counselor who is very concerned with college admissions. The first thing to understand is that your counselor has many different, often competing, priorities. A counselor's first priority—and often the benchmark by which he or she is judged—is getting as many students as possible into four-year colleges. This is why you will find that many counselors will urge students to apply to "safety" colleges which the students would not attend even if it were the only college to which they were accepted; but the counselor pushes the unwanted safety colleges because the counselor must be sure that every student is accepted somewhere. Sometimes, this priority will clash with your priorities. You may inform your counselor that you're applying to very competitive colleges and your counselor may be very discouraging because his priority is that you are accepted to any college, not necessarily the right college for you or a good college.

In most cases, your counselor's second priority is administrative ease and coordination of plans. Consider this example: your counselor is probably responsible for 150-400 students. If 80% of a class of 250 applies to college, then that's 200 students applying to college. Now each student will probably take the SAT (at least) twice, and most students will take the SAT IIs once or twice for a total of around 800 test administrations—not to mention AP and ACT testing. And each student will probably apply to, on average, eight colleges. Do the math: that counselor will have several thousand applications, test scores, recommendation forms, and transcript requests pour through her office in less than a year. Whew! It's easy to see why a top priority is organization!

This desire for organization explains why most counselors give you specific dates and deadlines for everything from when to take the SAT to when to submit your recommendation forms. Counselors in the northeast usually tell their students to take the May SAT, but in most cases, May is too late to take the SAT for the first time (in fact, you should always take the SAT earlier than May). Why do counselors continue to give out this apparently bad advice? Because they are trying to keep everything organized, and if the May test—and not the April test—is offered at their school, then they will tell everyone to take the May test. Similarly, they might require you to submit the counselor recommendation forms to them by December 1. Is that a date required by the colleges? No, it's an arbitrary date picked by counselors. You may be better served to apply earlier or later, but your counselor's priority is to keep everything organized, so everyone must follow the same directions regardless of what may help the individual student. You should thoroughly explore your options in every case and be sure that your choices reflect what's best for you. You do not want to anger your counselor, but your top priority is you, not administrative ease.

Your counselor's third priority is the individual student's needs. But as I mentioned, nearly all college counselors, even counselors at good prep schools, must deal with more students than they can reasonably manage. A private college counselor can successfully manage no more than thirty students (assuming that each student is applying to 5-8 top colleges). As you will learn after reading this book, the admissions process is lengthy and full of details; there is no way to navigate it successfully in a short period of time. Because of this, most high school counselors focus their time on their top 10-20 students—those students who are most motivated and most likely to be accepted to top colleges. The counselor's goal is to get a few top students accepted to Ivy—level colleges and get everyone else accepted anywhere. This may be apparent to you already; you may have noticed that your counselor has more time or is more interested in some students than others. Once again, this is not necessarily the fault of your counselor. With 150 or more students, there is simply not enough time in the day to consult fully with every student. So the top 5%-10% get most of the attention, and the rest are guided so that they apply to at least one sure-fire safety college. Counselors will deny this occurs, but experience and logic bear out this truth. If any counselor seriously believes that he fully services all the needs of 150 or more students, then either he is fooling himself, or he does not know of all the requirements of the admissions process, or both. I've heard many counselors—mostly from mediocre urban public schools—deny this observation. They truly believe that they are fully serving the needs of—in most cases—300+students per counselor. And yet I, too, have worked in these public schools, and I can attest that these counselors are usually less than competent. A simple review of the colleges to which their students are admitted corroborates my conclusion; in most cases, fewer than 30% of their students were admitted to competitive colleges, and often students aren't admitted because of a lack of information and guidance. (By comparison, 75%-95% of students from good public schools and prep schools are admitted to competitive colleges.) In most cases, students from mediocre, urban schools actually have a great advantage in the admissions process because top colleges recruit those types of students, and yet the counselors do not know how to take advantage of the situation.

However, this third priority is balanced with another priority: counselors, particularly established counselors, have a level of credibility with each college. If the counselor is good, then her credibility may be very high with a few top colleges. In fact, a counselor's credibility could be so high with a few top colleges that when the counselor submits an application for a student, the college will review it with the assumption that the student should be admitted. The college knows that the counselor will only permit students who are highly qualified to apply. While this is rare, this is the level of credibility that every counselor should seek.

There are also a few counselors who have little credibility with colleges. When does this happen? When a counselor permits too many students, particularly too many very under-qualified students, to apply to a college. Most top colleges have no interest in receiving applications just for the sake of rejecting an applicant; they would prefer it if the counselor discouraged grossly under-qualified students from applying. It is, in fact, a counselor's job to discourage under-qualified students from applying to top colleges and to manage the number of students who apply to top colleges. We all know that Boston College will not admit forty students from the same high school, but neither does Boston College wish to reject thirty-five students from the same high school. It's the counselor's responsibility to manage applications so that only qualified, interested students apply; in the case above, probably only fifteen of those forty should apply. But if the counselor permits forty students to apply to Boston College every year, and BC rejects thirty-five of them every year, then that counselor will lose credibility (and BC will become annoyed).

Counselors can also lose credibility if they try to sell the college on under-qualified students, perhaps stretching the student's achievements or ability. Colleges rely on complete honesty from counselors, so a counselor caught stretching the truth will lose credibility. The college admissions office will remember who the counselor was and report that information to other top colleges. Why would a counselor stretch the truth, and how would a college know? First, recall that counselors have many competing priorities. Perhaps the principal is upset because no one has been admitted to Harvard or Yale in a decade; she told the counselor to make sure that someone this year is admitted to one of those colleges. It seems irrational, but it happens. Counselors also stretch the truth in response to pressure from parents; maybe an overbearing, relentless mother said, "You better get my son into Penn, or you'll hear from my husband—and he's lawyer!" So the counselor pushes the under-qualified son a little too hard because she doesn't want to hear from the lawyer-husband! There are a million little ways to sully a relationship. Most college counselors have relationships with admissions personnel; they meet them, often, several times each year. If students from your high school are having great difficulty getting accepted to a particular college, it may be because your counselor has a poor relationship or little credibility with that college.

Most colleges track the progress of students so they will know how well students from different high schools performed. If they admitted a few students based largely on the counselor's assurance and these students performed very poorly in college, then the admissions office will no longer accept the counselor's assurances.

The moral of the story is two-fold: one, don't pressure your counselor to say anything that isn't completely true or to stretch an accomplishment in the slightest (this is true for parents as well—don't pressure your child's counselor!) because your counselor must maintain a bond of trust with colleges; and two, if you notice a strange pattern in the college admissions of the graduating classes ahead of you, the explanation may be one of the scenarios presented above. If this seems to be the case, you should relax because there's nothing you can do about it. (I suppose you could change high schools and some students do this, but it's not a real option for most students.)

I will delve into one seemingly extreme scenario. There are cases where high school counseling departments have very little credibility with several top colleges. In one recent case, a good high school found it impossible for their students to get accepted to several top colleges primarily because the school "dumped" students on these colleges for several years. This means that the high school counselor from this high school encouraged and promoted the same three colleges to every student, and each year about thirty students (out of a class of about 250) would apply to each college. While each college usually accepted 5-8 students from this school every year, the colleges eventually grew exasperated by the constant, indiscriminate flow of applications from this high school. Now, these top schools only accept the top 1 or 2 students from each class. The other students who might have had a chance of being admitted are now paying the price for the counselor's lack of judgment in previous years. At this high school, many students now transfer to private schools for their junior and senior year in order to improve their chances of being admitted to these top colleges. Some students study abroad their junior and/or senior year, an exciting option that allows them to apply from a different high school. But such drastic measures should only be considered in extreme cases and should be discussed with an independent admissions professional.

Most college counselors are not experts in admissions to top colleges. First, most college counselors did not attend top colleges, so they cannot provide you with first-hand knowledge and experience. I believe this sort of first-hand experience is crucial when going through the process of matching your personality and experience with a college. It is said that the best advice comes from experience (steeped in reflection), and to that end, most college counselors cannot give you the best advice if you're considering Yale, Williams, Drew, New York University, or similar colleges. (As an aside, one should not consider a master degree in counseling or a teacher certification relevant because nearly all such programs are not competitive, even at the best schools such as NYU and Columbia.)

I was surprised to learn that a much-lauded counselor at a prestigious prep school did not even attend a competitive college. (He attended Western Connecticut State!) Other counselors and administrators from around the country admire this man, yet the only colleges he attended were "open admission." His lack of experience became evident after I interviewed his students; most admitted that they didn't find him helpful, particularly in helping them understand the top colleges. As it turns out, this counselor's reputation was mostly due to the fact that the school's academic program, in which he has no input, is outstanding and highly regarded. It was the extraordinary efforts of the students, not this admissions counselor, which led to so many acceptances to Ivy League schools. So keep this in mind: most college counselors have a tremendous amount of book knowledge but no practical experience; they did not attend top colleges; and in some cases, they did not even attend a competitive college. If your counselor cannot provide you with first-hand knowledge of attending a top college, then seek out someone who can. Typically, you need that person's advice to help you discover which colleges best suit your personality, experience, and goals. Most college counselors can help you do this, but they use the college's own literature to match colleges to students, and as you will see later, college literature is very unreliable.

Most counselors took counseling courses in college (and are invariably "certified" in something); however, less than 4% of graduate counseling programs even offer college counseling courses, and very few counselors concentrate in college counseling. In a recent survey, only 30 of 125 graduate counseling programs offered any kind of training in college admissions counseling (even within other courses). This means that 76% of the graduate counseling programs surveyed offered no training whatsoever in college counseling. None. So although most counselors are trained in counseling, the vast majority has not taken any courses in college counseling. When it comes to admissions to top colleges, the majority of counselors are without first-hand experience and without training. In most cases, they learn the vagaries of college admissions while on the job. You may, at times, get the feeling your counselor doesn't know what he's doing; you may be right.

However, your counselor writes a very important recommendation that outlines your strengths and weaknesses as well as your academic performance and ability. You should be nice to your counselor: buy him or her a Christmas present, a birthday present, send her random flowers—whatever seems appropriate. Regardless of what you think of your counselor, it is not an option to express negative feelings. You should try to make your counselor's life as easy as possible by giving her forms early—well before the deadline! Make sure everything you give him or her is neat and presentable, in order, and completed (as much as you can complete it).

Your counselor (and the counseling office) can be of great assistance when it comes to forms and college information. The counseling office should have view books and course catalogues from nearly every college in America and several foreign colleges; it should have many copies of every form needed, including SAT/SAT II registration forms, the Common Application, and financial aid forms (these are all available online, but it's nice to pick up copies first from your counselor's office, complete the hard copy, then complete the online version). The counseling office should also be able to allay any confusion regarding the college admissions and financial aid processes, including forms and deadlines. Many admissions offices have parent volunteers to help with the burden of assisting so many students. Usually, these volunteers can effectively answer your questions about forms and deadlines. You should use your college admissions office when you're first starting the college search—you will be able to browse through many college guides and view books without making any phone calls. It's an easy way to get acquainted with the college world when you're beginning your college search.

You should try to meet with your counselor as early as possible (middle of 10th grade at the latest) to get an idea of what he or she thinks of you. Your counselor will need to write a very important recommendation for you, so his opinion is germane to your success. If your counselor's opinion of you and your work is anything less than enthusiastic, then you must find out why and fix it. How? Ask your counselor! ("Why do you think I'm an average student, and how can I improve?") Lousy students aren't necessarily bad; lousy students who don't care are. If your grades are bad, then any counselor would be impressed if you met with him or her and sought guidance on how to improve. If you've done less than stellar, then your counselor will be happy to help you improve. After all, your counselor's job is to get you admitted to a good college; they want to help you. If you're willing to work a little, then your counselor will be willing to do everything he can to help. Don't be afraid to be honest with your counselor ("I didn't do any work in that class and that's why I got a C") as long as you are now trying to turn over a new leaf ("But now I want to do everything I can to get straight A's—even in a few AP classes").

Meeting with your counselor early also has another bonus: you must make your counselor aware of your special and unique qualities. A great counselor recommendation will speak highly of both your grades and your extracurricular activities. How will a counselor know about your extracurricular activities unless you tell him? You should meet with your counselor regularly from 10th grade until the college application process is over so that you can improve your counselor's opinion of you, improve your chances of being admitted to a top college, and improve your counselor's understanding of what makes you unique. The bottom line: your counselor's recommendation is very important; your opinion of your counselor is not. You must make friends!

When the process is over, you should send your counselor a thank-you note and perhaps a small present. In most cases, you should do this regardless of where you were accepted. Think of this: what if you hate the college you attend? Then you will wish to transfer, and you will need your high school counselor's assistance. So even if you think your counselor did a lousy job, you may need him later—besides most counselors are over—worked and underpaid.

The High School. No two high schools are alike. Maybe that seems obvious, but it causes great confusion to colleges. Colleges have a very difficult time comparing high schools and inevitably believe that an A at one school isn't equal to an A at another school. Furthermore, your high school may not be "college preparatory," may not offer any or many AP courses, or may not offer many rigorous academic courses (but instead has a dozen so-called "culinary arts" electives). The quality of your high school is crucial, and you can't do anything about it.

If you are in a rather poor high school or school system, like the Chicago or Los Angeles public system, then you may actually be at an advantage. Oddly, colleges are particularly interested in attracting students who make it out of bad schools; this means you should be one of the top students in your graduating class, but don't let the lack of AP courses stop you from applying to top schools. If your school doesn't offer AP courses, then take extra SAT IIs. The point is this: do not let a mediocre or bad school limit your goals. I know of many students who are trapped in awful public schools, and they were actually recruited by top colleges. Most top colleges only get 2-3 applicants (if that many) from the Chicago school system, so every one is prized and accorded every advantage in the admissions process. A poor minority student from a Chicago public school could probably get accepted to a top college with an 1150 on the SAT (which may be 400 points above the average SAT score for that school). Every college is particularly interested in the academic superstars from poor, awful, inner-city public schools—and you can be that superstar. Ironically, the high school students who could benefit the most from earning AP college credits are those from poor, inner-city schools, which typically offer few (if any) AP courses; if such a student were aggressive in taking AP courses, he might be able to enter college as a sophomore, save $30,000 in tuition, and start earning a salary a year earlier.

A few students do actually transfer to private schools in their junior years because they believe their high schools aren't academically challenging. Usually, this is a good idea if it means that you will receive more personal attention, a wider choice of AP courses, and a more serious academic atmosphere. Similarly, some students who attend mediocre schools take a PG year ("PG" is post graduate, which is a 13th year of high school). That may not sound like fun, but it may mean the difference between attending the college of your dreams and the local state university. During a PG year, students can improve their grades, take rigorous academic courses, and round out their high school education.

You should ask your counselor for your high school's profile so you get an idea of what your school's average numbers are; this profile is particularly important if your school doesn't rank students. The profile will give you a very good idea of where you rank in your class. Is your 3.6 great, average, or poor? Most schools have two profiles. One is the "public relations" profile and is published for prospective parents (sometimes published by the PTA); it generally provides positive information and interesting tidbits. The other profile is usually more hardcore: it's full of numbers and statistics and will give you a very good idea of exactly where you rank in your class (even if your school doesn't officially rank). This hard-core profile is sent to colleges in order to evaluate you; it's also the profile that most administrators, boards of education, and mayors look at. If you simply ask for a profile, you will probably get the public relations version. You should ask for a copy of the profile that's sent to colleges along with your transcript—then you will get an idea of what colleges will think of your academic performance.

Students in private schools can look up their school's public relations profile in Peterson's *Guide to Independent Secondary Schools* (which is probably in your school's library). However, you should still ask for the profile that's sent with your transcript. The profile in Peterson's *Guide* is 70% marketing fluff.

The College Admissions Office. To a large degree, the application process is an effort by you to coordinate communication between your high school counseling office and the college's admissions office. You will need to call the college admissions office in your junior year to arrange for campus tours and to receive information. Contact them to arrange for an interview, to visit classes, or to stay overnight. Most admissions offices are managed by a dean and staffed by several admissions officers, administrative assistants, and technicians. Usually, these admissions personnel are younger recent graduates who are readers/regional specialists and older employees who have worked in the office for decades. The admissions office also employs tour guides, who are usually undergraduates trained to sell the college. Keep in mind that campus tours, usually done in groups of 5-20 prospective students and their parents, are not intimately connected to the admissions office. Most offices will note that you attended a tour, but that's it. The tour guide is not grading your behavior on the tour and putting a note in your file (unless, of course, your behavior is unusually horrific).

Here's one of the great ironies of the admissions process: most of the high-ranking admissions officers are not graduates of the colleges they represent and, in fact, probably would not have been admitted had they applied (and they may have). The full-time employees in most admissions offices consist of the two groups mentioned earlier: the young, eager graduates and the older, often cynical, employees who have worked at the college for several decades. Usually, the younger recent graduates work for 2-3 years and then leave, so they rarely gain a position of stature or authority. The admissions officers with stature and authority are the older employees who are typically not graduates of top colleges; these older employees not only have seniority, but they usually sit on all of the committees charged with carrying out the college's long-term goals. These people, who have not graduated from a top college, are judging you. So if you actually have a shot at getting accepted to a top college, then the two people you will deal with the most—your high school counselor and the admissions officer for your region—probably are not and could not be top college graduates.

To be blunt: if you have a good shot at a top college, it's more than likely you are more intelligent than your high school counselor and most of the admissions officers reading your file. Chances are you scored much higher than they did on the SAT, your grades are much better than theirs, you aced classes that they wouldn't even understand, and you're capable of writing an essay with subtleties that would escape them. The fact is: graduates of top colleges do not become lifelong high school counselors or admissions officers. Those jobs don't pay well, they quickly become monotonous and unchallenging, and the rewards are not great. Top college graduates in those fields usually get out within a few years (though they may go into a related field, usually in the private sector).

So does this observation have any practical implications? Yes, many. First, take everything your counselor says with a grain of salt. If he didn't attend a top college, then his advice should be all "nuts and bolts" (deadlines, facts, and so forth). Additionally, your counselor may suggest changes to your college essays with which you disagree. You may be right (and your counselor may be wrong), but, in most cases, your counselor's opinion is meaningful because your audience in the admissions office is similar to your counselor. If your counselor says that the subtleties in your essay escape him, he may simply be a poor reader. But then again, the admissions officer reading your essay is, most likely, also a poor reader. So don't take your counselor's opinion as an indictment of your writing, but his opinion will probably reflect the admissions reader's opinion.

Second, because most admissions officers are middle-income college bureaucrats who probably did not and could not be admitted to the top college they represent, they can exhibit some strange tendencies. While these tendencies are not necessarily prevalent, it's a good idea to protect your application against them. Some admissions officers are bitter people who think it is their job to right all the wrongs of the world; they resent the wealthy New York City student from the all-girls prep school who summers in the south of France. They will hold this student to the highest of standards they can justify in the hopes of rejecting her. Meanwhile, they will admit the middle-income Hispanic student from Brooklyn, even though neither he nor his parents speak Spanish, both his parents are college graduates, he lives in a $350,000 condo, he scored a 1220 on his SATs and has a B average in school. Simply put: when some admissions officers smell privilege (particularly white suburban privilege), they recoil. If they get the slightest indication of any sort of disadvantage, even if the student isn't truly disadvantaged, they will give that student every benefit of the doubt.

You should take this do-gooder mentality into consideration when completing every part of your application. Admissions officers usually do not review financial aid forms, but they do pay close attention to the parts of the essay that ask about your parent's background, education and employment. They will also notice where you live and what school you attend. Typically, the first reader is a regional reader, and this person will typically know the relative wealth of the communities within the region. If you're from a notoriously wealthy community (i.e. Scarsdale, NY), you attend a top high school, and your father is the CEO of a major company, then you will be tagged by the admissions readers; they will raise the bar very high for you, oftentimes so high that no one could possibly get over it. While most others will need a 1410 to be admitted, you will need a 1460. While a 3.8 gets most others admitted, nothing short of a 4.0 will be acceptable for people like you.

If your father is the CEO of a major company, there's no reason to state this on an application. For employment, simply put the name of the company. If they ask about his position at the company, simply say "management." If your father is a partner at a huge law firm, simply say he's a lawyer; there's no reason to tell the admission people that he's a partner. It will only be used against you. (In fact, in many cases, doctors and lawyers can reasonably state that they are "self-employed.") If your mother is a graduate of Yale medical school, then there's no reason to include "Yale" unless they ask. Simply put "M.D." under "highest degree earned." If your father is a chief advisor to a Senator, put "government employee" unless they ask for specific details. Do not make a point on your application of exhibiting your parents' wealth or stature. That is the fastest way to an admissions reader looking at your SAT scores and saying, "1450? Not good enough."

This advice is important in other areas too. You will be required to list your activities, including work experience, summer activities, and travel. If your family spends the summers at a resort in St. Tropez or at your ranch in Wyoming, do not list it unless you can conceal it as something other than a wealthy person's vacation. Leave off activities such as "horseback riding on Martha's Vineyard" and "yacht racing from Newport to Bermuda" unless you can cloak them. If a do-gooder admissions officer reads activities such as these and then finds no work experience, he will then expect the world of you. He will assume you have wealth and privilege, and will expect that you did something extraordinary with that wealth. While you must report your parents' employment and general background information, there is no need to list activities that will be used unfairly against you. If your list of activities reeks of money, then edit out the offending entries.

And finally (I suppose this is obvious by now), be careful about what topic you choose for your essay. That crazy incident that happened while on holiday on the Greek isle of Santorini is not a good essay topic. Your family's wealth is never a benefit on the application. If your family is inordinately wealthy, the development office will notify the admissions office. Under no circumstances should you display your wealth on an application. If you think it will come across, then I suggest getting a summer job, preferably at a menial job (and not at your parent's place of work). If a do-gooder admissions reader wonders about your economic status, one of the first things they will check is whether or not you've ever had a real job. The assumption is that a very wealthy child would never get a job, particularly a job at McDonalds or the supermarket. (Yes, most admissions officers will view a job flipping burgers quite favorably.)

The admissions officer reading your application may have had to work to pay for college, may have applied to the college he now works for and was rejected, and may begrudge those who can afford prep courses, tutors and nice vacations. Chances are, at least one of the people who reads your application will be someone like this. Since your application is, essentially, a sales pitch, these people are the potential buyers. Be sure that your application doesn't offend any of their do-gooder proclivities.

Is this a case of the inmates running the asylum? In some ways, yes. Most high school counselors and admissions officers are neither great readers nor good scholars; more often than not, they are products of mediocre colleges with undergraduate degrees in non-academic disciplines (such as education). And more often than not, they have some wish to "set the world right." While some are more aggressive than others, you should be aware that there are many activists in nearly every admissions office. Be clear and forthright in your essays, be careful about describing your background, and downplay any advantage you've had. If you're underprivileged, then be specific in answering questions about your background. If you're anything else (middle class or better), then you should be as vague as possible with anything that smells of money. It may seem odd, but when you're applying to college, it's an advantage if your parents didn't attend college, if you're poor, or if you've gone to a notoriously bad high school.

College admissions officers operate under much the same duress that high school counselors do: they have many, often conflicting, priorities. Admissions officers wish to be independent from outside pressures and wish to admit the "best" students. However, of the 1800 available seats in the freshman class, the athletic department wants 500 of them to go to their top recruits. The development department, which is charged with raising money for the college through the alumni association, wants 700 seats to go to the children of alumni. The Diversity Committee and African-American Studies departments insist that the admissions office accept 400 underrepresented minorities (which excludes these presumably over-represented minority groups—Asians, Jews, and Catholics), the music department needs two oboists and four violinists, and the Classics department will disappear unless three-dozen students who intend on majoring in Classics are admitted. To top it off, the university president just walked in to the admissions office and asked, "Why don't we ever admit students from Wyoming?"

If the admissions department accepts all the students on everyone's list, in addition to accepting the top 500 academically qualified students, they would mail out 3,500 acceptance letters. And they know that in an average year, 70% of the accepted students will enroll (2,450 students in this scenario). That's 650 students too many. The problem is that someone will be disappointed; some department won't get every student it wanted; some recruited students will be rejected in the end.

To illustrate how stressful the admissions process can be, consider this: in most cases, the wish lists from coaches, academic departments, and the development/alumni office are often top secret. Coaches do not share information with each other; departments keep the number of applicants they wish admitted secret; the development office makes every effort not to prematurely divulge how much money some families are donating to the school. If the baseball coach does not get all of his top recruits, he wonders if perhaps the football coach got too greedy and demanded too many recruits. Perhaps the basketball team got more players than it needed. The entire process is usually fraught with tension and secrecy, even within the same college.

Most admissions offices take seriously their responsibility to admit the "most qualified" applicants; if they don't, they hear complaints from professors that less-than-qualified students are being admitted. I've even heard complaints from Princeton professors about the quality of athletic recruits, so no college is immune to a persnickety faculty who demand the highest quality students. But the admissions office must admit some less-than-qualified athletes, some recruited minorities, a few legatees, and an oboist for the music department. And, of course, the admission department should aim for geographic diversity. It's one big juggling act—and a very tricky game of diplomacy and politics played out among departments of the college. No one is ever completely pleased with the outcome, and most are consoled by the admissions dean with the words "nothing else could be done."

If you read the admissions guidelines and mission statement of admissions offices, you will usually find double-talk and ambiguity befitting the most mercurial politician. I've long believed that the ambiguity of the statements published by admissions departments is not mostly aimed at students and parents. I believe that many admissions departments would prefer to lay bare their entire admissions process so that only the most qualified applicants would bother to apply. Admissions officers find little joy in sorting through thousands of pieces of mail from students who are grossly under-qualified. I'm sure a few colleges would like to publish their admissions formulae, their indices and their exact requirements so that instead of receiving 14,000 applications for 1,800 openings, they received 3,000 applications, and every one exceedingly qualified.

But the political atmosphere of departments competing for students doesn't allow the admissions office to be so candid. They must play a cat-and-mouse game with the precise parameters of admission not because they wish to keep applicants in the dark, but because they need to keep the athletic director in the dark as to why three of his top soccer recruits were denied admission. A little secrecy provides the admissions office room to maneuver through the minefield of departmental recruiting. Of course, this ambiguity also allows admissions departments to explain why a student with 1100 on the SAT or a C+GPA was admitted to an Ivy League college—this is why admissions offices say "there's no formula" and "we don't admit by the numbers." To a degree, both statements are true. But the fact is that most students are admitted based on class rank and test scores. Period. Colleges "don't admit by the numbers" when it comes to recruited students.

Through December, most admissions offices are helpful, prompt, and well-organized. However, once the applications start flooding in, things start to become hectic. It's wise to get all your questions to the admissions offices by late October, before the rush hits them.

Your Parents. Your parents should help you understand the meaning and benefit of attending college, as well as advise you on selecting a good college. Some parents are very helpful, while other parents are detrimental to the process. In most cases, the less your parents are involved, the better. Your parents should not call the colleges, harass your counselor, register you for tests and so forth. You should be doing all these things. If your parents are too involved, a college will often pick up on it—and it's not a good thing.

Your parents should help you weigh the pros and cons of each college, but they should not actually choose a college for you. If you enroll at a college that your parents choose for you against your will, chances are you will either transfer out or perform very poorly there. The college at which you enroll must be a college of your choosing.

This truth may annoy you, but the single best thing your parents can do for you is offer worldly advice. They understand the world better than you do (in most cases) simply because they've been alive longer and around the block more times than you. Listen seriously to them. If your parents attended a top college, then they probably have some indispensable advice for you. You may be awestruck by colleges; hopefully, your parents won't be and will be able to offer objective guidance. Your parents also know about you. In fact, your parents may know you better than you do! Ask your parents to describe you and listen to what they say. No one is more interested in your well-being than your parents are (of course, I'm assuming you have normal parents).

You. Here's the bottom line on the entire college admissions process: you and only you are responsible for everything. Yes, everything. If your counselor loses a recommendation form, you are responsible. If ETS doesn't mail your SAT scores, you are responsible. If your high school misprints your grades on your transcript, you are responsible. If you assume an attitude of complete responsibility from the beginning, you will avoid the many mistakes that some make.

You must take total responsibility for every aspect of the admissions process because, in the end, only you will be accepted to or rejected from the colleges to which you're applying. ETS has millions of customers; your high school counselor probably has 150-800 students to deal with, and your parents have many responsibilities—you need to take charge and make sure everything is in place. If you give your counselor a form to complete, follow-up a week or two later to see if it was completed. Do not assume anything!

What if someone makes a mistake? Perhaps your counselor loses a form or a teacher forgets to write a recommendation. First, don't get angry—mistakes happen, and in most cases, these problems are honest mistakes. (There are lazy or disorganized teachers, but you shouldn't ask them for a recommendation in the first place.) And don't forget that in most cases, you will need to continue to work with the person, so yelling at them will only hurt your relationship. And on the off chance you get to college and decide you don't like it, you will need your high school counselor and teachers to help you transfer to another college. So getting angry with someone will usually backfire.

Second, if a mistake happens, then you need to swing into action. Do not assume that the person who made the mistake will correct it. You must correct it! Here are a few tips so that you can stay on top of things:

- Always give people a deadline, even if it's several weeks into the future. Then follow-up near the deadline.
- Always remain calm; never yell at anyone.
- Create a checklist for every college. Checks items off as they are finished; do not assume that an item is finished unless you've personally investigated it.
- The sooner you start the process, the more likely mistakes will not be made or can be fixed. Students who start completing applications December 20th may run into some problems that can't be fixed by the application deadline.

Friends, Relatives, Coaches. There are many other people who may wish to help you. If you know anyone who has attended the college you wish to attend, you should discuss the college with him or her. This is true even if he attended the college 50 years ago—alumni usually receive mailers and updates from the college and may still be involved with college events. Either way, they can probably provide you with a bit of useful advice.

You should only involve others, such as family friends and coaches, if they have something substantive to add. A coach is great if you intend on playing a sport in college; a coach is not useful if he just want to "put in a good word for you," and you don't intend on playing a sport. The same is true of family friends, even friends who are alumni of the college you wish to attend. It's okay if you're using someone to write a formal recommendation, but it's cumbersome and often annoying to colleges if you're cramming your application full of extra recommendations. So use others for advice, but remember that only you are in charge of your future.

Private Counselors. In 1990, the head of Harvard admissions said, "Some of the best high school guidance people I know are now independent counselors." A private counselor (also called an admissions consultant) is someone you hire to assist you with the college admissions process; this person is in addition to your high school counselor and typically assists you with selecting colleges, writing admissions essays, completing application forms, preparing for interviews, and formulating an overall strategy. Most private counselors will also have a wealth of good information and advice for you. Here's all you need to know about private counselors: colleges despise them. Why is that important? Colleges strongly dislike private counselors specifically because these counselors give students a big advantage—and colleges think this is unfair. Of course, if God gives someone the gift of great athletic ability, which results in that student being recruited by top colleges, then that student has a significant unfair advantage too. Colleges approve of some unfair advantages and disapprove of others, depending on which way the winds of opinion are blowing that year. The bottom line: if you can afford a private counselor, then you should hire one.

Just as the gifted athlete needs to work in order to be recruited by colleges, you will also need to work to be admitted by top colleges. A great private counselor will not magically get you admitted to a top college; your grades, test scores and hard work will. But a counselor can turn a very good application into a great one. Most top counselors are former successful high school counselors, former college admissions officers, or other professionals who are largely occupied with the college admissions process. Unlike your high school counselor, most private counselors only work with 15-25 students at a time (instead of 150-400) and don't have a slew of unrelated responsibilities such as scheduling classes, writing hall passes, tracking sick days and excused absences, and so forth. All private counselors do is college admissions, which is usually why they are so good at it. There is simply no way any high school counselor can spend an adequate amount of time with every student. It's physically impossible. During the admissions season (Sept.-Dec.), I spend about 2-3 hours each week working with each student (which is why I can typically only work with 15-25 students at a time). It's simply not possible for a high school counselor with 200 students to spend this amount of time with each student as well as fulfill all his other responsibilities.

Most private counselors charge $200-$600 for a few hours of college selection advice; comprehensive fees for assisting you throughout the admissions process for 5-8 colleges can range from $1200 to $5000. Price does not always indicate quality. I suggest meeting with the counselor once to see if you think this person can really help you and proceeding with the counselor that inspires the most confidence. Getting references seems like a good idea, but many top college counselors do not keep reference lists readily available because their clients do not wish to be bothered. (If you paid $4000 for a private counselor, you probably wouldn't want to be bothered with a bunch of phone calls either.) Most top counselors respect the privacy of their clients, so references are not always an option.

It should be remembered that nearly all college admissions personnel have some degree of dislike for private counselors. Some private counselors take an active role in the admissions process (by calling the admissions office, for example); private counselors should, in almost every case, only work with the student and parents and be invisible to admissions offices. You should avoid private counselors who say that they work with admissions offices. The only exception to this rule is for students who are learning-disabled or physically challenged in some way. Colleges understand that these students may need more help than their high school can possibly provide, so they may not be troubled by the presence of a private counselor.

Test Prep Courses & Books. I review test prep companies later in the book, but for now I'll quickly address their place in the admissions process. There are many companies that provide SAT, ACT, and other prep courses and tutoring services. Do you need these services? Yes. Prep courses consistently prove that they significantly increase test scores; in fact, the evidence is so consistent that even the College Board/ETS (the people who own and make the SAT) have started providing for-profit test preparation. The bottom line: test prep works. Most courses range from $500 to $1000 and tutoring usually ranges from $1500 to $4000. Private tutors are the most effective; if you cannot afford a tutor or a course, then buy a book. But you must do something to improve your test scores.

About 80% of the techniques and advice you will get from test prep courses and books is the same. The difference is the emphasis and the qualifications of the teachers. See the section later in this book for a review of the different courses and books.

On-line Resources. You can do almost anything (and everything) on-line. But the only aspects of the admissions process that you should do on-line are (1) basic college research, (2) to get essay questions early, and (3) to search for financial aid information. Nearly every other aspect of the admission process should be done the old-fashioned way. (See the section later in this book regarding on-line applications.) A later chapter will cover useful online resources.

Chapter 8

Getting Started

"I have a friend who started the college admissions process when
he was 2 years old. I started it last week. So either he's wasted a lot of
time or I have no chance of getting admitted to Cornell."

Ready. Set. Panic. When should you start the college admissions process? The answer may surprise you: college-bound students should start the admissions process as soon as possible, preferably in the freshman or sophomore year. Here are a few mistakes students make when they start the admissions process late (end of junior year) and a few reasons why starting the college admissions process today is important:

- Most high schools require less to graduate than colleges require for admission, so you could enter your senior year without the courses necessary to apply to college—even many very good high schools do not fully inform their students of all the courses they need in order to apply to very competitive colleges.

- Different colleges are interested in different academic backgrounds, so the classes you take in your sophomore and junior years should correspond to the type of colleges in which you're interested.

- Avoid the "Culinary Arts" courses. Too many students take non-academic electives in 10th and 11th grade and then decide at the end of 11th grade that they want to apply to top colleges. The sooner you start thinking about college, the sooner you will start taking your course-work seriously—and a few cooking classes in high school can mitigate an otherwise good transcript.

- Your college counselor probably has between 80 and 400 students to counsel and probably does not have the time to adequately address all of your questions. Counselors usually focus on the top 10% of the class and try to help the rest as best they can. If you start early and use a private counselor, then you won't need to rely too much on your over-worked high school counselor.

- Don't take the SAT unprepared, and don't take it for the first time in May—you will end up gambling with a senior year score and may not be able to apply early admission.

- And students who don't plan ahead or seek the advice of a professional often make mistakes such as waiting until the end of their junior year to take a leadership role in an extracurricular activity, giving their first interview at their first-choice college, and requesting an alumni interview instead of an admissions office interview.

But perhaps most importantly, it's best to begin the college admissions process early in order to set goals. The sooner you set goals, the more relevant your high school work will seem to you. First, buy two college guides. I recommend buying two because most college guides contain ridiculous mistakes that you may not catch. Kaplan's recent college guide ranked the University of Central Florida (UCF) on the same competitive level as Columbia University. For college insiders, this was a bad joke (and an atrocious mistake), but you may not catch this mistake. UCF is a four-year "community" college, geared towards non-competitive and commuter students. It isn't in the same league as Columbia; in fact, it's one of the worst colleges in Florida. Similarly, Princeton Review's guide recently ranked Laurence College equal to Columbia; while better than UCF, Laurence was admitting nearly every qualified applicant—hardly in the same league as Columbia. And the *Fiske* guide stated something that can only be described as idiotic: it claimed that New College, the "honors" college of Florida (and a very good school) was named thus because it's new (as opposed to being old). In fact, New College is named after New College, Oxford. If you buy a few college guides, you will be more likely to spot these mistakes.

College guides are also tricky because while some guides are non-partisan, most are written by alumni or admissions officers of the college being reviewed. In fact, most college guides, including Princeton Review's and Peterson's, solicit payment from the colleges being "reviewed." Obviously, a review of a college written by alumni or admissions officers will not be objective and therefore not be very helpful. Many college guides have very cozy relationships with the colleges, so take everything you read with a grain of salt.

Make a list of a dozen colleges in which you're interested and their admissions requirements. (We will discuss both later). Once you have this list, you now have your set of goals. You know the grades, the test scores, and the extracurricular activities you will need to get accepted. I cannot stress enough the importance of setting goals. If you put this list of colleges and admissions requirements on your refrigerator in 9th or 10th grade, you will (probably) make the admissions process much easier for yourself—by the time you get to the fall of your senior year, everything will be in place.

Chapter 9

You in 12th Grade

"I never thought about being a senior when I was a freshmen. I wish I did. The admissions process would have been so much easier."

If you're in 11th grade or earlier, this chapter is for you. The "You in 12th Grade" exercise will help you discover your strengths, weaknesses, and help you better define your goals. Goal-setting is vital to being successfully admitted to college— in fact, being successfully admitted to a top college is more often the result of early goal-setting than academic ability or intelligence. Those who set their goals in 9th or 10th grade are more likely to achieve them in 12th grade. Ideally, you are starting this exercise in 8th, 9th, or 10th grade. However, completing this exercise at any point prior to your senior year will be very helpful.

The purpose of this exercise is simple: by completing a college application 2-4 years prior to your senior year, you will be able to pinpoint your weaknesses. This allows you to set goals to improve these weak areas. By knowing early exactly what top colleges are looking for and exactly what you can offer them, you should be able to evaluate and improve your chances of being admitted to a top college.

In this exercise, you will complete two college applications. The first one will be the application of someone who was successfully admitted to college. You will use a college directory to get all the information needed to complete this. The second application will be for you, using your current information. You will then compare the applications, find your greatest weaknesses, and start to improve them. This exercise will take all the surprise out of entering 12th grade and suddenly realizing that Princeton requires great grades.

1. Goal Setting: Choose a Few Colleges To Set Your Goals.

Buy a college directory and pick two or three competitive or top colleges in which you're interested. I know it's very early (you may only be in 8th or 9th grade), but try to pick a few colleges that seem to interest you. You're using these colleges for comparative purposes only; you're not committing yourself in any way. If you're not sure which colleges interest you, read the chapters "Looking At Colleges: Comparing, Choosing & Applying" and "The CASIS."

2. Tools to Set Your Goals: Get Two College Applications.

Go to your counselor's office and pick up two copies of the Common Application (if you're in high school) or go to www.commonapp.org and download a copy. You can also go to the web site of any top college and download their application (for example, at www.princeton.edu or www.yale.edu). If you have a specific college in which you're interested, then go to that college's web site and download their application. Using either the Common Application or a specific college's application is okay—just be sure to have two copies of the application.

3. You In 12th Grade: Complete One Application As If It Came From a Successful Candidate.

Put your name, address, and other personal information on both applications. Now, imagine it's the fall of your senior year, and you're applying to the best of the colleges you chose in Step 1. Also imagine that all of your statistics match the averages listed under this top college in the college guide. The average SAT score is a 1260, and you have a 1280; the average GPA is a 3.6, and that's exactly what you have! Using the college directory, complete one of the applications with the information from the best of the colleges in which you're interested. For example, if you're interested in Penn, U. Michigan and NYU, then complete one of the applications with the information listed under University of Pennsylvania in the college directory. What is Penn's average SAT score? Fill that in on one of your applications. What is Penn's average GPA? Fill that in also. For a few of the other items, refer to the chapter "You & The Top Candidates" in this book. That chapter will give you a good idea of what a top candidate will have under awards, honors, extracurriculars, and so forth. Fill in everything except for the essay. (Assume that the essay is great.) When you're done, you should have one completed application (excluding an essay) for your top choice college for which you used all the information from the college directory—it has your name on the top, but it has the academic and extracurricular information from an average person who was admitted. This application represents what you should be in 12th grade if you want to be a competitive applicant to that college. Regardless of the college, you should fill in at least 30+community service hours per year, 1-2 sports, 2-3 clubs with leadership roles in at least one of them, at least 1-2 AP courses, and at least 3-4 awards.

4. You Now: The Real You Completes the Second Application.

Complete the second application as if you were applying with all your actual information. Put in your name, address, and everything it asks for. When you arrive at test scores, use your PSAT scores, or if you're in 8th-9th grade, use your SATs from the Duke/Johns Hopkins Talent search (if you participated). If you have no test scores, I suggest obtaining a free SAT from your counselor's office, requesting one from ETS (www.ets.org), or buying the College Board's *10 Real SATs* and taking one of them. Fill in your current grades, extracurricular activities, honors and awards from the past three years. (If you've just started 9th grade, use your three middle-school years to complete the application.) Complete the section on extracurricular activities, community service, sports, honors, and awards, and write the essay. For the essay, write a rough draft, have your parents read it, and rewrite it until you're satisfied. This entire process may take as long as a month.

5. You Today and Tomorrow: Compare and Contrast.

Once these applications are complete, read the rest of this book. Then you will be able to compare the "You Now" application to the successful "You In 12th Grade" application. Take a bright yellow marker and highlight the parts of the "You Now" application that need the most work. Is it community service? Grades? The level of the classes you're taking? Check the college directory and find a few colleges in which you're interested; do you meet their application requirements? Are your grades average? Above average? How are your test scores? The following is a list of all the areas you may need to improve and what you'll minimally need to apply successfully to a top college; how do your areas compare?

1. Level of Coursework (honors classes leading to AP classes; AP classes; few or no non-academic electives).
2. Grades (A- or better).
3. Test Scores (85th percentile or better).
4. Sports (Active participant in 2 sports; leadership role in 11th/12th grade).
5. Community Service (50+hours per year).
6. Extracurricular activities (participate in 2 clubs, hobbies, or activities outside of school; potential leadership role).
7. Awards & Honors (recognized academic or extracurricular success in 3-4 areas).

List the top three areas in which you need to work, and create a plan to improve these areas. If you're in 8th-10th grade, you will probably have many areas that need improvement; this is okay (and to be expected). Your goal is to get everything in place by the beginning of 12th grade. Be patient, and set realistic short-term goals. Once you meet your goals, review your application again, and set new goals.

You should keep the "You in 12th Grade" application handy and repeat this exercise every summer. Complete a new "You Now" application each summer, and compare it to the prior year's application and the "You in 12th Grade" application.

Are you improving? Are your grades getting better? Is your essay better? Are you earning more awards? Your goal by the time you need to complete the actual application in the beginning of your senior year is to have your "You Now" application match the "You in 12th Grade" application as well as the ideal applications described in this book.

Here are a few notes to help guide you in this process:

I. If you're in 8th-9th grade, your test scores—the SAT in most cases—will be significantly lower than they will be when you take the actual test in 11th grade. You should add 150-200 points to your 8th or 9th grade SAT score in order to project your 11th grade score. For example, a SAT score of 900 in 8th grade would roughly translate to a score of 1100 in 11th grade. This translation system is far from perfect, but it will help give you an idea of what your scores will be 2-3 years from now. (Unfortunately, this means that those who score a 1450 in 11th grade are often scoring in the 1200-1300 range in 9th grade). Keep in mind that working with a SAT tutor for a few months in 10th-11th grade can add another 150-200 points to your score.

II. Although your test scores will be low, your grades will provide a fairly accurate indication of how you will perform 2-3 years from now. Students who get great grades in 8th-9th grades often continue to get great grades in 11th grade; similarly, if you're a C- student now, chances are you will be a C- student in 11th grade unless you make a concerted effort to earn better grades. Your grades will not automatically improve with the years; you need to work on them.

III. Similar to your grades, your current extracurricular activities, community service, awards, honors, and everything else gives a good indication of what your application will look like when you're in 12th grade. Chances are if you don't participate in extracurricular activities in 6th-8th grade, you won't magically start participating in them in 10th-12th grade. If your application is sparse in these areas, you need to start working on them right away. Now that you know exactly what colleges are looking for, start working now to give them what they want.

IV. The essay is the most difficult to judge, but you should write it. After you write the essay, read the chapter in this book on the college essay; this will help you judge your own essay. Have your parents read this book and your essay. The quality of the writing is important, but the subject of the essay is much more important. You should note that colleges are looking for individuality, honesty, maturity and leadership skills. These qualities are not developed magically. A little effort over a 2-3 year period will help develop these areas. If you have little (or nothing) to write about, then you need to set out to create something, put yourself in a leadership situation that shows maturity and initiative.

V. What should you look for in your application? First, look for areas you can improve. Second, look for areas of individuality that you can develop. What if your application looks awful? There's no need to throw in the towel; colleges aren't so much interested in stellar 9th and 10th grade years as much as they are interested in steady improvement. It's okay if your freshman grades are mediocre as long as your sophomore grades are much better and your junior grades even better. Just make sure that your grades are improving and your courses are getting more difficult. A few very strong grades in AP classes in 11th and 12th grades can mitigate a bad 9th grade. Preferably, your freshman and sophomore grades should be good, but if they're not, you still have a chance of making it into a top college as long as you dramatically improve. (Such improvement shows determination and maturity.) Check out the chapter "You Make The Call" later in this book for more guidance on this topic.

VI. Continue to refer to the "You Year By Year" chapter of this book as you complete a new "You Now" application each year.

VII. Take your completed application to your college counselor and ask, "How can I improve this?" Showing your counselor that you're seriously working on your college application early should be impressive; remember that your counselor needs to write a very important recommendation for you. The more you ingratiate yourself, the better that recommendation will probably be.

VIII. If you change your top college choice, complete another "You in 12th Grade" application using your new top choice's information.

IX. If you wish to push yourself a little or if you're approaching your "You in 12th Grade" application, then you should complete another "You in 12th Grade" application using the college's top statistics (instead of the average stats). For example, the college may have reported that their SAT scores for the 25th to 75th percentile of students admitted were 1200-1300, so you entered "1250" onto your "You in 12th Grade" application—but if you are nearing (or broke) 1200, then complete a new application using the top score (1300).

X. The primary purpose of this exercise is to get you to look seriously at a college application early. Too many students look at a college application for the first time in 12th grade and say, "oh, I didn't know they were going to ask for community service" or "gee, I didn't think they'd want four years of math." Often, it's too late to do anything. The sooner you look seriously at college applications, the less likely anything will surprise you. But do not obsess over this exercise; it should help you gain control over your future and relieve stress, not cause more stress.

Chapter 10

You Year-By-Year

"It would have been nice if the guidance office gave me a checklist in ninth grade. I kept finding out what I was supposed to be doing after it was too late. What, I should have taken AP U.S last year? Whatever."

Here is a brief list of the activities you should accomplish each year. This list is very prescriptive, but it shouldn't take the place of your common sense and proclivities (if you hate the piano, stop—don't do it solely for the purpose of applying to college.) This is the list so many students and parents tell me they wish they had. To get a good appreciation for what it takes to get admitted to a top college, read the entire list, regardless of what grade you're currently in.

9th Grade

1. Take the hardest courses you can, either honors or AP (if possible). Your coursework should enable you to take an AP course in 10th grade (if possible) and several AP courses in 11th and 12th grade and should include Algebra (or Geometry/Trig), a foreign language (preferably French, German, Latin or ancient Greek), a fine art, and a hard science with lab. Your school will probably also require an English and a history course. Avoid non-academic electives (the dubiously titled "Family Sciences" such as cooking, sewing, checkbook balancing, and so forth). In all cases you should take the most difficult courses available to you—even if your grades suffer a bit.

2. Find one sport you love and work as hard as you can. (It's great if it's a somewhat obscure sport, such as squash or luge.) Join the school's sports team, join a club team during the summer or during the off-season (a club team is operated in your community, not by your school), and travel, if possible, to national training camps. You may play more than one sport, but your goal should be to excel in one sport, hopefully becoming captain of the team in 11th or 12th grade.

3. Find one extracurricular activity you love, and excel at it. Similar to the advice above, you should participate both within your school and without. I recommend a fine art: play the violin, paint, throw pottery, sculpt. Take lessons from a professional, and try to gain recognition for your achievement. (Simply "playing the piano" doesn't really count: anyone can "play the piano." Enter competitions, play in junior orchestras, and record a "junior orchestra" CD.) If you have limited artistic inclinations, then find another "hobby." Often, the hobbies available to you will depend on many variables, including what part of the country you live in; they may range from boat-building and woodworking to origami and gardening. Just remember these rules: stick with it, excel at it, and gain outside recognition for it.

4. Pick one in-school activity, and excel at it. These activities are the ones that are specifically school-related, such as student government, debate team, and high school newspaper. Depending on your school, some of these commitments may not be very great, so feel free to pick two activities. The key here is to do it for all four years of high school. Student government, debate team, and school newspaper are three great choices; however, remember that your goal is to excel so that by the time you're a senior, you're the president of the student body, debate team captain, or newspaper editor.

5. Community Service. Many schools require you to volunteer—often as little as 15-30 hours per year—at a local charity. Even if your school does not require this, you should do it. I won't pontificate on how this service will make you a better person, but it will. The key is to find something that interests you: the inner-city food bank may be okay, but perhaps the local literacy program or museum interests you more. Nearly every activity has some charity related to it: like horses? volunteer to teach handicapped children to ride. You should aim to complete at least 75-100 hours of community service per year for each of your high school years (I know of no high school that requires more). If that seems like a lot of hours, consider that you can rack up 80 hours with only 2 full "work weeks" during your summer vacation. Many students take trips during their summer vacations to build churches in Guatemala or work in orphanages in Romania. Often, a two-week hurricane relief trip to the Dominican Republic can earn you 100-150 hours. Such trips are priceless.

6. Read. The best advice I can give you is to read as much as you can. What should you read? Big thick books that aren't made for the mass-market. In order to improve your reading skills—and "improve" means being challenged—you need to read books that have some complexity. Books made for the mass-market are designed to be simple so that everyone can easily understand and enjoy them. It's okay if you read a book that's very complex, and you don't fully understand it. After you read it the first time, go back and read it again. Some of the novels you

are required to read for English are good; some are not. Unfortunately, many of the books you read in English class are not very complex. For fun but challenging books try Fielding's *Tom Jones*, Cervantes's *Don Quixote*, Thackery's *Vanity Fair*, and Dickens' *Pickwick Papers*. For something a bit more modern, pick up anything by Graham Greene, and for a real challenge, read something by Henry James. Your reading need not be limited to fiction. If you prefer history, you should read books that are well-written; unfortunately, historians are not always good writers. For interesting, well-written history, try Paul Johnson's *Modern Times* or J. M. Roberts' *A History of Europe*. For straight vocabulary improvement, I would be remiss not to mention Norman Lewis' *Word Power Made Easy*. This book is somewhat boring (as any vocabulary book is), but it is the undisputed best book of its kind and has been since first published in 1949. Just remember that improving your vocabulary takes time, and the more time you have, the more you can improve your vocabulary. And finally: improving your reading skills will improve your PSAT and SAT scores and will also help you in (almost) every other facet of life. It's a simple truth: great communicators get more for themselves in life, get more done, and are better understood. Don't let poor reading skills and a poor vocabulary limit you. You can solve both problems by reading good books.

7. Find out if you have the same counselor for all four years of high school. If you do, then your current college counselor will write your college recommendations in a few years—get to know the counselor and be extremely nice. Always behave well, be motivated, and be involved. Buy this person gifts for the holidays and at the end of the school year. (You can't really buy them gifts in your senior year, so the time to do it is in 9th-11th grades.) You need to kiss this person's derriere! If you don't have the same counselor for all four years, then you should still be nice because this person is probably putting a few notes in your file, and your senior—year counselor will probably review this file. Either way, a good impression goes a long way.

8. Complete the "You in 12th Grade" exercise.

10th Grade

1. Continue to take the most difficult courses you can, including many honors courses. Try to take one AP course (usually modern European history). You should also take a foreign language, a hard science with lab, and Geometry/Trig or Algebra II. Your courses should be preparing you to take AP U.S. history next year, Calculus (honors or AP) in 11th or 12th grade, an AP science and foreign language in 11th or 12th grade, and AP English in 12th grade. Once again, steer clear of non-academic electives (other than physical education and the fine arts) and the soft-sciences (which is anything other than biology, chemistry, and

physics). Your school may require a health or nutrition course; if this is unavoidable, c'est la vie.

2. Continue the sports, extracurricular, and community service recommendations suggested above. And yes, continue to read.

3. Take the PSAT if it's offered at your school. (Remember, this is a fake PSAT, so it's only practice.)

4. Plan to do something interesting or impressive over the summer. Take a course at the community college. Travel. Compete in a regional or national event. Start a business. Get an internship at a laboratory. Learn to scuba dive. Volunteer at a political campaign. Write Op. Eds for your local newspaper. Anything—just don't sit around the house. Many people ask me: does a job count? It depends on what it is and why you have it. No college will be impressed that you worked at the GAP to earn money so that you could travel to a Dave Matthews festival. However, if you needed to work to help support your family or if you held a particularly impressive job, then your employment will help your chances of getting admitted. Remember: no typical hourly job that you have for typical reasons will help you get into college, particularly if you only held the job for a few weeks over the summer. If you do get a job just to earn a little extra money (and to get employee discounts), then try to hold on to the job as long as possible, preferably throughout the school year. Colleges are always impressed with students who earn good grades in difficult classes while holding down a 15-hour-per-week job. See #7 and #8 under "9th Grade" (above).

11th Grade

1. You should be in all honors courses and AP U.S. history. If possible, it's beneficial to take one more AP this year (a math, science and/or foreign language). If your school doesn't allow juniors to take AP courses, complain vociferously. You should be preparing to take 2-4 AP courses your senior year (for a total of 3-9 AP courses). Continue taking hard-science courses (with labs) and foreign languages. Eschew non-academic electives and soft-science courses.

2. Consider the colleges to which you're applying, and your potential major at these colleges. Plan your course work accordingly. I will discuss this planning in detail later, but the idea is: most colleges will ask you what your intended major is, and they will admit candidates with a wide variety of intended majors (many English and bio majors, a good dose of math majors, a few Latin and fine arts majors). It's advantageous for female applicants to say their intended major is "chemistry" instead of "English" because the college will get an overabundance of female English majors. However, you cannot claim that your intended major is chemistry if you've never taken chemistry (or only taken one chemistry course

and received a C- in it). The "Intended Major" strategy is worth considering when choosing your courses for 11th grade.

3. Prepare for and take standardized tests. Prepare for the PSAT. Take the PSAT in October. Prepare for the SAT from November to March and take the SAT in January or March/April. Take the SAT II Writing, Math, and a third one of your choice in May/June. See the chapter on testing for more information.

4. Tour your 4-10 top colleges. While many students tour colleges over the summer, it's highly preferable that you tour colleges during the academic year. (More on this in a later chapter.)

5. Continue the sports, extracurricular, and community service recommendations suggested under "9th Grade." And yes, continue to read.

6. Travel. Go anywhere. Colleges respect students who have traveled (particularly without your parents, on academic or community-service trips, and for extended periods of time). If possible, spend a semester (or year) of high school abroad. If you have the money, spend a semester or summer in Florence studying art. If you don't have the money, drive to Quebec or Mexico—just get out of town. You can take inexpensive classes over the summer at schools in Canada and Mexico. You can volunteer on archaeological digs in Mexico. Or you can work on Indian reservations in Oklahoma (if you're from Connecticut, then Oklahoma counts as a semi-foreign country). The point is: go somewhere and do something. This helps build real awareness of other communities, helps you develop maturity, and lets colleges know that you can function outside of your usual environment. And once again, it helps if you go without your parents (sorry, mom), and don't take the 5-star hotel package.

7. Do everything within your power to make your counselor love you! This person will write the all-important counselor recommendations, so their opinion of you is very important. If they don't think very highly of you, your applications will suffer tremendously. Buy your counselor lunch, flowers, a Ferrari (if you can afford it and they'll accept it). In any case, treat this person nicely no matter what your opinion is of them.

12th Grade

1. Take as many AP courses as possible—at least 2-3. You should be taking (or have completed) courses in calculus, physics, chemistry, biology (the sciences all with labs), U.S. history, European history, four years of English and four years of a foreign language, and at least two years of a fine art. In addition, your school will probably require physical education, a health/nutrition course, and some sort of world/third world/multicultural history. As usual, avoid the soft-sciences and non-academic electives. If you need to take another course and no academic courses are available to you, investigate the possibility of doing an independent

project or taking a course at your local community college. Your school should give you credit for doing one of these. (If you do an independent project or take a course at the local community college, do not pursue the conspicuously indolent; at your community college, take "The Art of Russian Verse" not "The Art of Russian Cooking.")

2. Take the SAT or SAT IIs in Oct/Nov if you need to; call colleges in July for applications. Narrow your college list to 5-8 colleges (at most). Start writing your application essays and considering who will write your recommendations by early September.

3. Continue with the sports, community service, and other activities as recommended. Ideally, you are captain of some team (football, field hockey, debate), president of something (student government, French club) and/or a leader of something (newspaper editor, chair of student activities committee). You should have 300-400 total community service hours (9th-12th grade) and have been recognized in one extracurricular activity (a fine art or hobby).

4. As odd as this may sound, it's highly beneficial to have accomplished something unusual. You want something on your application that will stand out, something that will stick in the minds of the admissions officials. This unusual accomplishment may be a sport (luge), a musical instrument (the lute), or spending a semester in an unusual country (Lithuania). Having great accomplishments will help, but having a unique accomplishment is even better. How do you know if something is unique? Look around your high school: do other students have similar accomplishments?

Chapter 11

Comparing & Choosing

"There are two kinds of colleges, right?
Good ones and community colleges in Iowa."

As you investigate different colleges, you should keep a few things in mind. First, colleges will ask many questions of you; don't be timid in asking many questions of them. Colleges will want to know everything about you and, if you are applying for financial aid (most students do), everything about your parents' finances. They will poke and prod you in order to determine whether to accept you. You should poke and prod back in order to determine whether or not to pay $75,000-$160,000 for a piece of paper (the diploma). Obviously, a college education should be much more than a piece of paper, but you need to determine this truth before attending a college. You don't want to realize it upon graduation.

Tens of thousands of students transfer out of college every year. This migration happens because many students realize they've made bad choices. Transferring involves going through the entire admissions process all over again. Take your time and be aggressive now so you won't need to go through this entire process again once you're in college.

To a private college, every accepted applicant is the equivalent of a $100,000-$160,000 sale. Only house sales deal with greater sums of money (and real estate commissions are usually only $10,000-$20,000). You should treat the admissions process as a buying experience, and the product costs as much as a typical house. (The average home in American costs about $140,000, which is about what an average education at a top private college costs.) If you were buying something for $100,000, you would really investigate it, right? You would ask tons of questions to be sure you're getting something that's worth $100,000, wouldn't you? No one would buy a car or a house without knowing anything about it and neither should you buy an education without thoroughly investigating all of your options. Despite what private colleges say, price does matter.

How do you decide which colleges to apply to? It's difficult and time consuming. Here are the steps to consider.

Type of College. First, decide if you want a liberal arts education or a specialized education (tech, religious, and so forth). The most recent major studies on the correlation between attending a top university and one's salary in later years show that, in fact, there is no statistically significant correlation. So going to Princeton over Penn State won't make you more employable or wealthier. If you're a Pennsylvania resident, why should you spend the extra $100,000 and attend Princeton instead of Penn State? The answer is: to get that most fundamental but ineffable part of Western culture we call an "education." In the collegiate world, this is referred to as a liberal arts education. Here are descriptions of the many different types of colleges.

Technical Colleges. If you wish to acquire specific skills or skills related to specific vocations, you should attend a public college. If you want a technical education, you should save your money and attend the cheapest, large public university you can find. Public universities almost invariably provide technical and vocational education as well as or better than private schools and at a fraction of the cost; in the long run, a technical education from a private school does not benefit you more than a public education would. However, something should be made clear: if you attend college to get a technical or vocational education, then you are not being educated; you are being trained.

This leads to a logical but (perhaps) controversial conclusion: I can think of no reason why one should attend a highly competitive technical college, such as M.I.T., Stanford, or Cal Tech as an undergraduate. If you can get admitted to one of these colleges, then you can get admitted somewhere far better. If M.I.T. or Stanford has a highly specialized program you wish to enroll in, then do so as a graduate student.

Research Universities. The other major kind of college is the "research" university, called such because it focuses its resources on graduate research. Private schools such as Harvard and Johns Hopkins and large public schools such as University of Michigan and University of California at Berkeley are research institutions. In most cases, the best professors at these colleges do not teach; they conduct research. Often, they do not even work on campus. Research schools attract large numbers of highly qualified graduate students and billions of dollars in public research funds. (Johns Hopkins alone gets almost a billion dollars in public research funds.) These schools also attract top professors by paying high salaries and requiring them to teach very little or not at all. The result is classes with 300-1200 students being taught by other students (not professors). (It's no wonder that so many students skip the classes and buy the class notes from local bookstores or online vendors.) In fact, at most research schools it's possible to complete your first two years of college and never be taught by a professor. The advantage of a research school is obvious: money. Research schools usually attract the most money for technological and medical research and therefore usually have the best facilities. Research schools shouldn't be completely discounted, but don't be surprised if you attend the University of Florida and your Introduction to Economics class has 700 people in it. For the undergraduate, research schools always do a second-rate job.

The same sixteen colleges have dominated the field of "research" for the past three decades: Harvard, MIT, Yale, Columbia, Cornell, U. Penn, Johns Hopkins, U. Chicago, U. Minnesota, U. Illinois, U. Michigan, U. Wisconsin at Madison, U. Washington, U.C. Berkeley, UCLA, and Stanford. These sixteen colleges dominate the process by which billions of federal research dollars are awarded and—not coincidentally—also receive the most money (in essence, they award the money to themselves). When push comes to shove, these colleges will side with the graduate schools that vie for billions of dollars in grants over an undergraduate college that, on a good day, may generate $250 million in revenue. The notable exceptions are U. Chicago, Yale and Columbia, all of which have developed safeguards that protect their undergraduate programs from pernicious grad-school cannibalism.

A few trends prevalent at research colleges will put the problems in perspective. At many of the most renowned research universities, such as Harvard, the number of professors employed by the university has grown between 200% and 300% from the 1950s to the present. During the same period, the number of graduate students has increased by 45% to 110%, and the number of undergraduate students has increased by 12% to 18%. So over the past forty years, the typical research university has significantly more professors, many more graduate students, and a few more undergraduate students. Now consider this: the number of undergraduate courses taught by professors has actually decreased during this period. How can a university have so many more professors (200%-300% more) and more undergraduate students and yet offer fewer courses? Additionally, consider that at most research universities, less than 30% of your tuition is used for paying your professors. At research universities, most of your tuition is not spent on paying professors and most of the professors simply do not teach at the college level.

The problem becomes obvious when one actually investigates a college's course catalogue. In a recent year, if you walked onto Harvard's campus as a freshman and intended to major in modern European history, you would have discovered that the course catalogue boasted an impressive 71 modern European courses. Perhaps you knew about these 71 courses because you read the catalogue before applying to Harvard. Perhaps this was why you chose Harvard over

Haverford and Williams. But when you arrived on campus, you discovered that 32 of the 71 courses aren't actually being taught that year. Of the 39 Mod-Euro courses that were actually being taught that year, only 20 of them were actually being taught that semester. Of these 20 courses, only 11 were taught by tenured professors, and three of those 11 were intended for graduate students. So of the 71 courses listed in the catalogue, only eight were actually taught by tenured professors and were offered that semester for undergraduates. Only eight courses? All of a sudden, Harvard's history department seems no bigger than that of the very small liberal arts colleges you rejected (Swarthmore, Williams, Haverford). When fewer than 12% of the courses listed are actually offered and taught by tenured professors, you begin to wonder about Harvard's priorities. Unfortunately, this sort of disregard for undergraduate education is the norm for most large research universities. I should note that I picked an academic area (Mod-Euro) that is average. Some academic subjects can even be worse. Harvard has been known to have as few as one (out of 42-51) of its undergraduate American history courses taught by a tenured professor, and at many colleges, no introductory economics or math classes are taught by professors. Harvard's student-written annual course catalogue has often lambasted the quality of teaching ranging in everything from the history department to the physics and philosophy departments.

Problems like this are prevalent even at colleges that are not renowned centers of research. New York University (NYU), an unwieldy collection of schools and programs that rivals any bumbling public university, offers over 200 regular sections of its expository writing course each semester. Of these 200+sections, none are taught by tenured professors. That's correct: zero. In the interest of fairness, though, I should report that of approximately 230 sections, a few are actually taught by non-tenured instructors. How many? About ten, which leaves the other 220 sections to be taught by graduate students. NYU asks $25,000+per year from you for this.

This problem is not confined to "writing" courses. One can search high and low and find innumerable courses taught by students or "part-time" professors. At the University of South Florida (USF), many humanities classes are taught by students in master programs (who are typically 21-24 years old). And when a college wishes to become a research institution, the first priority is to jettison "teaching." Rensselaer Polytechnic wants to reinvent itself as an internationally recognized research institution. The goal of its "Rensselaer Plan" is clear: hire top information and biotech researchers, require them to do little teaching, and let teaching become a secondary concern. As one commentator put it, "until recently, the focus at Rensselaer had been on teaching." For research universities, good teaching is not a priority. From prestigious Harvard to lesser-known USF, students and part-time professors are teaching classes that tenured professors formally taught. These colleges are hiring more professors but spending less on teaching (about 30% of a university's expenses are classroom-related). At many of the larger research universities (such as the University of Texas and the University of Wisconsin), it has been (and usually still is) possible to earn an undergraduate degree without ever taking a class with a professor. All of these universities have two things in common: they are or aspire to be significant research universities, and they all have large graduate schools. *Caveat emptor.*

Women's Colleges. Women have another choice when considering colleges. Although there are very few all/mostly-male colleges (lawsuits have largely abolished them), there are still about 60 women's (or mostly women) colleges. While attending a women's college may seem an unattractive option, these colleges usually prove to be good investments. Graduates from women's colleges consistently score higher on graduate entrance exams than do female graduates of coed colleges, and women are many times more likely to major in economics or the sciences at women's colleges than at coed colleges. If you're a woman interested in science or math, you're more likely to find a friendly environment at a women's college; on average, about 80% of graduates of women's colleges take four years of science and math (the average woman at a coed college takes only two years of science and math). Graduates of the top five women's colleges, Barnard, Bryn Mawr, Mount Holyoke, Smith, and Wellesley, account for almost 50% of all women who hold doctorate degrees in math and engineering.

Although over 95% of all American colleges are coed, it's the women's colleges that produce, per capita, the majority of female Fortune 1000 board members, lawyers, doctors, scientists and engineers. About 32% of all female Fortune 1000 board members are graduates of women's colleges. Of course, these numbers are a bit inaccurate because the majority of women who graduated from "top" colleges prior to the early 1970s are likely to have attended a women's college because most of today's "top" colleges were still all-male. (Most of the Ivies and other top colleges became coed in the 1960s and 70s.) Debate continues over the reasons for the seeming success of women's colleges, but the conclusion is that they produce successful women more often than coed colleges do.

The primary criticisms of women's college that I hear from high school students and parents is that such colleges tend to be characterized by liberal, extremist feminists, lesbians, female chauvinism, and/or misanthropes. On top of all that, it's hard to find a date on Saturday night (if you're heterosexual). To some degree or another, these charges are usually true. Despite their claims to the contrary, women's colleges tend to be remarkably lacking in diversity and are characterized by the same chauvinism that characterized all-male colleges in the past. In considering women's colleges, one should judge them by both their successes and their obvious limitations.

Service Academies. The service academies are colleges that are supported by the federal government and train graduates for service in the military, military-related, or other service-related fields. The three top service academies are the United States Military Academy, better known as West Point, the United States Naval Academy, better known as Annapolis, and the United States Air Force Academy. There are lesser-known academies such as the United States Merchant Marine Academy (better known as Kings Point) and the United States Coast Guard Academy. In all cases, the federal government pays for most fees, including tuition. In some cases, students are paid to attend the academy. (The Army pays West Point students about $7,000 per year; Kings Point students are paid while they are on-board ships; Coast Guard students are provided a stipend of about $29,000 paid out over four years.)

The top service academies boast the lowest acceptance rates of all colleges; lower than Harvard or Princeton or Stanford. Typically, the acceptance rates are less than 10%. (Coast Guard's is often the lowest at 5%-7%!) As part of the application process, the President of the United States or a member of Congress must nominate you.

The top service academies are very different from other colleges. First, upon graduation you will be a commissioned officer and have to serve for about five years. Next, you must respect order and discipline. The academies take their charge very seriously: they are in the business of shaping and developing your mind, body, and character. To that end, these academies tend to expect or require things of its students (who are typically referred to as "cadets") that other colleges wouldn't even consider: participation in campus clubs, extracurricular sports, and community service organizations. The academies don't just find these things nice; they find them necessary. I must admit that I find it refreshing that some colleges are still concerned with issues of character.

The campuses of the academies are stunning (of course, I suppose it depends on what you prefer). Annapolis is a beautiful town on the water in Maryland, while West Point is an Academy/Fortress carved out of granite on the banks of the Hudson (just north of New York City). Few colleges can compare with these remarkable locations. (As an aside, both Army and Navy compete in the Ivy League in some sports.) If you think of the Post Office when you think of Federal service academies, you would be surprised by Annapolis and West Point. Very few (if any) colleges can compete with these two when it comes to the beauty of the campus and the architecture of the buildings.

The academies tend to be tech schools, specializing in technology and engineering (sort of a MIT or Stanford with more discipline). Cadets typically are required to wear uniforms, exhibit a great degree of maturity, and take their studies seriously. One of the more interesting sides to being an engineer from an academy is the engineering projects you will be able to work on once you graduate (at which point you are, for example, a second Lieutenant). The military has long been one the greatest sources of technical innovation, and many academy graduates quickly find themselves working on some of the most cutting-edge technology in the world. Academies also tend to have highly-respected specialists in history (History of Tactical Warfare, History of Rocket-propelled Artillery, et cetera).

If you are disciplined, very mature, have great credentials, and are considering engineering, then I highly recommend researching the academies. They are, by far, the best value for the money (because they are free) and do the best job of developing the mind, body, and character. (Of course, given West Point's beautiful chapel, they probably develop the spirit fairly well, too.) However, you must visit them to get a feel for the atmosphere; it is very different from anything else you've ever experienced and is not right for many people. You will find very serious students saluting professors, walking around in uniform, and carrying themselves with a degree of maturity unparalleled in America. You will see museum displays of famous battles, cadets practicing marching formations, and no umbrellas in the rain. (A soldier does not need an umbrella.) You will also find about 85% of the students are men (which is not unusual for engineering colleges), so women are strongly encouraged to apply.

Religious Colleges. There are religious colleges such as Wheaton, Pepperdine, Gordon, and Westmont. Religious colleges seem like an anomaly today, but nearly all colleges, including Princeton and Yale, were very religious schools a century ago. Today, "religious college" means that the college actively incorporates some religious beliefs into its mission, which in most cases includes an applied concern for the values and character of the students. Generally, the education at most religious colleges is similar to that at non-religious colleges for the simple reason that religious colleges hire professors with a broad range of backgrounds—they don't hire religious professors exclusively. The significant difference at a religious college is that the campus art gallery will be less likely to have a pornographic exhibit and there will be fewer Planned Parenthood posters on campus. The majority of good religious colleges are Catholic (or related faiths, such as Jesuit): Georgetown, Notre Dame, Loyola, Boston College, Villanova, Fordham, Catholic University, Fairfield University, and Providence College.

Business Colleges, Liberal Arts, & the Real World. I strongly recommend that students attend a college that will educate them broadly in the liberal arts tradition; however, this occasionally leads to the concern that such a liberal arts education may be useless upon graduation. For example, a few students who wish to go into business or earn a MBA after college think that they need to take courses in (or major in) business, finance, accounting, and/or marketing. This is not true. In fact, the opposite is true. Many of the top candidates for entry-level jobs in Manhattan are Princeton and Yale graduates, and the closest major to "business" at either school is economics (a traditional liberal arts major). Most top MBA programs will tell you that they prefer candidates who did not major in business at college. If you want a top entry-level job in business or to attend a top MBA program, major in any of the humanities and sciences and take a few math and economics courses. The most important factor isn't so much your major in college; it's your grades. Keep in mind that often the prime candidates for business jobs are Princeton, Yale, and Swarthmore graduates who didn't—and couldn't—take accounting, marketing, or management courses.

The average college graduate will have ten or more jobs in five or more careers in his or her lifetime. Your undergraduate education will need to be broad enough to support your changing interests. It's likely that whatever career you think you'll pursue when you graduate will not be the career you'll be pursuing when you're 35 years old. In fact, it's healthy to assume that you won't know what you will be doing when you're 35. Your undergraduate education will need to be adaptable to different careers, and a liberal arts education is the most adaptable.

Chapter 12

Things That Matter

"You want to know what I look for in a college? Pretty girls in the view book. If there are lots of pretty girls in the view book, I apply."

Parents and students are swamped with information about colleges: college directories, magazines, and view books all offer a variety of facts and figures. Some of the information is useful, much of it is useless, and occasionally it's simply inaccurate. Here is a list of things that matter when considering colleges.

Location. Geography will play an important role in the college selection process. First, you should narrow down the parts of the country where you would be interested in attending college: Northeast (New Jersey, Pennsylvania, New York and New England), Mid-Atlantic (northern Virginia to Delaware), South (Mid-Virginia to Florida and west to the Mississippi), Midwest (Ohio west to the Dakotas and south to Kansas), Southwest (Texas and environs), West (California north to Washington and east to Colorado).

Here's a rough sketch of some characteristics of each area:

Northeast. The Northeast is the powerhouse of private universities. Without a doubt, the Northeast has the most impressive collection of private colleges anywhere in the world, from small and distinguished Williams and Amherst to prestigious Yale and Columbia. Most of the colleges have the "classic college" look—beautiful campuses with red brick or neo-Gothic buildings. The exceptions to the "classic campus" are the several Northeast colleges that are in cities, often in undesirable neighborhoods (Yale, Vassar, Columbia, Penn). Northeastern colleges are known for their long-standing traditions, century-old rivalries, and famous alumni. The Northeast's failure is in its public colleges— dollar-for-dollar they are probably the worst collection of public colleges in the country. (The reason is obvious: unlike the rest of the country, the Northeast only recently saw the need for public colleges due to the overwhelming success of its private colleges.) If you're looking for a college in the Northeast, it's advisable to stick with a private one.

Mid-Atlantic. These colleges range from Johns Hopkins, a school so focused on its graduate research that the founding president didn't even want undergraduates, to St. Johns, a great-books school greatly concerned with the undergraduate education. The Mid-Atlantic is mostly known for its DC-area schools: Georgetown, George Washington, American, Catholic, U. Maryland at College Park, and George Mason. If you're interested in politics, policy, or law, these Mid-Atlantic schools may be right for you.

South. Despite its unearned reputation for being backward, the South is the powerhouse of public universities: University of Virginia, College of William and Mary, University of North Carolina at Chapel Hill, University of Florida, New College, and James Madison University. There are also many well-known private schools: Duke, Washington & Lee, Wake Forest, Davidson, Vanderbilt, Emory, Tulane, University of the South, and the University of Richmond. The private schools in the south, with the exception of Duke and Emory, tend to be more traditional (meaning you can't major in the History of the Toilet in Southwest Mongolia). Many southern schools still maintain "old south" traditions such as formal dances and honor codes. If you're looking for a good public school or a traditional private school, the south is the place for you.

Midwest. The Midwest has an eclectic bunch of schools, the powerhouse being Rockefeller's baby, the University of Chicago—one of the finest schools in the country. The Midwest also has the diploma-mill U. Michigan (50,000+students and counting), the best Protestant college in Wheaton, and some wonderful private schools like the Ivy-caliber Northwestern, the remarkable Hillsdale, and the excellent Kenyon. Most private Midwest colleges tend to be conservative/traditional, reflecting the values of the people of the Midwest, while most Midwestern public schools have vocational tendencies that focus on the "useful." Midwestern colleges offer a big advantage to you if you don't live in the Midwest: Midwestern colleges are eager to attract non-Midwestern students. There simply aren't many students from the Northeast, South, or West dying to attend college in Illinois or Ohio, so geography may be to your advantage. (More on that later.)

Southwest. The Southwest is mostly two schools: the University of Texas at Austin and Rice. There are many other respectable schools, from Texas A&M to Kansas' two universities (Kansas State and U. Kansas), but it's rare that a competitive student, particularly one from outside the state, would be interested in any of them. Both UT-Austin and Rice are decent schools; UT-Austin's big advantage is the city of Austin (the so-called live music capitol of the world). If you're in the Southwest and want to stay there, chances are you're aiming for UT-Austin or

Rice. If you're not in the Southwest, then chances are you're not interested in going to college there.

West. Quite frankly, the West has too many schools, most of them over-rated. >From the University of California system (very over-rated) to Stanford (also over-rated), one can get lost in all the schools and over-look some of the better schools. The West's strength is obvious: technology. From Stanford to Cal-Tech, technology is king. The West's other strength—if you can call it that—is Hollywood. UCLA and USC both have excellent film and entertainment-related programs. (The other big-hitter in the film-entertainment field, and probably the best undergraduate school in the country for film, is NYU.) The West's weakness is traditional, caring, student-focused, liberal arts and humanities-based education (small classes, real professors, actual discussions—no 800-student classes). It's unfortunate that with all the wealth and the intelligent students in the West, it has no equivalent to Yale, Princeton, Middlebury, Amherst, or Swarthmore. Reed, Pomona, and Colorado College are the West's best colleges. (For those in California irritated with these comments: Stanford is a fine school, but if you can get admitted to Stanford, you have a good shot at getting admitted to U. Chicago, Columbia, and Yale—all much better schools.) If you're in the West, aim for Reed, Pomona or Colorado College (or Pepperdine if Malibu strikes your fancy). If you're considering Colorado College, you should keep in mind that it's one of only two colleges in the country where students take only one course at a time.

Other Considerations. There are other geographical considerations, such as weather, accessibility, and distance from home. The best way to assess these issues is to visit the campus during the academic year. This way, you will discover if you can withstand the cold of Cornell or the bucolic cow-tipping plains of Notre Dame. You also need to decide if you would prefer an urban, suburban or rural school. Many students come to me with both Cornell and NYU on their list of schools, and I tell them that if they like one, they will probably dislike the other. Cornell is extremely rural—hours from anything. While NYU is the ultimate urban college—so urban it doesn't even have a campus.

Most students strongly prefer small, suburban or urban campuses with traditional buildings. Nearly every study of campus community finds that small, private, rural colleges with traditional campuses (like Dartmouth) have the strongest communities. Similarly, NYU's high freshman dropout rate is no doubt due to its ultra-urban environment: many students find out the hard way that they'd prefer a school with a traditional campus. While I think there's nothing more exciting than an urban campus—NYU, Columbia, Yale, Georgetown—you should be very careful choosing an urban school because the overwhelming majority of students prefer a traditional campus. (An aside: Georgetown's campus is somewhat traditional, though small, and DC really isn't a typical big city, but Georgetown does have unattractively modern high-rise dorms, a hallmark of an ill-planned urban campus.)

Visiting the campus will also give you a feel for the surrounding community. For example, you will want to assess whether or not a car will be necessary (as they are at many large public colleges). From experience, it is often desirable not to have a car at college (not to mention that many colleges don't permit freshmen to have cars). If the campus and surrounding community are small enough so that everything is within walking distance, a car may actually be cumbersome. You will find that on many campuses you will be required to park a great distance from your dorm, and countless college seniors have tales of enormous parking tickets and fines that had to be paid before they could graduate. And finally, the primary crime committed at colleges is theft, so the fewer valuables you bring to college, the better—and obviously, the most valuable thing you can bring is your car.

Assessing the larger community in which a college is located seems relevant, but I think the importance of such an assessment can be overrated. For example, I know many students who decline to consider Vanderbilt because they think Nashville is "too Southern." While this may be true, it's difficult to subscribe to the notion that one should discount a college because the larger community—the surrounding neighborhood—may be undesirable. If one followed this advice, one would discount colleges ranging from USC and UC Berkeley to Chicago, Penn, Vassar, Columbia, Yale and numerous others because of the undesirability of the surrounding neighborhoods. There is a balance between judging the college on its own merits and gauging the safety and vitality of the surrounding neighborhoods, but I do not think it productive to discount a college *a priori* because "Nashville is too Southern" or "New Haven is a rust-belt town." Those comments may be true, but it could still also be true that the best college you can be admitted to is Vanderbilt. (I happen to think that Yale is the best college in the country, so clearly I think that the quality of the surrounding town can be rendered meaningless by the quality of the college.)

This is not to imply that the surrounding town shouldn't be considered: certainly, there are exciting places to live (Boston, New York, Atlanta) and boring places to live, and this should be factored in after you consider the college on its own merits.

Size. Colleges range from the small (Drew, Colby, Kenyon, Pomona, U. Chicago), to the medium (Yale, Princeton, Boston College), to the large (Penn, Cornell, NYU), to the ridiculous (UT Austin, U. Michigan, U. Florida, Purdue). Small colleges are those that have fewer than 4,000 students. There are many colleges, such as Swarthmore, that have fewer than 1,500 students. (Think about this: your high school may have more students!) Medium colleges range from

4,000 to 9,000 students; large have 9,000 to 20,000 students, and the ridiculous have more than 20,000 students (often closer to 50,000).

The size of the college can be crucial: it is the difference between a personal learning experience and an indifferent diploma mill. You will be a number at U. Michigan—what else would you expect from a college with more than 50,000 students? (The average town in the United States is smaller.) In fact, most small and medium colleges believe that the size of the student body is so important that they work very hard to keep their colleges small: Williams and Yale could admit twice as many students, but they don't because they believe that a small student body is vital to their educational mission. I would go so far as to say that there are only two reasons to apply for (and pay for) a private college: 1, to get actual professors in every classroom; 2, to get personal, individualized attention. Neither of those happens at large public universities. If you don't care if you're taught by a graduate teaching assistant and are known as a number, then save your money and attend a large public university. At a large university, you will be responsible for educating yourself and will save a lot of money. My guess is that about 5% of high school seniors are actually capable of being fully responsible for educating themselves. But if you prefer small classes, interactive professors, and personal attention, then you have no choice but to attend a small private college. Keep in mind that one of the primary reasons you wish to apply to a private college is to be a part of a community, which means that it makes no sense to apply to a large private college. My advice is to stick with colleges with fewer than 9,000 undergraduates: if you want large, go to a school with 7,000-9,000 students; if you want small, go under 2,000. Everyone else, look between 2,500 and 7,000 students (which includes the majority of private colleges). If you go higher than 9,000 undergrads, then you're not likely to get what you paid for—you might as well attend a public college and save money!

The best way to get a feeling for the size of the college is to visit the campus during the academic year. It's important to visit while the students are still there. (We will discuss campus visits in a later chapter.)

Reputation. According to a recent survey, the top college selection criterion of college freshmen was "reputation." What does these mean? No one knows. The reputation of a college is some witches brew concocted from your parents' advice, your friends' opinions, something you heard on the radio, something your older sister once said, a few reviews you read in books, a silly "Best Party School" survey, a comment made by your college counselor, and the record of the college's basketball team. There is no relevant measurement of reputation, no guidelines regarding this criterion that seems so important to high school students.

And yet I'm going to contradict some of the advice I've given you (which is why choosing and applying to college can be a pain): sometimes, nothing else matters but the college's reputation. Harvard is the #1 college brand name in the world, so Harvard does not need to be concerned with the quality of its undergraduate education (and it's not) because it knows the brand will sell. You will probably get a better education at St. John's College or Washington & Lee, but it's hard to turn down the prestige of a Harvard degree. If you're going to college for an education, then be aware that sometimes the top "brands" have the lowest quality (because they're not selling quality; they're selling the brand name). If you're going to college in order to go to grad school or get a high-paying job right after graduation, then the college's reputation will be important. Think of blue jeans: if you wish to quickly impress someone, you will buy over-priced designer jeans; but if you want jeans that will last, you will probably buy less expensive (but more durable) jeans. Quality in education is much like the world of designer blue jeans: the reputation of the label doesn't necessarily correspond to the quality of the material.

Colleges have other types of reputations: male-friendly, extremist, low-school spirit, great parties, and so forth. Many of these reputations are earned. For example, colleges such as Antioch, Brown, Dartmouth, and U. Michigan (Ann Arbor) all have reputations for being antagonistic towards men. In most cases, this reputation is well-earned. For example, Antioch has a campus rule that requires "willing and verbal consent" at each stage of intimacy (sort of like getting someone to sign a waiver as you round the bases). Such a rule results in a very stilted, abnormal environment for relationships. (Frankly, it's just weird.)

Other schools have reputations for being very male-friendly (Davidson, Princeton, Vanderbilt, Washington and Lee). Some schools are known for poor (or no) school spirit (Emory), others known for being traditional (Hampden-Sydney), and still others get a bad reputation for banning Napster even when it was legal (NYU). It's worth noting and investigating these reputations; usually, they have a bit of truth to them.

Social Life. There are two sides to your college experience: academic and social. This may seem obvious, but too many students (and parents) don't fully consider the social side. College will be a place you will live for four years, learn a lot, and (hopefully) grow up. The environment that surrounds you is vital to your success—it should be a place you love and enjoy. It's not surprising that students who don't like the social climate of their college often do not perform very well academically.

So how do you find out about the social life at a college? Well, it's impossible to really know until you live there (as it's impossible to really know what any place is like unless you live there). It's useless to ask the admissions office (they'll say, "It's great! We just spent ten billion dollars on a new gym complete with a dozen coed clothing-optional hot tubs!"). The first step is to visit the campus and stay overnight if possible. Talking to people you know who recently attended the school is sometimes helpful, but it can be prejudicial. If your older friend is at Wake Forest and hates it, that means that Wake Forest isn't right for your friend. This information may not apply to you (unless you're exactly like him). It's foolish to say, "I'm not applying to Brown because my friend goes there and she hates it." The opinions of students and recent alumni are potentially helpful, but they are also only one piece of the puzzle.

Staying overnight, attending classes, going to parties, and loitering around the campus on a Friday and Saturday during the school year can be very helpful. You should be able to get a good feel for campus social life. For example, you may discover that everyone deserts the campus during weekends and goes to the nearest big city (which isn't conducive to building a close community) or you may find that most stay on campus and party (New College, Dartmouth), which tend to build friendships (and rumors).

Campus clubs and organizations are also a sign of campus life. However, it's important that you actually investigate the club's activities. Nearly every college view book or directory lists dozens (if not hundreds) of clubs ranging from the Eco-Lesbians for Dolphin-Safe Tuna Club to the Libertarian Student Union (not to mention a newspaper, College Republicans, Rugby club, and so forth). However, many of these clubs may only exist on paper. You may find out that the club you're interested in is, in fact, only two boring anthropology majors who meet once a semester over a pizza, or the campus newspaper is only one guy with a camera. While on campus, seek out the leaders of the club(s) in which you're interested, and talk to them. If possible, attend a club event. The admissions office should give you the information you need. By directly investigating the vitality of clubs, you will get a decent idea of campus life.

Greeks: either you love them or hate them. On most large public universities, fraternities and sororities dominate social life, which means either you're in a frat or sorority or you go bowling on Friday nights. Private colleges vary widely: some of them have no frats (Harvard, Georgetown,), some have quasi-frats (Princeton, Yale), and some colleges have high frat participation (Cornell, Dartmouth). Typically, a "high frat" college is one at which more than 30% of students join a fraternity or sorority. The "quasi-frats" can vary widely, ranging from Princeton's odious Eating Clubs to Yale's wonderful residential college system. The hallmark of a leading eating club is exclusive snobbery, whereas the foundation of the Yale's residential colleges is inclusive community.

So how do you find out the "frat content" of a college? If you ask the admissions office "Are frats a big deal here?" you will get some version of "Not really." Either the actual answer is no, or the admissions office doesn't want to admit that frats are a big deal. Fraternities and sororities are often the cause of embarrassment, and admissions offices won't be quick to share embarrassing information. Even at high-frat schools, the admissions office will give you some version of "There are frats if you're interested, but there are numerous other social and living options for upperclassmen who aren't interested in frats." Translation: Frats are a big deal, and either you join one or you spend Friday night ordering pizza from Dominos and watching *Sabrina the Teenage Witch* re-runs. How do you find out the truth? First, find a junior, senior, or recent graduate of the college, and ask them; unless they work for the admissions office, they will give you a fair and reasonable answer. Second, ask the admissions office what percent of upperclassmen (juniors and seniors) join fraternities and sororities. You can then take this number and compare it with the other colleges you're considering. You should translate the answer like this:

- Less than 20% of upperclassmen in frats and sororities: not a big deal; substantial social life exists outside of frats.
- 20%-30%: not bad, but you will probably "loose" some freshmen friends to frats unless you join too.
- 30%-50%: not much social life outside of frats; you will want to join one (or get a satellite dish to amuse yourself while all your friends are at frat parties).
- Over 50%: frat city; you should either love frats or not apply to this college.

Whether or not you would like to join a fraternity is a complex question I cannot answer for you. While many fraternities are of the *Animal House* variety, colleges are aggressively trying to reform the Greek scene by (typically) limiting or banning kegs, restricting alcohol during rush weeks, punishing hazing/initiation rites, and often requiring parties to be registered and/or monitored. The social life the Greeks engender usually is of the superficial, Mardi Gras sort, but they do tend to provide some semblance of community at large universities where there otherwise is none.

Another question to ask admissions offices and current students is whether or not a large number of students stay on-campus or in town over the summer. Usually, if a large number of students stick around over the summer, then the college and/or the town have developed a desirable collegiate community. I find it suspect if all the students immediately evacuate the campus and the town once final exams are over: what's wrong that everyone is so interested in getting out? If a large number of students stay in the area over the summer, then that tells you that a community has developed that extends beyond the classrooms. Obviously, this is a good sign.

And finally, the political climate on campus may affect the social life of the community. Political activists on college campuses have birthed untold inanities, from protesting the campus newspaper by stealing and destroying all the copies (Cornell) to requiring students to sign a "dating agreement" prior to going on a date which spells out what each person can and cannot expect from the other (Antioch). And in many cases, the professors on campus tend to be activists, chasing the latest theoretical fad and exorcising the newest demon in society. Some campuses are notoriously activist—Stanford, UC-Berkeley, U. Michigan, Duke—and almost always in the worst way. And never assume a campus is "liberal" or "conservative" in its activism. Two of the more liberal campuses are Princeton and Dartmouth—few applicants realize this upon applying, and discover this fact after enrolling. You can ask current students and recent graduates about the political climate, but this may be fruitless because different people will have different opinions: the liberal activist may think the UC Berkeley campus isn't political enough. You should pick up a copy of the campus newspaper when you visit, and hopefully you have a well-informed counselor who can teach you the ways of campus politics.

Crime. One of the topics that colleges do not wish to discuss is campus crime. In fact, colleges only started reporting crime statistics in the past few years because federal law required it. Before the government required campuses to reveal their crime statistics, it was almost impossible to find out a campus's crime rate. In fact, the mandatory detailed reporting of manslaughter, hate crimes, and weapons offenses only dates back to 1998 and 1999. Even now, the best source of information about crime on campus is from the FBI; colleges collect and report this information, but they are not interested in disseminating this information. Recently, the U.S. Education Department created a web site for campus crime statistics (http://ope.ed.gov/security), but the statistics on that web site are jumbled and, in many cases, clearly inaccurate. How did this problem arise? Colleges claim that the reporting process is too confusing or that they didn't have enough time to "add up the numbers." The same people who are responsible for organizing the lives (and living arrangements) of tens of thousands of undergraduates can't seem to add 500 (or so) arrests made for weapons and drug charges. More than one government official has suggested that colleges are less than interested in reporting accurate crime statistics (despite the laws that require them to do so and the $25,000 per instance fine if they don't).

The only way to get reasonably accurate information about crime on campus is to have an informed college counselor who can get his or her hands on the statistics. Colleges are required by federal law to provide a crime summary to those who ask for it, but they often make this process cumbersome and lengthy. For example, they may require you to request the crime report in writing. Usually, the easiest thing to do is to ask for the crime summary while you're visiting. (By the way, the FBI refers to it as "crime" whereas most colleges refer to it as "security.")

College campuses are usually very safe, but they can also be prime targets for criminal activity. For example, thieves take advantage of the close-knit community and relaxed security on some college campuses to easily steal televisions and stereos. Crime matters for one simple reason: most teenagers have yet to develop the responsibility necessary to avoid being a victim. Your parents worry about you; you live in a safe suburb; your house and car have alarm systems. None of this may be true on a college campus. (Your parents may still worry about you, but they won't lock the door for you at night.)

The most dangerous college campuses tend to be large public universities such as Michigan State and UC Berkeley. Campuses can also be dangerous because of the neighborhoods they are in (some of the neighborhoods around Yale are known to be dangerous). Most colleges, particularly private colleges, are very aware of the potential for crime on their campuses and in their communities and usually employ private security firms.

Many colleges, such as UC Berkeley and U. Miami, suffer from being in or near unsafe neighborhoods and being either powerless or unwilling to do anything about the crime in the area. What is often most disturbing about this situation is that, often, the college owns and controls much of the real estate surrounding the campus. For example, there is a park near the UC Berkeley campus that is a notorious home for all sorts of derelicts, alcoholics and drug-dealers. Although many students have asked Berkeley to do something about this problem, the college refuses; this is particularly galling when one considers that the college actually owns the park.

You will want to make sure you feel safe and comfortable at college (and that you will feel safe parking your car and bringing your stereo). How do to find out about the crime on and near campuses if colleges are so unwilling to be honest on this subject? Visit the campus; walk around the campus and around the surrounding neighborhood at night. (Many colleges will offer to "shuttle" you to the campus in lieu of you driving yourself; kindly decline this offer. Drive to the campus yourself. You should find out if the surrounding neighborhoods are safe.) While visiting the college, pick up both the college newspaper and the local neighborhood's newspaper; this will help you get a good idea if the area is "high crime." Often, the best people to talk to are the campus security guards. They are often not employed directly by the college and have not undergone any training from the admissions office. In most cases, they will be candid. While security guards don't know what goes on in the classroom, they usually have a very good idea of what campus life is like: crime, parties, emergencies, and so forth. If you feel a little strange talking to the guard at the front gate about these things, ask your parents to talk to him. Finally, ask a few current students (who aren't employed by the admissions office) and recent grads about crime on campus.

One last word: the most common crime on campus is theft (mostly committed by other students). So I suggest not bringing anything highly valuable to campus until you've lived there at least one full semester. You need to know what your roommate is like, what the campus is like, and what the surrounding area is like—unfortunately, roommates do sometimes steal. If you have a $2000 stereo, leave it at home until your sophomore year.

Professors' Salaries. This may seem like an odd area of inquiry, but think about this: colleges boast about their new multi-million dollar gyms and the big-name speakers they bring to campus (at $70,000 each), but they don't often discuss how much they pay the teachers that will be in front of you in the classroom. Since teachers, like everyone else in a free market, are attracted to high salaries, it seems obvious that the colleges offering the highest salaries typically have the best teachers. It may also surprise you to know that many of the teachers at top universities make less than $20,000 per year. In fact, you could go through your entire freshman year and never have a teacher who makes more than $20,000 per year (teaching a full load of classes). When you discover this kind of information, you will probably be irritated to learn of the new $30 million gym and the new $4,000 teak trash cans. Why don't colleges spend more money on hiring good teachers? Because they don't think good teaching will attract you like big-name speakers and shiny new buildings do.

The problem in finding out average teacher salaries is obvious: colleges control this information. Colleges are unregulated; therefore, they don't readily report this information unless they think it to their benefit. While this information is reported in a few obscure publications, the only way a typical applicant can get it is to have a good college counselor.

Obviously, you should avoid colleges that are at the bottom in average teacher's pay. But assessing a college's average teacher salary should be balanced by the amount of access you will have to those teachers. Many top colleges lure top teachers with high salaries and the promise that they won't be required to teach much (if at all). Many of the highest paid college professors in the country don't actually teach.

The other side to teacher's salaries is teaching assistants. Teaching assistants are graduate students, many of whom are 21-25 years old, who are paid little (or nothing) to teach classes. They usually have little or no teaching experience, and teaching is usually not their primary focus (and often not even their only job). A few decades ago, TAs were only used to assist professors by researching for them, proofreading, grading exams, and assisting in classroom management. But now, as many as 50% of the classes at some universities are left totally in the hands of

TAs. Sometimes TAs teach in exchange for being able to take graduate classes for free (an academic barter system) and sometimes there are paid stipends, usually about $12,000 per year. Imagine, your college teacher may only be making $12,000 per year! (Until recently, Ph.D. students at Yale, who are assigned to teach undergraduate courses, were paid just $11,400 per year.)

This abuse of the TA system is why many people get very upset about the use of teaching assistants. Many TAs are good, but students and parents expect a little more for the enormous price of tuition. Your high school cost less than your college, and yet your high school teachers may have been paid a lot more. Certainly, a college that uses $12,000-per-year teaching assistants should not be charging $25,000 per year in tuition. (One of the great ironies—and mysteries—of college tuition is that colleges charge so much more now than they did just ten years ago, but they are spending so much less on teacher salaries. Where does all that money go? Yeah, sports teams, shiny new buildings, expensive view books and rock star professors who don't teach.)

Under no circumstances should you spend $25,000-$30,000 per year to be taught by 24-year-old graduate students who have almost no teaching experience and are more concerned with their own graduate studies than with you. It should be noted that many TAs in the sciences, math, and engineering come from foreign countries and hardly speak English, and yet these grad students are put up in front of hundreds of undergraduates. (In fact, over 50% of all engineering, chemistry and physics graduate students are foreigners.) Many universities take little notice of whether their TAs actually speak English; they are only concerned with staffing their classes with the least expensive teachers they can find. (I've heard many Harvard undergraduates complain about incomprehensible TAs who either don't speak English or are such poor teachers that no one can comprehend what is being taught—or both.) At most larger Ivy League colleges, TAs teach as many 25% of all undergraduate courses.

The only way to completely avoid TAs is to attend a small, private liberal arts college that has no graduate school (or a very small one). Colleges such as Bowdoin, Middlebury, Haverford, New College, Pomona, and Drew use real full-time professors to teach all their courses. Overall, these small liberal arts colleges will offer better teaching, better classes, and a better education, whereas at most large public universities, you will receive little direction and attend large classes taught by underpaid and overworked TAs. (Technically, only a university can have TAs because TAs are graduate students culled from the graduate school and colleges don't have graduate schools. But this is just a technical point that often isn't true. For example, undergraduates at Harvard College are taught by TAs from Harvard University. However, it is true at colleges that have no graduate school connected or affiliated with them, such as Amherst College.)

Specialties & Majors. If you wish to specialize or major in something very specific, such as industrial engineering or Scottish Common Sense Philosophy, then you should investigate the college's specialties. (In the above example, you'd want to consider Cornell for engineering and Brown for philosophy.) Most college English, history, philosophy, religion, art history and engineering departments have strengths and weaknesses. And small, private colleges are bound to have more extensive weaknesses.

If you are interested in specific scientific, technological, or medical areas of inquiry, then large public universities will be much more likely to accommodate your interests. The problem with majoring in a narrow, specialized area at a small college is that often the college's ability to accommodate you rests on the shoulders of a single professor, and when that professor leaves, so does the major. For example, a small private college may offer a concentration in genetic engineering, but they may have only one professor who actually teaches genetic engineering. If that professor leaves, so does the entire field of genetic engineering. Similarly, if that professor does not teach a semester, then there won't be any genetic engineering courses offered that semester. (It would be rare for such a professor to teach continuously for four years.) No college can make guarantees that any single professor will be at the college in the future. If genetic engineering is your area of interest, you would be better off attending a larger college that has at least 4-5 professors who regularly teach genetic engineering courses. In conclusion, if you're very interested in concentrating in a specialized field, it's important to discover whether the college offers that area of concentration and how many professors actually teach courses in that area. All colleges publish course catalogues and most publish them online, so you should peruse these catalogues to investigate the courses offered and the areas of expertise of the professors.

If you're interested in studying U.S. history, British literature, or pre-medical studies, then nearly every college (other than technical ones) will be able to provide you with a solid education. However, it's still worthwhile to peruse the course catalogue to see what's offered; you may decide that you prefer one college to another because of the specific courses that are offered. For example, you may find that Duke's English department concentrates heavily on feminist and queer theory, Marxist gyno-reflexive interpretative poetics, and identity deconstructionism—none of which interests you. If you simply wish to study British Renaissance poetry without the clouds of radical theory over your head, then you would be disinclined to consider Duke. Therefore, investigating the course catalogue of every college should help inform your application decisions and may engender new questions about the college (which you should direct to the admissions department or the academic department in question).

One final note on course catalogues: most colleges publish course catalogues every 2-3 years, and they publish a description of every course that could possibly be taught. This means that many (if not most) of the courses published in a course catalogue will not be taught in any given year. Often, course catalogues are more suggestions or intimations of what *may* be taught than actual descriptions of what *will* be taught. If you find 1 or 2 courses in which you're very interested, you may be required to wait 2 or 3 years before these courses are actually offered (if ever). The danger is this: you may find a college that offers, for example, 70 English courses in its course catalogue, and you find 5 that interest you. This seems okay, but it may take 2 years before some of those courses are offered, and some of them may never be offered. Each course described is often only taught by one teacher, and if that teacher leaves, the course may never be offered again. If that teacher takes a sabbatical, a leave of absence, or a maternity leave, then that course may not be offered that year. It's dangerous to choose a college (or a department) because of a small number of desirable courses. In the above example, those 5 courses may all be taught by the same teacher, and that teacher may leave the college the year you arrive. Then you're stuck with 65 other courses that don't really interest you. So if you decide you like a department, be sure you like the majority of the courses offered.

Inside Information. Inside information includes all those things you hear about a college that aren't published. You hear things from friends, parents, teachers, and hopefully from a well-informed college counselor. In fact, your college counselor should be a fountain of inside information on colleges. Some inside information is available in chat rooms, but it's not very trust-worthy. In order for the information to be credible, you should know and trust the source. Good inside information should be like talking to someone who drives the car you're thinking of buying and can tell you their opinion. Such opinions aren't definitive, but they are helpful.

Such inside information may lead you to the fact that Williams College has banned beer pong (and other drinking games): if you're caught hanging around a ping-pong table with a beer, you could be suspended from college. Or perhaps you'd learn that the University of New Hampshire has had "search and seizure" problems: some students feel the school unlawfully searches dorm rooms and seizes "evidence" to be used in disciplinary hearings. You might even learn that Princeton's famous professor Peter Singer seems to think that sex with animals (bestiality) is okay; in fact, Professor Singer thinks that bestiality is only a taboo that will soon go away once conservatives and the church stop ridiculing it. In Professor Singer's writings on bestiality, he shows a particular fondness for orang-utans. Ironically, Professor Singer is an undergraduate professor of ethics. (I suppose that would be funny if it weren't so perverse.) Even more shocking is that

Princeton President Harold Shapiro went out of his way to hire Singer. This sort of "inside information" may cause you to think twice about applying to a college that thinks that people like Singer should be teaching.

Inside information can help you get a feel for a school, so ask around because most schools aren't publishing this sort of information in their view books.

Sports Division. If you wish to play sports at college, then clearly you need to know everything there is to know about the team and the college's sports program. Most college coaches (or their assistants) are approachable and affable to serious potential recruits. If you are a serious potential recruit, then a coach may be your greatest ally at the admissions office. If you have any potential (and interest) in playing college sports, then it would be to your advantage to contact the college's athletic director as soon as possible. One word of warning: college athletics is very serious business. In most cases, you will be required to make an enormous commitment to the team, which will inevitably infringe on your academic pursuits. (Sports programs will deny that they diminish a student's academic achievement, but they are myopic; most athletic sports programs are so demanding that they require a tremendous amount of time and energy that would otherwise be spent on academic activities.)

Collegiate sports may be important to you even if you don't intend to participate. Despite the fact that many professors dislike highly popular sports programs (football, basketball) and recruiting-intensive admissions offices (the Ivies), most students believe that collegiate sports add to the overall college experience. Students from Boston College to the University of Florida will attest to the ways that sports teams improve the social atmosphere. It's certainly the case that a greater sense of community spirit improves the overall social life—and you can feel this difference on college campuses. You can go from a spiritless school (Tufts, Emory) to a school full of spirit (Boston College, University of Georgia) and almost immediately notice the difference. While having a successful sports program isn't a necessity, I believe it adds to the overall college experience and is one of many factors that should be considered.

Freshman Dropout Rate. The freshman dropout rate is another little fact that no college wishes to discuss, and yet it may be a commentary on all of the previously mentioned selection criteria. A few college guides publish a variation of a freshmen dropout rate (how many freshmen do not return for their sophomore year). Typical freshmen dropout rates range from 4%-7% for top colleges, which means that 4%-7% of the freshmen class does not return for their sophomore year. Many of these students do not return for personal reasons that have nothing to do with the college, but some of them transfer to another college because they did not fit into the college community. It's perfectly normal for a few freshmen (about 3%) to drop out of even the best colleges.

However, a high freshman dropout rate should set off alarms. It may not mean that the college is bad, but it may mean that the college either misrepresents itself to students or that the college is unusual, and students have trouble acclimating. For example, New York University has an unusually high freshmen dropout rate (about 15%). This fact should be reason to pause: why do so many freshmen decline to return to NYU? It's a very competitive college; surely, those freshmen worked very hard to get admitted. The most likely answer is that NYU is a very unusual college in that it has no campus; it's a collection of buildings in a densely populated section of this country's largest metropolis. Obviously, this sort of setting might scare away freshmen from Iowa (or even suburban New York). If you want a traditional college experience, then NYU will let you down. An additional reason could be NYU's housing, which is notoriously atrocious, and the Manhattan real estate market leaves undergraduates with few (if any) options to leave NYU housing. I wouldn't be surprised if a few hundred NYU freshmen declined to return for their sophomore year because of the extremely poor housing situation. Another example is Cornell, which has the highest freshman dropout rate among the Ivies (about 6%). The reason may be the location: applicants who take a 2-hour tour during the summer find a pleasant, tranquil campus. However, during the academic year they find themselves hours from any city and surprised by the severity of the winter.

Although you should use high dropout rates as warning signals, you should also keep in mind that top colleges do everything possible to keep these rates low-often artificially low. For example, it's almost impossible to drop out of Harvard or Swarthmore; the administration will do everything possible to maintain your status as a student. While this kind of support is nice, you should note that colleges don't want their dropout rates to increase. (Most colleges look at this from the perspective of graduation rates: the percent of students who graduate within four, five, and six years of matriculating). If you're failing several classes at Swarthmore, you may leave for a semester, but Swarthmore would prefer you to come back and finish your degree than transfer to another college. So while freshman dropout rates are helpful, they won't tell you much about the most competitive colleges because those colleges actively and aggressively manage their dropout rates. (This is also why some say the hardest part about Harvard is getting in; once you're in, they won't let you leave until you've graduated.) So use high dropout rates as a point of inquiry, but don't assume that a low dropout rate at a very competitive college means that few drop out.

The Course Catalogue. The course catalogue is (usually) a thick book that lists every course the college offers over a 1-2 year period as well as academic requirements for majors, minors, and independent studies. The college's course catalogue is one of the most substantive ways to judge a college: are the courses offered adequate and do they meet your academic needs and interests? In a sense, the catalogue is a detailed list of what you're paying for—an education. Whereas the view book is mindless fluff and marketing hype, the catalogue gives you serious details. Some colleges will gladly mail you a course catalogue, some colleges will be annoyed, and some will actually attempt to charge you. (NYU will tell you to go to the bookstore and buy it.) Personally, I wouldn't attend any college that won't mail a course catalogue for free. (This would be like Ford trying to charge you for a brochure. It's crazy.) Either the college is cheap, or they're embarrassed by what's in their catalogue (or both). Why would a college be embarrassed? Because they may have an entire page on "Erotic Film Studies" (a.k.a. Porn Studies) or "Queer Marxism and the Politics of Masturbation" (a.k.a. Big Government and Porn) or "Gender Dogma and the New Vaginal Paradigm" (a.k.a. Pseudo-Intellectual Female Liberation and probably some porn).

I'm not joking—these courses all actually exist. Middlebury recently offered a course in strip dancing. Another fine Middlebury course featured the eroticism and misogyny of the films of Brigitte Bardot. The University of Michigan has offered sports management courses that test students' knowledge of Michigan Stadium admissions policies. ("What is the primary means of admission to the stadium?" and "Does a hand stamp allow readmission to the stadium?") At Auburn, undergraduates take courses in how to talk to visitors at parks ("Outdoor Recreational Communication Technology"). Auburn sounds like they are taking lessons from Kent State's course on camp counseling which examines the role of the camp, the campers, and the counselors.

The University of Florida offers "Exceptional People in School and Society"; this course has a blustery title, but all that gold turns to gild when you discover that the highlight of the course is reenacting episodes from the *Jerry Springer Show*. If reenacting a Jerry Springer episode seems a bit dangerous (or if your chair-throwing skills are a bit rusty), then perhaps American University's "Presidential Campaign" course is for you: no text or other substantial readings are required. Your assignment is to watch television. You may supplement this with listening to the radio, chatting on the Internet, or, for those aspiring scholars, read a magazine. (If you're at American and can't find this course, it's #302.001H. That "H" stands for "Honors." That's right, "Presidential Campaign" is in American's Honors Program. Apparently, American offers courses that require less.) These courses seem rigorous compared to the courses offered at the University of Massachusetts at Amherst where students can take Frisbee courses for credit. But even a Frisbee course seems strenuous when compared to some of the offerings at the Ivies. Never to be outdone, America's top colleges offer some of the most dubious courses for credit. My favorites include Brown University's "Rock n' Roll Is Here to Stay" (heavy doses of the Rolling

Stones and the Beatles) and the in-depth seminar on Rastafarianism (I'm not sure if a bong-lab is required). Another choice morsel of vacuity is Harvard's "Coins of the Roman Empire" (no midterm, no final, no reading). One Harvard student told me, "Coins is only challenging if you never go to class." Another student commented, "Fortunately, that class is designed for second-graders, so it's fairly difficult to get anything lower than an A." One of Harvard's most popular courses is "Justice" which includes a little reading of Aristotle and John Locke. So far so good. But the course focuses on debating the issues of homosexuality, in-vitro fertilization, affirmative action and other *de rigueur* left-wing agenda items. All of a sudden, Aristotle and Locke seem like ornamental accouterments of an academic quota system: include at least two dead white men in your course and then you can talk about anything.

When I mention the fatuous "Environmental Justice" major to parents ("if trees could sue, how much would they sue for?"), parents often seem to think that I'm joking. The courses and majors offered at many colleges are simply mind-boggling. As a final example, let's look at Emory University's Religion/Environmental Studies course #329. This course, taught by Professor Bobbi Patterson, focuses on helping students understand trees by attempting to become trees. Students write phenomenological studies of one-square-foot plots of land, hold reflection circles, tend communal gardens, learn forest meditation, and take an oral history of a spiritual environmentalist. I'm not sure what any of this is, but for the price of a year at Emory (about $30,000), you can find out. Professor Patterson's great insight is that "when it's been cold," her students are unhappy, but when "the sun comes out two days later," students are happier.

Many colleges don't actively publicize course catalogues because they are worried that you or your parents will see this and (rightfully) ask, "Why would anyone pay $30,000 per year for this crap?" The bottom line: get the course catalogue and go through it.

In addition to the course catalogue, there are an increasing number of independent web sites that publish course critiques and evaluations for professors. Colleges generally despise these web sites, but until colleges publish their own objective evaluations, then these web sites will flourish. Please note that these web sites are usually unregulated and maintained by college students; often, but not always, they are very accurate. Course evaluation web sites include grade-it.com and collegestudent.com. Harvard's famous Confi Guide was known as a rebellious outpost of truth but has become much more tame (and a little less useful).

Chapter 13

Worthless Information

*"I thought I had Toni Morison up the ying-yang in English class,
then I went on a campus tour and all the guide talked about was
how Toni Morison spoke here, taught here—yada yada yada. I thought
I was going to be Toni Morisoned to death."*

Using view books, web sites, sales letters, postcards, campus tours and interviews, colleges fill you with information about the college: *the new $50 million gym is almost done, we've invested $4 million in new computers, Tom Brokaw spoke here last week.* We've just reviewed what's important in gauging a college; now we will review what's not important. Colleges—unregulated and aggressive—are very selective about the facts they tell you. Much of what they try to sell you is irrelevant when actually attending college.

Student/Faculty Ratio. Everyone loves the student-to-faculty ratio. Is the college with only 6 students per faculty member better than the college with 11 students per faculty member? The answer is: I have no idea and neither do you. Further, there's no way of getting an answer to that question. Why? Because the numbers that colleges report are completely misleading (that's a nice way of saying a lie). To arrive at a student-to-faculty ratio, colleges take the total number of faculty members on the payroll and divide that by the total number of matriculated students. Now that seems logical, but if Harvard's student-to-faculty ratio is 13:1, then why are there many 300+student classes?

Here's why: say there are 2,000 faculty members at a top university of 20,000 students (ratio of 10:1). At any one time, 400 of the faculty members are doing "research" or on sabbatical (meaning they don't teach), 200 are on leave for some other reason, and 100 are currently teaching at another college (though counted as faculty members at both colleges.) Of the 1,300 faculty members remaining, 500 of them are senior faculty who teach only one class per semester (at most) and teach only small upper-level seminars that are limited to the top juniors and

91

seniors. Now we're only left with 800 faculty members to teach 18,000 students (I've subtracted out the 2,000 top upperclassmen who take classes from the 500 senior professors). Now the student-to-faculty ratio is 23:1. And of those 800 faculty members remaining, 500 of them are graduate teaching assistants (grad students) and adjuncts (academic coolies) who make less than $25,000 per year. So the ratio of students to professors (not grad students or adjuncts) is 60:1 (18,000:300), and that's why you get so many 300+classes at colleges that claim to have a student-to-faculty ratio of 10:1.

The above example isn't true at all colleges, but no college (that I know of) reports student-to-faculty ratios faithfully; they don't reveal how many professors actually teach. The problem is far worse at universities that rely on the cheap labor of graduate students and adjuncts who teach in place of the professors who are off doing "research". For example, Swarthmore cannot replace professors with cheap grad students because they don't have grad students. However, colleges from NYU to Harvard and Yale rely heavily on their grad students. Many of the famous professors at top colleges don't teach, teach only very exclusive senior seminars, or teach 500-1000 student lectures. (In fact, many top professors are often lured away from one college to another with the promise that they won't be required to teach or will have to teach only one lecture per semester.) The actual 30-student class of freshmen and sophomores is taught by a grad student or adjunct.

To provide a specific example, let's look at the famed University of Wisconsin. In a recent year, Wisconsin had 2,027 professors on its payroll, but only 1,318 actually taught classes. So only 65% of Wisconsin's professors actually taught a class. To make matters worse, these 1,318 professors only taught, on average, 4-6 hours per week (6 hours of teaching is equivalent to teaching no more than 2 classes). The result? Despite rapidly increasing enrollment, Wisconsin actually had fewer professors teaching classes and fewer classes offered each semester, which is why many students have reported graduating from Wisconsin without taking a single class with fewer than 100 students.

There's no way of knowing what the true student-to-professor ratio of a college is, and there isn't much you can do about the situation other than to avoid research schools and universities with large grad schools (which means avoiding all public universities and most of the Ivies). What you should do is avoid considering the student-to-faculty ratio when comparing colleges; it's meaningless and most colleges can invent and invariably defend any ratio they wish.

The student/faculty ratio is supposed to give you an idea of the quality of teaching, but it is not a qualitative measurement, and as a quantitative measurement, it is highly inaccurate. In addition, most of the best teachers in the country aren't famous and, in many cases, aren't at the top colleges. If the top colleges wished to convey the quality of their teachers, then perhaps they would publicize the highly respected Carnegie Foundation's annual survey of top professors. Top colleges don't publicize this report because their professors rarely receive recognition for teaching; for the year 2000, only one of the 48 professors singled out for recognition taught at a top college (Dartmouth). The Professor of the Year at an undergraduate college, according to the Carnegie Foundation, teaches at the College of the Holy Cross. Odd—isn't it?—that the top colleges are so eager to publicize bogus student/faculty ratios but are rarely recognized for employing top teachers.

Size of Library. Colleges with large libraries like to boast about the number of volumes they have (and the number of subscriptions, microfiche, and so forth). It's truly one of the sillier boasts that colleges make. Harvard's library is seven times larger than Dartmouth's; is Harvard seven times better that Dartmouth? Penn State's library is bigger than Swarthmore's. Does it matter?

Sure, you need to have a good library, but any library with 500,000 or more books should provide everything an undergraduate might need. Besides, quantity does not predicate quality, and this is particularly true with libraries. I've been in awful libraries with 1.5 million volumes and wonderful libraries with only 400,000 volumes. In most cases, only graduate students require the obscure resources that a seven million-volume library might provide.

In addition, local, hardcover resources are less vital in the era of the Internet. (And in many cases, you may be inclined to attempt to buy a book from an Internet bookseller from the comfort of your dorm room than to trek to the library and brave the endless stacks.) Also most libraries have arranged inter-collegiate loan privileges for its students, so you may borrow books from other colleges or public libraries. Between the Internet and inter-library loans, you should be able to get any book (or article, essay, or other piece of information) you're interested in, even if your college's library does not have it. Often, getting information from the Internet or from interlibrary loans is actually preferable than getting it from your own college's library. One of the great banes of college life is the hefty library late fines (often hundreds of dollars) you will pay—yes, I'm assuming you will have late fines because nearly everyone does. There are no late fines for getting information from the Internet and most interlibrary loan periods are much longer (often an entire semester) than your college's loan period. If you check the book out from your college, you will need to return it in three weeks (or pay the fines); if you check it out via interlibrary loan, you can keep the book for three months.

Ultimately, it makes no difference if college A has 700,000 books, college B has 1.7 million books, and college C has 6.2 million books. Chances are you will try to get the information from the Internet or from interlibrary loan anyway.

Research Dollars. Many universities pride themselves on the hundreds of millions of dollars they win in research grants (usually federal and corporate). In most cases, these research grants are used to conduct technological and medical research. Most of the research is conducted through the graduate schools, so you may be wondering why you should care about research grants.

The benefit in research grants is that the money is used to buy very expensive equipment, which is often available to upperclassmen. Usually, the colleges with the best-equipped labs also have extensive graduate research projects, which in turn are funded by multi-million dollar grants.

But this upside is balanced by an even greater downside. Universities like research money because, in part, they can attract eminent professors; these professors do not teach (they "research"). In turn, these research programs enroll and employ large numbers of graduate students; it's these students who teach. So large research universities tend to have a high number of professors who do not teach and a high number of graduate students who do teach. To compound the problem, over half of all graduate students in hard-science and engineering programs are foreigners; it's common to have a chemistry teacher who doesn't speak much English, has little (or no) experience teaching, and is far more interested in his research than in grading 400 chemistry exams.

In the final analysis, the amount of research funding a college has is meaningless. It may be beneficial to undergraduates in a few cases, but it's more likely to be detrimental to your undergraduate education. The bottom line: the more research money a university has, the poorer its undergraduate teaching will be.

Shiny New Buildings. Some colleges, like Emory, are loaded with shiny new buildings. Some are necessary, such as dorms and classrooms. Some are extravagant (such as a $40 million lacrosse field house designed to resemble I.M. Pei's Louvre glass pyramid). Colleges love to show off their shiny news buildings in press releases, on their web sites, in their view books, and on campus tours. Your campus tour will take you past every shiny new building on the campus (along with the oldest building—all the buildings erected in the 1960s and 70s will be skipped).

Often, when a college creates a plan to enroll more and/or better students, the first thing they do is sink some money into a prominently placed shiny new building (or two). Colleges consistently assume that students will be attracted to a shiny new building like a moth to a porch light.

However, how these shiny new buildings are paid for is a dirty little secret. Wealthy colleges with large endowments and annual alumni contributions have no problem paying for the new $40 million gym, but the vast majority of colleges do not have easy access to millions of dollars. Often, they raise the necessary capital by selling bonds. This may not seem bad, but these bonds are rated the same way all corporate bonds are rated: by measuring cash flow. In order to maintain a good rating, colleges must keep revenue high by increasing enrollments and expenses low. One of the primary means by which expenses are kept low is teacher salaries; another area involves denying tenure to teachers. In fact, bond ratings are often lowered if teacher salaries increase or if more teachers are given promotions. So a few shiny new buildings may translate into a concerted effort by the college administration to employ less expensive (and often lower quality) teachers.

As an example, the University of Virginia recently had the rating on its $220 million in outstanding bonds upgraded because of increased revenue. The rating on Clark University's $30 million in bonds was upgraded because of increased revenue and solid profits of 3%. (By the way, in the non-profit world "profits" are referred to as "surpluses.") While Eastern Michigan's $103 million in bonds were upgraded because of increased revenue and profit margins ranging from 2 to almost 5 percent. A college increases revenue by increasing enrollment (accomplished by good marketing) and increases its profits by lowering its variable expenses (teacher salaries, clubs and organizations, special projects, and so forth). One of my favorites is a recent upgrade on $38-million bonds from Southwest Texas State; the bonds were upgraded, in part, because Texas State can now charge an "unlimited student fee" to pay for the bonds should the university be unable to otherwise pay them. Can you imagine the student reaction if Texas State actually attempted to impose that "unlimited student fee?" Students would quickly realize that those shiny new buildings often carry a huge price tag.

There's no way for a typical college applicant to know all the details of a college's new buildings, but shiny new buildings shouldn't impress you. While college A may have constructed several new buildings, college B may have opted for keeping the same old buildings but hiring better (and more expensive) professors. Which one matters more for your education? Obviously, you would prefer to have better professors than a gym with a retractable roof. If you wanted to join a gym, you could have spent $500/year by joining an area gym instead of $25,000/year on tuition. If your college doesn't have a great gym, you can always join the local town's gym. However, if your college doesn't have great professors, what are you going to do? (Suffer through bad classes, that's what.) In many cases, colleges erect buildings so they can publish pictures of them in their view books and impress students on campus tours. Don't be impressed.

Special Speakers. The view book will list them, the web site will have pictures, and the campus tour guide will speak of them: famous people who walked across campus just last week. The list might include Tom Brokaw, Maya Angelou, and the former President of Botswana. It all seems so amazing until you realize that anyone willing to spend $50,000 can get a famous speaker; if you were willing to spend the money, you could get any number of former Prime Ministers to come to your house and cook eggs for you. A few colleges, such as Harvard, Princeton, and Yale, can often get famous people on campus for nothing. But most colleges are required to pay an enormous speaking fee, and in many cases, the speaking fee (for a 30-50 minute speech) is more than the annual salary of most of your teachers. When a college wants to enroll more students, the second thing it does (after erecting shiny new buildings) is hire a few famous people to come to campus. These famous people add credibility and prestige to the college. (The cost of someone famous? General Colin Powell, $60,000; former president Bush, $80,000; former president Clinton, $90,000; former Prime Minister Lady Margaret Thatcher, $65,000. Of course, it depends on the college and the event: Colin Powell was recently paid $200,000 to speak at a Tufts lecture series. I guess it takes a lot to get a General to travel to Medford, Massachusetts.)

The problem is: in most cases, the famous speakers that colleges bring to campus are nothing more than publicity stunts—very expensive publicity stunts. If you wonder where all your $25,000 in annual tuition goes—especially when your freshman writing teacher makes $11,000 per year—this is one of the answers. And yet having a speaker on campus is no more interesting than watching him or her on television (and you probably will get a better view by watching on television). Personally, I wish colleges would stop paying $15,000-$200,000 speaking fees and spend the money instead on hiring better and more teachers. It's ridiculous that a college would pay $30,000 for a one-hour speech, and then force you into a 500-student chemistry class with a graduate student teacher (not a professor) who has no teaching training, poor English skills, and is making $11,000 per year. Sometimes it's hard not to be impressed by the list of special speakers, but remember that anyone with the money can hire a famous person to speak—and if you want to watch famous people speak, watch PBS or C-SPAN.

A Great Football Team. Colleges spend (and lose) millions of dollars on big-name football and basketball programs. Why? Because they believe that a top-ranked football team will attract more students. Many professors do not like having top-ranked teams at their college because they feel it develops an atmosphere disrespectful to intellectual inquiry. Perhaps so. But the bottom line is: colleges know that many students consider and apply to their school because of a nationally recognized sports team (usually football or basketball). While prominent sports programs can significantly add to the campus environment, it would be foolish to choose a college because of its sports programs. The success of a college's sports teams could be a factor, but it should never be a deciding factor.

View Books & Web Sites. College view books and web sites are developed by consultants, produced by marketing teams, and judged by their effectiveness just as is any sales tool used by any business. However, college marketing is unregulated. View books and web sites usually promote the useless (special speakers, a winning football team) and hide the useful (quality of the teachers, actual student-to-professor ratio, actual class size, crime statistics). If a view book or web site publishes facts, use them with caution. Otherwise, ignore the view book and web site. To understand a college, you need to visit the campus. Yes, there are nice pictures of the campus in the view book, but those pictures are usually staged and airbrushed by professionals (even at most of the top colleges), often at the cost of tens or hundreds of thousands of dollars.

Chapter 14

Campus Visits

"BU's tour was a riot. Pat and Paul were hilarious.
I'm not applying there, but I'd pay $5 to take that tour again."

Visit Early. Visit Often. You should make every effort to visit several college campuses, even colleges that aren't your top choices. You will learn much about colleges by visiting them. And you must thoroughly visit any college to which you're applying early decision. Because early decision is binding, you must know the college well. If you cannot visit a college, do not apply early decision to it. In addition, colleges view the visit as a sign that you're truly interested; if you have the money, then the college will expect you to visit. Many colleges reject an applicant of it appears that the college isn't the applicant's first choice. Emory has boosted its yield to 33% from 23% simply by favoring applicants who had the most contact with the school. Connecticut College accepted only 18% of students who made no contact with the school (other than sending in the application), while Connecticut College's overall acceptant rate is around 35%. Anyone who clearly has the means to visit a college will adversely affect his application if he does not do so.

Visiting colleges is so crucial because you will live there for four years. Many overlook this obvious fact: would you decide to live anywhere for several years without visiting first? Half of college is academic, and half is social, and visiting the colleges will provide you with a better idea of both halves. In addition, almost all of the information you receive from a college prior to visiting comes from the college's admissions and marketing offices; it is biased. Your visit to the college will provide you with a good first-hand, unbiased evaluative experience.

When? You should try to visit colleges during the academic year. Unfortunately, most students visit while on spring break or summer break. (Most college spring breaks align with high school spring breaks.) Seeing the college with students will significantly aid your evaluation; also, if you visit the college while it is in session, you will be able to sit in on classes. More on that later.

Two other important reasons to visit while the college is in session are weather and the local town. The first may seem trivial, but if you're from Maryland or New York City and you visit Cornell in July, you may not know the kind of weather you will be required to live through. Ithaca, New York (where Cornell is located) is lovely in July, but chances are you won't be there in July if you attend Cornell (or Ithaca College). Often, colleges located in very cold climates have higher dropout rates precisely because of the extremely cold weather (which often lasts for many months). To make an informed decision, you should know what the weather is like during the academic year. The second reason is also important: many college towns are extremely different during the academic year. Stores may close or limit operating hours during the summer; many businesses in town sell different items during the summer. The entire town may have a different feel when the college is in session. Visiting during the academic year will provide you with the most accurate feel for the college experience.

If you intend to visit colleges while you're on spring break (during your junior year), then try to visit those colleges that won't be on spring break. You may need to take a few days off of school in order visit colleges; this is okay and should be approved by your counselor and parents. Once again, if you visit a college while it's not in session, then you are not visiting the college; you are visiting a collection of buildings. If you need to take off a Thursday and Friday from school in order to visit a college while it's in session, then do it. Many colleges, particularly smaller liberal arts colleges such as Swarthmore, are completely deserted over much of the summer, so visiting while school is not in session is pointless. At larger colleges, urban colleges, and public universities, most of the summer students tend to be special students, such as adult students. The atmosphere on campus will be completely different and probably less desirable than the atmosphere during the regular academic year.

Take the Tour. When planning a college visit, call the admissions office and inquire about tours. Some colleges give tours seven days per week, while others may only give tours three or four days per week. Make reservations if necessary. Parents and students should take the tour—as long as the parents remember that their job is to provide a mature, informed voice to the discussion, not to dictate orders. Ultimately, the student is the one who will live at the college, so the student must be the one who is comfortable with the campus.

The official tour may be led by someone from the admissions office or by a student (a volunteer or employee). In most cases, it's highly preferable to deal with admissions office employees, but student-given tours are the exception. In many cases, student tour guides will say things that admissions officers never would. For example, the tour may require a trip through a nice dorm room (most do), and the student tour guide will tell you the truth: you probably will never be able to live in that nice of a dorm room. (This happens on the NYU tour.) Student tour guides are more likely to be candid and to provide unique insights into the college.

If you have a student tour guide, then ask questions! *What college was your first choice? Why did you choose this college? Did this college live up to your expectations? What department is best? What department is worst? Do teaching assistants teach many classes? What's your biggest class? What's your biggest gripe about this college? Do you spend the summers here? Is there much crime? Is the academic pressure great? Do many students transfer out? How is the campus food? How is the registrar's office? How is the administration? How are the campus clubs? Do you belong to any clubs? What do you do on Saturday afternoons?* Your guide's job is to tell you all the great things about the college, but most guides are honest enough to tell you the bad things too—you just need to prompt them.

The one significant caveat to the campus tour is this: do not assume that your tour guide is representative of the college community. Upon returning from visiting Drew University (Madison, NJ), one student said he would never apply to Drew "because it's a bunch of poor theater homosexuals." While Drew does have a strong theater program, its student population is neither predominately poor nor homosexual; in fact, I would describe Drew as one of the more conservative colleges in the North. I asked the student how he arrived at such a conclusion about Drew, and he said his tour guide was a theater major who constantly lectured the group about his plights as a lower-class homosexual. While this may seem odd, it happens more often than you think. Sometimes politically active campus groups target the admissions office and other times it happens by accident, but regardless of the circumstances, admissions offices are never going to deny someone employment as a tour guide because of their sexual preferences or even suggest that tour guides should not discuss their sexual preference (lest the college want some sort of sordid protest on Parents' Day). You may get an activist tour guide whose mission is to attract like-minded applicants and scare away the rest. In defense of admissions offices everywhere, I suggest that you never presume that a tour guide represents the whole of the college community.

Most official campus tours are highly scripted (which is why you need to insert your own questions). The buildings you see and the things you're told are all designed to make the maximum positive impression. The goal of the tour is to get you to apply. Period. Campus tours are designed to seem forthright, but regardless of the seeming candor of your tour guide, remember that tours are scripted.

Your Own Tour. Because of that, you should always take your own campus tour. Before or after (preferably after) the official tour, wander around campus. Poke your head into buildings, and explore every corner from the dorms and the Commons to the student center and the classrooms. Check out the classrooms in the basements of buildings (which many colleges have and are often awful), seek out the freshmen dorms (which are usually the worst), and eat in the commons. The official tour will give you a good idea of the basic layout of the campus; your unofficial tour will help you better understand the college. But plan carefully because your unofficial tour may (and should) take up to 2-4 hours; you may live at the college for four years and spend as much as $160,000, so take your time and make an informed decision.

As you walk around campus, be as critical as possible. This may seem cynical, but the fact is that many colleges spend more on grooming their campus and constructing shiny buildings than on things that actually effect students (such as teachers). Most college administrations are very aware that their survival depends on recruiting high quality students each year, so they make sure that every tree is pruned and every petunia is carefully planted. Do not be impressed by the landscaping; in fact, be wary of it. Do not be impressed by the shiny new building. Think about it: after you live on campus for a few weeks, the effects of the petunia gardens and shiny buildings will wear off, so if you chose the college because it's "pretty," you'll soon be disappointed. A college will nit-pick your application trying to find a reason to reject you. You should nitpick the college trying to find a reason to reject it. You are probably starting with 12-20 colleges on your list, and you should cross off at least half of them—so start looking for reasons!

Most importantly, you should get a feeling for the campus atmosphere (which is why visiting during the academic year is important). I know this sounds nebulous, and it is. There's no formula for gauging a campus atmosphere, which is why bringing your parents is usually helpful. But you should try to assess the atmosphere and your response to it: if you're bookish, do you feel comfortable on a jock campus?; if you're a minority, do you feel comfortable on a campus that has few (or many) minorities? Does the campus seem too small and make you feel cloistered? Or does it feel too big and impersonal? Does it seem bleak and dreary? Or too lightweight? Too politically radical? Too confrontational? Too unfocused? Too antisocial?

How does one gauge these things? It's difficult. As you walk around campus, read the signs and flyers posted on bulletin boards, pick up a copy of the campus newspaper, and relax in the student center. Listen to what students say—in the campus center, in line at the commons, in classes. Do not be blinded by things you've previously heard or believed: now you're actually on campus, and now you're seeing the real college.

Visiting classes is another vital part of the campus visit. Most colleges will permit you to sit in on a class. In many cases, you may choose from a list of many classes. You should try to choose a class you're interested in taking should you attend the college and in which already have some knowledge so you will understand the conversation (for example, U.S. History, American literature, or a language). Sit in on the class for as long as you can, preferably in its entirety. Do not be asinine by asking questions and goofing off: you are a guest of the college, so you should behave as a guest would. If you're unsatisfied with the class you attend, you may be able to attend another class. At its most basic level, this is what you're paying up to $160,000 for: teachers teaching. Obviously, a college education has many sundry components, but the most fundamental and overlooked one is the quality of the teaching.

Many students are actually surprised at what they find on campus tours. One student, who scored a perfect five on the U.S. History AP test, said the U.S. history class he visited at Duke disappointed him. He sat in on two other classes and continued to be disappointed. He subsequently applied to and was accepted to Yale. Another student felt that the Princeton tour gave him the impression he was touring a high school—a very good, large prep school. (He currently attends Columbia.) Yet another student felt Bates was too small and too much like his current high school. If you do a thorough job investigating, your campus visits will have a few surprises for you. Inevitably, you will find many of the things you've heard or read about a college to be not quite true. So when you visit a campus, forget everything you've heard and read, and experience the college anew. After you leave, take some time to assess your visit and summarize your thoughts. Ultimately, the questions are: do I want to live here for four years, spent as much as $160,000 here, grow up here, and assign to this college the awesome responsibility of educating me? If you're hesitant about the answer, you should visit other colleges.

How Many Times? I recommend that you visit every college on the short-list once during your junior year to take the tour, look around, attend classes, eat in the cafeteria, chat with some students, read the college newspaper. You may visit as many as 10-20 colleges during this first look. Then narrow down your list to 5-10 colleges and visit them again early in your senior year. Stay the night in the dorms, sit in on more classes, go to an interview. This second visit should allow you to narrow your lists down a little more and prioritize your list. I find this second visit, usually 5-12 months after the first visit, to be crucial. Your opinion about the colleges on your list will evolve, and you will get a much better idea of what's right for you. Remember, you're making a $100,000+decision, so take your time and be informed! (Besides, by visiting twice, you're showing the admissions office that you are very interested in the college!) At the very least, you should always visit your top 2-3 choices and your early decision college (if any) twice.

There are those who believe it is better to make the second trips to the colleges after you've been admitted. You may make a third trip to colleges once you've been admitted, but my experience shows that a second trip (and overnight stay) 5-12 months after a first trip will really help you prioritize your college choices and show the admissions office that you're very interested. There's no point in showing an admissions office you're very interested after you've been admitted!

Wear a Belt. Finally, as with all your interactions with colleges, you should be on your best behavior. Do not wear jeans and a T-shirt; do not smoke or chew gum; do not use slang or swear; do not wear a big nose-ring or a Metallica bandanna. You may see college students do all of these things, and you may do all of these things once you're in college. But for now, you must be on your best behavior. Also, don't be surprised if there are tourists on your tour. Sometimes, tourists from Alabama and Japan may want to tour Harvard even though they don't have any children interested in the college. Some colleges are famous and many have famous buildings (or battle fields or statues or something).

Videos. Many colleges understand that visiting in-person is a time- and money-consuming endeavor that not everyone can afford. In this case, they offer video versions of the campus tours. The problem with videos is that they are finely tuned marketing tools, even more so than campus tours. A video produced by a college usually isn't very honest or helpful and won't give you the same sense of the campus as an actual visit will. You should make every effort to visit your top 2-3 choices, and you should never apply early decision to a college you haven't or cannot personally visit. If you cannot afford to visit a college that's a great distance from your home, then you probably shouldn't apply to that college. If money is an issue, then apply to colleges within a day's drive so you can give yourself the benefit of visiting them.

There are some campus-tour videos produced by independent companies; these companies produce these videos precisely because college-produced videos are very biased. While many of these independent campus-tour videos are very good-much better than those produced by the college—they still do not replace actually visiting the campus. You may choose to purchase a few independently produced videos to help you narrow your college list, and then actually visit the few colleges you've chosen. Using videos to help you narrow a college list from fifteen to six colleges is a good idea, but then you should actually visit those six colleges. Most high school counseling offices or libraries have college-tour videos, so you usually do not need to purchase them.

Chapter 15

The CASIS

> "I'm supposed to figure out where I want to go to college and
> what I want to do with my life, and I can't figure out
> what shoes to wear to the movies tonight."

The process of comparing colleges and thinking about academic interests and potential careers may seem overwhelming. If you are stuck and aren't sure where to start, the CASIS may be the answer. The CASIS (College Assessment, Skills and Interest Survey) is a 45-minute survey that asks the student questions about college, habits and interests, and high school work. All of that information is then compared to a database of over a million responses from other students. The CASIS survey looks for patterns in responses and matches them to the patterns of people who are successful and happy in their careers. The student's academic performances and test scores (if any) are indexed using the standard (AI) common admissions index. Then the CASIS matches this career data and academic performance information to colleges that best suit the student.

The CASIS report lists 3-5 recommended colleges and 2-5 "stretch" colleges. These stretch colleges will give you an idea of where you can go if you improve. What exactly do you need to improve? The CASIS report will tell you what the weakest part of your college application would be if you applied right now. The CASIS report also gives you a list of recommended careers and will report your current academic index.

The CASIS report is not an ending point: it is a starting point. It helps give you direction: which colleges to consider, which careers best suit your skills and interests, what your academic index is, and what your greatest weakness is. The CASIS report also helps link high school performance to college acceptance to careers. This information is very useful for 10th graders through seniors making college decisions in the fall.

The CASIS is unique because it's the only survey that recommends colleges and careers, and it's the only survey designed exclusively for college-bound high school students. Morganroth Forbes LLC developed the CASIS in consultation with me and many other college and career professionals in order to provide students and parents with useful information that will significantly facilitate the process of selecting and applying to college. The CASIS may be ordered from Morganroth Forbes (email them at CASIS@Mind2Mind.org).

Chapter 16

You & the Top Applicants

"Jenny McKorgle. Don't get me started. 1580 in the SAT. 5s on
AP Bio and Spanish. Class President. AIDS hotline counselor. Top
scorer on the lax team. Plus she's a genius and her mom is Hispanic, so
she's like a minority, right? She's applying to Harvard. I have no chance.
I guess I'll go to BC or something."

An early part of the application process involves evaluating your grades, test
scores, and extracurricular activities. How will you compare with other students
applying to top colleges?

Don't Go To Extremes. Unfortunately, students tend to swing to the
extremes: either they think they are wonderful and will be admitted everywhere,
or they think they are awful and won't be admitted anywhere. The first problem
is more common than the second. You may have an A average in honors courses,
an AP course or two under your belt, and so forth. Perhaps your mother and your
teachers all tell you how smart you are and your younger brother thinks you've
descended from Olympus. The problem? You may only apply to colleges out of
your league and find yourself headed to the local community college. (Yes, this
happens all the time.)

Most students and parents are not capable of providing a highly objective
opinion of a student's chances of being admitted to top college; providing this
objectivity is what a college counselor is for (however, do not get angry at your
counselor if he informs you that your chance of being admitted to Princeton is
zero). Students who think they are wonderful usually forget the fact that almost
everyone else applying to Yale will also have a 1430 SAT score, a 4.1 GPA (out of
4.3), 7 AP courses, and four SAT II scores of 720 or higher. You may be the top
ranked student in your school (the valedictorian), but you need to remember that
the Ivies reject over 50% of valedictorians. Too many students set themselves up
for failure by over-reaching. What's worse is that you may waste many hours

applying to colleges to which you don't have a chance of being admitted; meanwhile, your applications to colleges to which you have a chance of being admitted are sloppy and late. You only have so much time and energy: spend it on colleges to which you have a chance of being admitted.

Occasionally, the opposite is true: students underestimate their chances of being admitted because they don't want to deal with rejection. Once again, this is a problem with objectivity with which your counselor should be able to assist you. Receiving a one-page rejection letter from Penn is quite painless as long as you don't put all your eggs in one basket.

Never Just One. A crucial bit of advice: never put all your hopes into one college, particularly a highly competitive college. There is a bit of luck in getting admitted to any top college—even if you do everything else correctly. The only way that rejection will truly sting is if you convince yourself that "I'm a Princeton girl" and then are rejected by Princeton. When I'm advising students, this flexibility is the one rule that I don't allow to be transgressed: I refuse to work with students who are transfixed on one (and only one) college. How can you avoid this? Here are a few steps.

- Keep in mind that a bit of luck goes into successfully being admitted to any top college. Competition is so stiff that Princeton rejects hundreds of highly qualified students each year because it simply doesn't have the dorm and classroom space. In many cases, it's almost impossible to differentiate between the students who are rejected and those who are accepted.

- Never pick one college to rest all your hopes on; since being admitted requires a little luck, you should always have two or three top picks.

- If you apply early decision, remember that you're applying early not because this is the only college you want to attend, but because it's to your advantage. So if Yale rejects (or defers) your early decision application, you can then apply to Cornell without remorse or regret. Unfortunately, while early decision is usually advantageous to the applicant, it also conditions applicants to think that only one college is best for them. Yes, you can only apply early decision to one college, but that shouldn't suggest to you that only one college is best for you.

- When you visit a college, don't go to the campus bookstore and spend $300 on paraphernalia. (In fact, I suggest avoiding the campus bookstore during your tour.) If you buy a Princeton T-shirt and wear it everywhere for a few months, then you're setting yourself up for possibly being greatly disappointed. As a rule, don't attach yourself to a college before you've been admitted. (This is another area in which colleges could be more helpful, but since it's to a college's advantage to encourage applicants to attach themselves emotionally to the college, colleges encourage it.)

A Reality Check. So what does an average applicant who's been accepted to a top college look like? This is crucial information that you need in order to perform a reality check. First, his grades are almost all A's with a GPA of 3.8 or higher (on an unweighted 4.0 scale). His high school transcript has 20 or more "solids" on it. (A solid is a rigorous academic course, which excludes non-academic courses and soft-academic courses such as typing, vocabulary, and many computer and soft-science courses.) A dozen or more of the courses are honors or advanced, and he has at least three APs and often has as many as eight. He's in the top 10% of his class, though if his SAT and SAT II scores are very high (750 or higher), he could be in the 10%-12% rank range. His SAT scores are 670 or higher in each subject, and he has three SAT II scores of 650 or higher. He participates in sports, a club or two, and some community activities. And he has 30+hours of community service in each of his high school years.

Keep in mind that this description is *typical*, not exceptional. An "exceptional" student, which is not unusual at Yale, Harvard and Princeton, has a 3.9 GPA with nine AP courses, a 1520 on the SAT, is a nationally recognized violinist, and helps rebuild churches in Guatemala in his spare time.

Most students who are not accepted to a top college usually have one (or more) of three problems: low grades/ranking (B or lower or lower than a top 20% ranking), low standardized test scores (below 650 per subject), nothing going on outside of the classroom. Most college rejections boil down to class ranking, standardized test scores, or extracurricular activities. A good candidate for a top college excels in all three areas.

Chapter 17

Getting Information

"I called Georgetown to ask for an application and I just know I
sounded like a drooling idiot, like I was calling from some psychiatric
prison or something. They don't record those conversations, do they?"

How many? The first and perhaps most obvious question regarding getting
information from colleges is: *how many colleges should I contact?* Your friend calls
40 colleges while your older sister seriously considered only 4 colleges. What's the
magic number?

By the middle of your junior year, you should have a broad list of 10-20 colleges in which you're interested. After a bit of research, a few visits, and some
comparative analysis, you should have no more than 10 colleges on your list by
the end of your junior year. You should contact these 10 colleges for view books.
By the beginning of your senior year, you should have no more than 8 colleges on
your list (usually 5-6 colleges is sufficient). Your contact with colleges may be
extensive, but if you're only dealing with 5 colleges, it's manageable.

The details. Your initial contact with a college may be attending an information session presented by a college representative at your school or attending a
local college night. It's usually assumed that these information sessions are
intended for seniors, but I think juniors should attend an information session
for any college in which they're interested. The earlier you do this, the sooner
you will be able to start comparing colleges and formulating questions. Most
information sessions consist of a brief talk by the representative, a video, and a
question-and-answer period. If you're going to attend an information session, be
sure to look up the college in a college directory and jot down a few notes. You
should walk into the information session reasonably informed about the college,
and you should be able to ask a few good questions. (See the chapter on interviews to get ideas for questions.) Keep in mind that the representative is usually
an admissions officer; it's unlikely the representative will notice most students,

but any particularly poorly behaved student will probably get noticed. After you ask a few good questions, provide the representative with your information so the college can place you on its mailing list. And most importantly, take notes. (You should take notes even if you can't think of anything to write down—note-taking will make you look serious and mature!)

You may get invited to a college reception at a hotel; the college's representative will give a short talk, a video will be shown, and perhaps an alumnus or two will wax eloquent on their alma mater. If you're very interested in the college, you should attend. Otherwise, it will be a waste of time. You should not ask tough questions at such an event, and everything you will hear you can get out of the college view book-biased praise for the college.

Finally, there are college nights (or college fairs) where 30 to 300 colleges set up booths and sell their colleges. This is a great opportunity to get a ton of information from colleges; most of the colleges will have view books, applications, and tons of pamphlets available for you. You won't need to call them or e-mail them to get all this stuff. I suggest attending a college fair in order to acquire 20-30 view books quickly and easily. You may talk to the representative if you like, but as in all other cases, these representatives are skilled salespeople and aren't likely to tell you anything other than what's printed in the view book. In addition, a college fair isn't a good time to ask tough questions because the representative usually needs to deal with many people at once. Save your tough questions for the college information session at your high school or for your college visit. Some students feel college fairs and college visits to high schools are important events at which they can market themselves. In most cases, this isn't true. Most regional college representatives simply can't and won't remember most of the students they meet. Only the very bad ones (and a few extraordinary ones) will be remembered, so don't break your back trying to be impressive.

You need to contact each college to which you're seriously interested in applying. If you've given your name (and other relevant information) to a college representative during a college fair, information session, or some other engagement, be sure the college actually has your information and has spelled everything correctly. It's most common to start contacting colleges in the fall and winter of your junior year to inquire about campus visits. At this point, you're only making initial contact to arrange for a campus tour; it's not necessary to get an application, as the application you will complete in the fall of your senior year will be different. You may, however, wish to get a view book. You should particularly ask for brochures or pamphlets on particular subject departments, sports or other specialties of the college. Most colleges—particularly those that are aggressive marketers—will have brochures covering every major academic department. Getting these extra brochures will allow you to investigate the college better and will exhibit an informed interest in the college (which the college will note!).

You should also get a course catalogue from the college; the course catalogue allows you to investigate the details of the sort of education the college offers. (See the section above on course catalogues.)

In all cases, parents should never contact the college. The prospective applicant should make all contact. Repeat: parents should stay off the phone. Many colleges track this sort of thing, and the last thing they want to see is that an applicant contacted the college zero times whereas the applicant's mother contacted the college twenty-two times. This is a sign to the admissions committee that perhaps you don't really wish to attend that college, and the committee will do you a favor by rejecting you. Regardless of the issue or concern, only the applicant should contact the college.

It's usually best to contact top colleges via telephone, in person, or in writing; you can introduce yourself and request an interview and view book. Some colleges respond to e-mail inquiries, but for all their investment in technology, most colleges either do not respond to or often mishandle e-mail inquiries. For now, you should stick to the old-fashioned telephone or snail mail. If you're worried about your phone manner, call your father or mother at the office while they're at work and role-play. While a great phone impression usually does nothing for your application, a terrible phone impression may. Admissions offices have extensive databases of applicant information, and you never know what they might put in your file. ("Said 'duh' a lot on the phone, and asked if I could 'get jiggy' with sending him an application.") Colleges will note anything you mail to them, so your written correspondence must be perfect. In all cases you should start the process early, and you should make a good impression on everyone—from the janitor to the receptionist to the president of the college. Everyone counts, and you never know!

If you're an American living in a foreign country, then you need to send all mail via regular manila envelopes (or whichever color you prefer). Don't use the blue airmail (*par avion*) envelopes; the college mail-house usually assumes that blue airmail is from foreign students, so they sort this mail differently. If you use the airmail envelopes, you will be considered a foreign student and bureaucratic bedlam will ensue.

If you formally contact an admissions office once, in the spring of your junior year for example, you will usually receive an application (and other mail) from them. However, if the first week of August has arrived and you haven't received anything from the college, do not hesitate to contact them again. Colleges do lose information, and mail sometimes gets misdirected. (Do not assume, as some paranoid students and parents do, that the college has vetted you. No college will discourage you from applying after a simple phone call.)

Most colleges first mail applications in late July, while some wait until early August. You should contact every college to which you are interested in applying by mid-August, requesting a view book and application. You should visit every college by October of your senior year, so you may wish to arrange these visits in August/September as well.

Colleges mail many things to applicants; some are aggressive, and some are odd. After the PSAT, you may receive information from some colleges you've never heard of or didn't request information from; these colleges bought your information from the College Board—yes, this is the information you provided when you took the PSAT. This information may include your name and address, PSAT score, race, religion, grades, intended major, financial aid status, and so forth. Minority students with good grades and high PSAT scores will usually receive information from good colleges such as Washington & Lee, Harvard, Stanford and Wake Forest who are interested in attracting minority students. High-scoring students of all sorts will receive assorted information from obscure colleges. In most cases, you will probably be flattered to receive the information, and in most cases, you won't even consider applying to the colleges that send you unsolicited advertisements. When you start to receive this mail, put a box in the corner of your bedroom and toss the letters and brochures in it. After a few months, you may have a fairly large collection of unsolicited mail—keep this collection as a reminder that many colleges want you. If a college rejects you, take solace in the number of colleges that you rejected.

There are a few pieces of unsolicited mail to which you should pay attention: letters that solicit you as a special admit. If an athletic director or minority recruiter from a good college contacts you before you've contacted them, they probably bought your PSAT information from the College Board. You should, in most cases, politely respond by saying "Thank you for your letter; I will consider such-and-such college." Include any questions or comments you may have. If a good college contacted you first, then clearly they are interested in something about you and look favorably upon applicants like you. Take advantage of this if you are interested in the college.

Most colleges will mail you an application and a view book; some colleges will also mail a letter, a postcard (with campus tour information), or an admissions "newsletter." In all cases these mailings should be viewed as advertising of which college view books are often the most egregious example.

The "view book" is the brochure or sales catalogue of the college, except that it usually contains little or no useful information. They cost millions to produce and exhibit every hope of what the college will become. Therein lies the rub: view books often show colleges as they wish to be, not as they are. Perhaps you will find MIT's view book full of whimsy (as its recent version is); needless to say, MIT's student body is far from whimsical, and yet that's probably what the marketing study concluded: some brilliant students don't apply to MIT because they view it as grim, oppressive, and toilsome. So MIT created a sales brochure that's a cross between *The Simpsons* and the J Crew catalogue. Does this help you? Not at all. It's useless. Once you visit the campus, you'll find a great deal of that childlike fancy disappears into labs of students staring at beakers and oscilloscopes.

A recent view book from Vassar actually looks like a GAP catalogue, and I wouldn't be surprised if they modeled their view book on GAP ads. Most view books are more useful as case studies in modern education marketing than they are as providers of helpful information about the college. You will want to request one in order to exhibit your interest in the college, but you will also want to disregard almost everything in it. In most cases, the more helpful information in the view book is important application information and deadlines, and listings of majors, concentrations, and special programs. All the lovely pictures and witty repartee are efforts to convince you to apply, not to honestly inform you.

If you want to do some quick research on colleges before calling them, you should use the Internet. First, go through the college's web site (and in most cases you will be able to download the prior year's application). Second, go to independent sites—some are good and some aren't, but if you search enough you should be able to find some useful information. Just remember that much of the information about colleges—student/faculty ratio, size of library and endowment—is useless. In addition, your counselor's office should have a catalogue from nearly every college in America and several college guidebooks. Use them; they're free and readily available.

If anything goes wrong in your contact with colleges—perhaps they mail a brochure to you but misspelled your name—you should definitely call them to kindly report the problem. A little misinformation can go a long way, and most colleges are eager to correct problems before they become huge issues later. (Once the admissions season begins in November, colleges prefer to focus on reviewing applications than on correcting spelling mistakes.) If you're moving, give them your new address; if a college thinks you're a minority but you're not, let them know; if an athletic director is interested in you but you severely broke your leg, send him a note. To repeat: don't hesitate to report an actual problem to the colleges.

Finally, there are several "hi-tech" ways to conduct a college search and communicate with colleges. For example, the College Board offers a program called ExPAN, which allows you to search through colleges, send a letter of inquiry, and apply using the common application via computer. It's quick. It's easy. It's the wrong way to conduct a college search. If "quick" and "easy" are priorities to you, then perhaps you should not attend college (a bachelor degree is neither quick nor easy). You are about to spend four years, and $100,000+on one of the most important parts of your life, so take your time, take the slow and hard route, and do it right. You should look through college guides and view books, contact colleges yourself (not through some automated computer program), and apply using their own applications. The assembly-line approach will lead to poor decisions and poor applications.

Chapter 18

Grades, Classes & Transcripts

"I took a health class in 9th grade and it shows up on my transcript as *Human Sexuality and Reproduction*. Colleges know I was forced to take that, don't they? Otherwise, they might think I'm a pervert."

What classes should you take? What are good grades for top colleges? What should your transcript look like?

These are all questions that parents and students ask. First, you should note that at many competitive colleges, grades are only one-third of your academic index. Your SAT and SAT II scores may comprise two-thirds of your academic index, so if your grades are a little low, then ask your counselor which colleges rely heavily on test scores. Then work hard to get the highest SAT and SAT II scores possible.

Transcripts, which list your grades (and usually state or county testing scores) may or may not be a vital part of your application. Despite what colleges say, there are occasions when transcripts are not really used. I will go into this in more detail later, but for now, you should keep in mind that colleges do not completely trust transcripts. There are a handful of high schools that colleges completely trust, but the rest are often viewed with a little suspicion. For example, let's say your average grade throughout high school is a 93; is that a good average for the high school? It depends. If the average for all students in your graduating class is a 91, then a 93 isn't very good. However, what if you knew that the average grade for your high school was a 79? Then a 93 is well above average. Basically, your high school counselor must give the college a context within which to understand your grades; typically this context is provided through ranking or grade distribution charts (which is a slightly vague way to rank). If your high school counselor gives neither a rank nor grade distribution, then a top college is likely to judge your academic merits almost entirely on your standardized test scores.

Some colleges, like Princeton, do not consider your freshmen grades. All colleges will look very closely at your junior year grades and, unless you apply early, your senior year grades. The most important characteristic they are looking for is a trend of improving grades. You should get a copy of your transcript and ask your counselor for a context for your grades; are your grades far above average, a little above average, average or below average? Is there a trend of improving grades? (Your classes should be getting more difficult, and your grades should be improving.)

Before we get into the details of what colleges do with your transcript, let's first look at the classes you should take (or have taken). Admissions offices often refer to "solids," which is any serious academic course; this obviously excludes art and cooking classes, but it also excludes health, nutrition, and vocabulary classes. The most competitive colleges often don't consider soft-science classes (psychology) or highly specialized classes (the Political History of Marching Music) to be solids. Most top colleges look for a minimum of twenty solids on your high school transcript.

Obviously, you need English (4 years), math (4 years), history (3 years), science (3 years), and a foreign language (3 years). These five subject areas comprise the foundation of your "solids." The above list only includes seventeen solids because this is a list of minimums; you should have four years of history, science and a foreign language. Ideally, you choose a foreign language from among the following (in order of preference): Latin, ancient Greek, modern German, modern French. Your sciences should include chemistry and physics (don't take four years of biology variations). In English, you should have thoroughly covered major American and British authors, and in History, you should have a thorough knowledge of Ancient, European, and U.S. history. And hopefully you studied calculus in 11th or 12th grade.

Aside from the above-mentioned Latin, chemistry and calculus, taking a course in debate, forensics or rhetoric is very helpful (both in the admissions process and in "real-life"). Your high school may not offer debate/forensics/rhetoric as a course; if it doesn't, join your high school or county forensics club or debate team. If your high school does not offer debate/forensics/rhetoric as a course or as an extracurricular activity, complain to your principal (perhaps throw about the assertion that you're being robbed of an education). Then, start your own debate/rhetoric club. Debate, forensics, and rhetoric, which comprise the areas of public speaking, analytical argumentation, and critical analysis, are pursuits that will benefit you far beyond the application process. A great many successful people look back on their high school and college endeavors and single out these areas as being the most responsible for their later success. Unlike the chess club, debate/forensics/rhetoric is not an area relegated to the nerdy and date-less. It will make a very positive impact on your college application and your life. (No, chess club does not particularly help your college application—not unless you place in a major tournament.)

To make a quick point about Latin: colleges like it because it is a language of scholars. If you attend a Princeton commencement, you would find that the salutatorian address is given in Latin (even today). Colleges respect students who pursue academic subjects for academic reasons, and Latin is one of the most respected subjects.

Grades. Your grades should be as high as possible; I know this sounds ridiculously obvious, but the point is this: you cannot get C's even if you're in all AP and honors classes. You must earn A's with an occasional B. "Occasional" means, at most, one out of five classes is a B. If you're earning B's and C's in very hard classes, you need to drop a hard class or two. Most colleges will not weight your grades or ranking enough to make up for a B- or C average, even if your classes are very hard. The one exception is high schools which significantly weight grades and ranking, particularly on a scale higher than 5: at such schools, a B- in all AP classes may be a 4.1 GPA, and because colleges usually don't reconfigure your grades to compensate for weighting (or lack thereof), then your 4.1 is a good GPA. (More on this later.) The point is this: you cannot have a 3.0 GPA, even if you are taking very difficult courses. Colleges may, on occasion, consider a 3.5 viable because of the extreme difficulty of your classes, but anything lower than a 3.4 is usually not viable regardless of the difficulty of your classes.

A note about odd grading systems: many high schools do not use a standard A-F or 100-0 scale grading system. Some schools, particularly prep schools, use odd systems such as 1-12 or strange letters (H's and M's for example). If you attend one of these schools and your school is competitive and reasonably well known, then every top college will be acquainted with its grading system no matter how strange it may be. If your school is small and not so well-known and uses a strange grading system, then you may either wish to ask the admissions office directly if they are familiar with your school's grading system and/or talk to your counselor. Your counselor may suggest limiting your applications to colleges who have previously admitted students from your high school (on the assumption that these colleges are the ones who understand and appreciate the school's strange grading system.)

Weighting & Ranking. Basically, weighting is when a school gives you more credit for an advanced, honors or AP class than for a regular class. For example, regular classes may be on a 4.0 scale (4=A, 3=B, 2=C) whereas AP classes may be on a 6.0 scale, so an A in a regular class earns you 4 points, but an A in an AP class earns you 6 points. In schools that weight grades, the valedictorian (#1 ranked student) will usually have a grade point average (GPA) above 4.0. Because the valedictorian takes many honors and AP classes, her honors classes may grade on a 5.0 scale, and her AP classes may grade on a 6.0 scale, so a student who takes no honors or AP classes will have no chance of earning a GPA above 4.3.

Weighting exists for an obvious reason: an A in a cooking course is not equivalent to an A in AP chemistry or AP Latin. By weighting, the school is giving you more credit in calculating your grades for difficult courses. In theory, weighting is good.

Ranking is a school's way of rating your performance when compared to other students. Much like weighting, its goal is to give credit to students who work extra hard. For example, if a student tells you he has a B average, you may think that's not very good. But what if you learn that the student is taking AP chemistry and AP Latin, and is ranked 15th in his class of 150 students. That would change your mind. Ranking helps outsiders (such as admissions officers) determine if your academic performance in high school is above average, average, or below average. Once again, what if you discovered that the person with the B+average is taking all AP courses, including AP chemistry, physics, Latin, and French, and is ranked 2nd in his class of 950 students. Now you would have great respect for that B+student, and you may think that he could get accepted to an Ivy League college. We all know students with A averages who take all easy courses and students with B averages who work very hard in very difficult courses. Ranking helps outsiders understand which student is which. In theory, ranking is good.

Of course, this assumes that your school has a weighted ranking (or ranks from a weighted average). A weighted ranking is one in which students who take more difficult courses get more credit. If a high school's rankings or grades are not weighted, then the student who has a 4.3 GPA (an A+in every class) is most likely going to have the #1 rank, even if he took the easiest classes at your school. Unweighted rankings punish hard-working students because they often have lower grades than students who take very easy classes. In many cases, high schools with unweighted grades and rankings will have top students who don't take a single AP course.

To confuse things further, there are several different ranking systems used; each may be weighted or unweighted. Some schools have exact rankings, which means in a class of 370 students, all the students are ranked 1 through 370. Other schools rank by deciles, quintiles, or quartiles. Ranking by deciles means that the students are put into rankings by groups of 10%—so the top decile are students who are in the top 10% of their class; the second decile are students who rank above 80% of their class but below the top 10%. Quintile rankings categorize students in groupings of 20%, and quartile rankings categorize students in groupings of 25%. Many schools do not give an exact rank; they use one of these broader rankings scales. If you rank in the second quintile, then your rank would be in the 20%-39% range in your class.

If this isn't confusing enough, many high schools have pre-determined ranks. This is often the case with academically poor schools that are trying to "trick" the system. (Texas public schools are known for doing this.) Pre-determined ranks work like thusly: any student with a 4.0 or higher is ranked #1 and is valedictorian; any student with a 3.9-3.99 is ranked #2 and is the salutatorian, and so forth. With this system, schools often graduate 30 valedictorians (all ranked #1) and 40 salutatorians (all ranked #2) out of a class of 500. Obviously, this sort of scheme greatly annoys admissions offers.

The problem for admissions officers is that there are dozens of different ways to report grades and ranks. Some schools use a 4.33 scale, while many others use a 5.0 or 6.0 scale (and still others use a 7.0 or 8.0 scale, and I suppose we'll see a 9.0 or 10.0 scale soon). Some schools give exact ranks, while others use deciles, quartiles, quintiles or some other method. And still other schools have pre-determined ranks which allow them to rank 10% of their graduating class as #1 or #2. And finally, there are dozens of prep schools, many of them the best in the country, which do not give any type of grades. For example, Friends Academies (Quaker prep schools) give an array of H's in lieu of the usual As, Bs, and Cs while other prep schools give grades on a 1-12 scale. What do colleges prefer?

Colleges would love to have a standardized grading system and most would strongly prefer weighted grades on a 5.0 or 6.0 scale and exact weighted rankings. Unfortunately, every high school is determined either to do what's easiest for them or to do what they feel will benefit the greatest number of students. Exact weighted ranks are most beneficial to top students at larger schools: if you're #8 in your class of 500 students, then you don't want your school reporting that you're in the "top 20%," which could mean you're #99 in your class. And if you're taking many AP courses, then you shouldn't be competing for the #12 rank in your class with a student who has the same grades but is taking only easy classes (and no honors or AP classes). In either case, the top student would fare much better if the grades were weighted to reflect honors and AP classes and the rankings were exact.

If you attend a smaller school (fewer than 200 students per graduating class), then you may have a problem. Most colleges consider rank as it relates to the number of students in your class, so being ranked #10 out of 500 students is more impressive than being ranked #10 out of 65 students. For this reason, most smaller prep schools don't give exact ranks (or any ranks). In most cases, rankings are taken at face value for classes over 300 students (regardless of whether your school has 350 or 700 students in the graduating class), but the quality of rankings tend to be mitigated if your graduating class has fewer than 300 students. So it's very beneficial for schools with 300 or more students per class to give exact rankings, and it's probably beneficial for schools with 200-300 students per class to give exact ranks. For schools with fewer than 200 students per graduating class, it's probably best to drop exact rankings.

In almost all cases, admissions offices at top colleges find grades useless; they must have some indication of your academic performance in the context of your class in order to know what to make of your As and Bs (or Hs). In fact, some colleges won't even consider your grades if your school doesn't give some indication of rank. This "indication of rank" is what most prep schools do; while they claim they don't rank students, in fact, they do give admissions offices a very good idea of your rank because they need to in order for the college to consider your grades. How do they do this? They will write something like "Jane has a 3.7 GPA, which considering the difficulty of her classes, is better than about 93% of her class of 92 students but certainly not a good as the top 4% or so." Read between the lines: Jane's 3.7 GPA puts her in the top 5%-7% of her class. So her prep school has just ranked her without really ranking her (she's about the 6th ranked student in her class), and now the admissions officers know what to make of her grades (i.e. they're very good). When they look at her transcript quickly, they should find several honors and AP courses, which will corroborate the counselor's statement. If your school doesn't rank at all, then your counselor will write something on your transcript or recommendation that suggests where your standing is in your graduating class.

Since colleges prefer to work with rankings instead of GPAs, the big question is this: what do they do with the rankings? Many colleges have tables that they use to convert your rankings, SAT scores and SAT II scores (if required) into an index. For example, say you ranked #1 out of 400 students. The college may give you 80 points for this rank (the most points available), then add the average of your SAT math and verbal score minus the last zero; so if you scored a 680 and a 720, the average is a 700; so the college will give you 70 points. If three SAT IIs are required, the college will average those and remove the last zero; so if you have a 680, 700, and 720, the average is 700, so the college will give you 70 points. So you have 80 points for your ranking, 70 points for your SAT, and 70 points for your SAT IIs for a total of 220 points. So your academic index will be a 220. At many larger colleges, you may be admitted or rejected based solely on an index such as this one. Competitive colleges may automatically reject the bottom 20% of students using the index, but will in most cases consider the extra curricular activities, essay, and recommendations of the remaining 80% in conjunction with this index. If your high school only ranks in deciles, quintiles, or quartiles, then most colleges will use the median number; if you're in the second decile (top 11%-20%), the college will plug in 15% for you. If you're in the first quintile (top 1%-20%), the college will plug in 10% for you.

For example, if you're in the top 14% of your class and your school uses deciles, you would be in the second decile, and the college would peg you at 15%. If your school used quintiles, then you would be in the first quintile, and the college would peg you at 10%. So deciles would hurt you, but quintiles would help you; this explains why so many schools use quintiles and quartiles (and not exact rankings or deciles, both of which are more precise). While quintiles and quartiles hurt the very top students, they help the middle students and significantly help the lower students. So quintile and quartile rankings are a sort of academic welfare for lower students: they raise the ranking of lower students at the expense of the top students.

What's important to note is that in many cases, your actual grades aren't used at all. In addition, SAT and SAT II scores may comprise two-thirds of your academic index, whereas AP scores aren't considered (and can't be considered because many schools offer few or no AP courses). Unfortunately, this illustrates how important SAT and SAT II scores are, despite the claims made by most top college admissions officers who insist that they care more about grades and extra curricular activities than test scores. And finally, since this sort of indexing does not take into consideration your AP scores, the primary benefit of taking AP classes is to get the additional weighting in your GPA. Read the chapter on academic indices to get a more detailed explanation.

If you delve into the depths of admissions statistics, you may find that the statistics seem to contradict some of the statements above and certainly paint a grim picture. For example, for a recent Penn admissions year, of those applicants whose school provided a rank, 78% of those admitted were in the top 5% of their class. This would seem to suggest that you need to be in the top 5% of your class to get admitted to Penn. Furthermore, the admissions rate for applicants whose schools provided a rank was 25.3%, whereas the admissions rate for applicants whose schools did not provide a rank was 27.6%. This would seem to suggest that being ranked is undesirable.

However, we can make sense of these statistics by a simple fact: most top high schools (and nearly all prep schools) do not rank. Most of the schools that do provide a rank for their students are large, mediocre public schools. So the admissions rate for unranked applicants is higher because a disproportionate number of those unranked applicants are from the nation's best high schools. These phenomena help explain why the Penn admissions rate for valedictorians—the #1 student in the class—is only 58%. You would think that the #1 student from almost any high school would be admitted to Penn, but if you attended a mediocre high school where less than 40% of the students even apply to a competitive college, being ranked #1 may not be a huge accomplishment. This also explains why nearly all ranked students need to be in the top 5% to be admitted to Penn—because most of these ranked students are graduating from mediocre high schools.

What if your school doesn't rank at all? If your counselor provides some assistance in understanding your grades, as they should, then most colleges will use a table to convert your grades, and then plug your converted grades into a formula along with your SAT and SAT II scores. If your school does not rank or provide an indication of rank in any way, then the college will convert your GPA into a usable indexed number. Usually, colleges will use freshman through junior year grades; some colleges only use sophomore and junior grades (and may add in senior grades if they have them). Either way, your sophomore and particularly your junior year grades are the most important. (Your junior year grades are particularly important because they usually need to be as good as or better than your sophomore grades. Colleges do not look kindly on declining grades.)

Colleges rely so heavily on rankings and standardized tests because they do not trust high school transcripts: they don't know if your grades are inflated, if your courses are unusually easy, or what the agenda of your high school's board of education is, but they do know that they can compare every applicant's SAT scores.

So what's best for you? If your high school ranks, then you need to concentrate on that: get the best rank possible. If the rankings or grades at your school are weighted, then take as many classes as you can that carry extra weight (honors and AP classes). It should be noted that many top college indices only convert grades on a 4.0 scale, while some convert them on a 5.0 scale. This means that at many colleges, including many Ivies, a 4.3 (an A+ on the 4.0 scale) is the top grade; if your school has a weighted 6.0 scale, then a 4.3 may only be a B- in AP classes. These means that a B- in all AP classes on a weighted 6.0 scale will translate into the top possible index. Conclusion: if your ranking or grades are weighted, you must take as many weighted classes as you possibly can in order to get the highest numerical grade or ranking that you can. A grade of B- on a 6.0-weighted scale (all AP courses) will be much better than a grade of A on a 4.0 scale (no AP or honors courses), particularly because many college indices top out at 4.3.

If your high school does not rank or weight at all, then the advice gets a little tricky. If your school does not rank, then it will actually be detrimental to take many AP courses if it means you will have a B (3.0) average. Most colleges do not take into consideration if your grades are weighted or not: if they see a 4.8 GPA on your transcript, they use that; if they see a 3.6 GPA, they will use that. In the end, getting the higher number is sometimes a little more important than taking the difficult classes. However, you cannot completely avoid hard classes. Your counselor and the college admissions office will discount a high GPA if it isn't buttressed by at least a few difficult classes.

So if your high school weights grades, take as many weighted (honors and AP) classes as you can. If your school doesn't weight, then mix a few easy classes into your schedule to help maximize your GPA and/or ranking. Keep in mind that an "easy" class should still be a "solid." Don't count "The World of Mexican Baking" as an easy class, because Princeton won't count it as a class at all.

If you are confused about whether your school ranks, you should ask your counselor. And if your school doesn't rank, you should ask your counselor what she would write about your courses and grades. As noted above, your counselor will need to provide an indication of rank (usually called a Grade Distribution Chart), even if the school doesn't officially rank. Ask what your indication of rank will be and ask what you can do to improve it.

Bottom line: if you rank in the top 20% of your class, you have a shot at being successfully admitted to a top college; if you rank in the bottom half of your class, you have almost no chance.

Chapter 19

Extracurricular Activities, Honors & Awards

"My school doesn't require community service, and I
think it's kind of yucky. I'd rather take painting classes
this summer. You think Princeton will notice that
I don't have any community service?"

What? Extracurricular activities are typically defined as everything you do outside of the classroom. These activities aren't listed on your transcript. They may range from sports teams to school clubs, from church groups to music lessons. In theory, extracurricular activities include everything from working in a soup kitchen to lingering at the mall. Obviously, colleges are only interested in the important, meaningful activities (which, if you're wondering, does not include lingering at the mall). I mention extracurricular activities throughout this book because they are very important. Top colleges admit very few students based on their academic report alone; extracurricular activities are the third most important item on your application, after your grades/rank and test scores.

Just Four Things. Colleges look for four characteristics in extracurricular activities: maturity, leadership skills, determination, and continuity. They want to know that you can participate in the community at large, can recognize and assist in ameliorating community problems, and can contribute to the welfare of others. Playing on the school's soccer team is nice, but what does it show about you? Similarly, being class president is nice, but it doesn't help you too much if it was simply a popularity contest. You need to engage in activities that require responsibility and a serious determination to succeed. Always bring out the community-service angle in everything. Colleges think it mature when you help others (instead of yourself), so the question with everything is "how does this help others?"

Too Many Is a Bad Thing. The key to having a great list of extracurricular activities is not to have too many and to exhibit continuity. Do not list fifteen activities; if you do, colleges will think that you only joined clubs so that you could list them on your application. Even if you actually participated in fifteen clubs, don't list them all; it gives the wrong impression. Joining every club in school just so you can pad your applications shows a lack of maturity and honesty. When colleges are reviewing your extracurricular activities, they apply a score to them and/or enter them into a computer database. The college will usually ignore any activity in which you were only a member or only participated in for one hour per week. In short, they ignore (and in effect delete from your application) activities such as "French Club" or "Amnesty International" or anything in which you were only a member or only participated in an hour or so per week.

Colleges are looking for students who participate in 1-2 sports and 2-3 clubs and excel in them, hold a leadership position, are officers, and so forth. Colleges also want to see a few hours of community service. Community service is essentially any unpaid, non-credit work you do for the community. You should try to participate in the same clubs, sports and community service activities throughout high school; continuity exhibits maturity and dedication.

Even the very best colleges do not list extracurricular activities and community service as required items, but you should treat them as if they are required. For example, if you do not have 30-50 (or more) community service hours per year, you will be one of the only applications to Princeton who leaves this box blank on the application. Yes, you do want to stand out during the Princeton admissions process, but you don't want to stand out in a negative way. The admissions officers will almost always admit an academically weaker student with strong extracurriculars over an academically strong student with no extracurriculars. If you don't list any extracurricular activities, colleges will assume that you spend your free time watching television and loitering at the GAP. About 90% of applicants to top colleges have some community service (20-30 hours per year). Having 25 hours of community service will neither help nor hurt you; it will make you seem normal. However, if you have no community service, it will be noticeable. The only time you should make a big deal out of your community service is if you have 150+hours per year or if you did something extraordinary (i.e. worked for the Red Cross in Bosnia to help provide vaccinations to war-orphans). If you have 20-60 "normal" community service hours per year, simply list it on your application and move on. Under no circumstances should you make a big deal out of community service that was required by your high school in order to graduate. Colleges think nothing of required community service hours.

Some extracurricular activities cost money—traveling to the Caribbean to take an on-board marine biology class or participating in a student U.N. program in The Hague. What if you don't have the money for these items? First, there are always very exciting and/or impressive things to do that don't cost much. Second, you can always work a little over the school year and save your money for a trip over the summer. In most cases, you can do a great student trip for just $800-$1200. Third, and perhaps most importantly, colleges do not measure everyone by the same yardstick. Colleges expect affluent students to do much more than others. If you don't have much money or many opportunities, colleges simply expect you to do the best with what you have. Not everyone needs to travel to Nepal over the summer to kayak competitively, but under no circumstances should you do nothing.

Work works well. The same advice holds true for employment. Do colleges like students who work? Sometimes. Holding down a steady job (for 2+years) shows maturity. If you worked during the school year out of necessity, then colleges will be impressed (even if it hurt your grades a bit). However, if you worked during the school year because you wanted to buy some neon lights for your new car and working hurt your grades, college will think you're an idiot because you thought neon car lights were more important than good grades. If you work from necessity—you or your family needs the money—then you must express this in your application. Make it very clear that your socio-economic situation required you to work. If you work because you simply want a little extra money, then don't make a big deal about it. Colleges are not impressed about a job you had so you could buy a few extra CDs, particularly if you only had the job for two months. (Short-term jobs are rarely impressive.) My advice is that if you don't need the money, then working should not be a priority—don't work during the school year, and only work over the summer if you can fit it in after doing other community activities (such as community service). If you want or need to work, then try to maintain the same job for a long period of time (a year or longer).

If you are going to get a job, try to get something interesting, perhaps something that relates to your interests or develops your diversity. (Colleges love diversity.) For example, if you come from an affluent background, working at the GAP will do little for your application. However, if you work at a construction site, colleges will be impressed. You will probably be able to pull a good essay out of that. (Besides, many unskilled construction jobs pay fairly well.)

The Bottom Line. You must do something after school, on weekends, and over the summer. If you go home and rot in front of the television, you are handicapping your application. Colleges think extracurricular activities are almost as important as grades and test scores and rarely accept applicants who don't have extensive extracurricular activities. The do-gooders at colleges particularly appreciate extensive community service activities and tough jobs (like construction work). One of the best things you can do if you come from a privileged background is to work fifteen hours per week at a tough job. And what if you took a $30,000 trip to Paris, then jetted down to a beach on Zanzibar? Leave that off your application. Do-gooder admissions officers do not appreciate extracurricular activities that reek of money and privilege, so be selective in what you choose to do and choose to include on your application.

Honors & Awards. All colleges will also ask you for a list of honors or awards (academic or extracurricular). Most high school students initially believe that they don't have many honors or awards. My first suggestion is to ask your mother. Mothers will typically remember every little award you've ever won. The rules for reporting awards are as follows. First, anything can count as long as you put it under the correct heading; one part of the application may ask for "Academic Awards" while another may ask for "Extracurricular honors." Be sure to put everything where it belongs. Second, you may only go back to ninth grade; that Good Citizenship award you won in second grade doesn't count. Third, regional or national honors/awards are far more significant than local honors/awards; the larger the pool of potential winners, the more significant the award.

You should sit down with your parents and list every award and honor you've won since ninth grade. Then put this list in order of significance; on most applications, you will be able to list your top 5-9 awards/honors. Which ones should you choose? As mentioned, stick with the regional or national ones, the most competitive ones, and the most academic ones. You should include awards/honors that correspond with your academic strengths, intended major, and extracurricular interests. You do not want to include awards/honors that appear out of the blue. If you win the County Chemistry Contest, but you aren't a great chemistry student, have not taken honors or AP chemistry, and have no demonstrated interest in chemistry, then there's no point in mentioning this award.

There are some awards/honors that are so commonplace that they aren't worth mentioning, such as *Who's Who*. (*Who's Who* is a for-profit company.) There are some honors, such as National Merit Commended or Semi-finalist/finalist Scholar, that mean much less than most think. Top colleges see many national merit scholars, and they reject more than half of them. If you are a National Merit Scholar, you should include it, but don't think too much of it. However, National Merit "Commended" Scholar may not even be worth mentioning. Some other honors, such as the AP Scholar's program, which honors students who take three or more AP tests and score a three or higher on each one, is a fairly significant honor. (Keep in mind that many applicants to top colleges will have good scores on seven or more AP tests.) Other awards/honors worth mentioning include honors (or cum laude/dean's/principal's) lists for high grades, departmental honors at your high school, NCTE writing awards, regional math competitions, winning major sports events, winning (or placing highly) in any major academic contest (debate, Latin, physics), and any significant community service award. If your high school does not give awards (some religious schools do not), then you should state this on your application or the admissions office may wonder why you didn't win any awards in high school.

Chapter 20

Recommendations

"My coach says he'll write me a great recommendation.
He says I have brass balls."

The Counselor Rec. Every college asks for one or more recommendations. One will always be from your counselor and is typically included with a copy of your transcript. The counselor's recommendation will usually divulge any conduct problems you have had (that aren't on your transcript), a little about your course work, and an indication of your rank within your graduating class. Counselors at prep schools and at more rigorous public schools will usually write a more detailed and personal description of your strengths.

Colleges depend on these counselor recommendations to help them understand who you are, your level of academic success, your maturity, honesty and motivation. It's your counselor's job to be candid with the college; the admissions officers trust that your counselor will tell the truth. A counselor who isn't very honest can ruin a high school's reputation with a college.

Therefore, your counselor has a significant degree of influence. (In the case of recommendations, the counselor I refer to is your high school's counselor in charge of college guidance, not a private counselor.) At many large public schools where there may be one college counselor for 300 students, the counselor's recommendation may be perfunctory. You should make an effort to be very helpful and kind to your counselor because they are probably overworked. Do not assume your counselor will know everything about you or do anything extraordinary for you; you should be well-prepared, plan ahead, and do everything that you are able to do yourself. Well-prepared, pro-active students and parents will make the counselor's job much easier, which usually results in better, more informative recommendations. In fact, some counselors use the college search process as a way to gauge your organizational skills and interest in college. If you arrive at your counselor's office and declare, "I haven't really thought about college, don't know where I want to go, and don't have much time for this stuff," then it's likely that your counselor will refer to you as "disorganized, uninterested, and lacking effort" in the recommendation he writes for you. Be as helpful as possible to your counselor, and in turn, he will be helpful to you.

You should keep your counselor informed of your college decisions: which colleges you're visiting, which colleges you're most seriously considering, and so forth. Some counselors will have deadlines for giving them recommendations and transcript request forms. Remember: your counselor is writing an important recommendation for you, so you must meet every deadline. Or even better, give everything to your counselor before the deadline. The more time you give your counselor, the more time she will have to think about all of your wonderful qualities.

If you are a nervous student, you should consider hiring a private counselor. While a few high school counselors don't mind students camping out in their office diurnally and don't mind moms calling every other day to ask more questions, you do not want to become a thorn in your counselor's side. If you have a question that is answered in a college guidebook, then get the answer from the college guidebook. If you want someone to hold your hand throughout the process, hire a private counselor (many of whom are former college counselors or admissions officers). But don't drive your high school counselor crazy, or they may not write the best recommendation for you.

The foremost purpose of the counselor recommendation is to give the college a context for your course work. Did you take easy or hard courses? Are your grades below or above average? The second purpose is to let the college know of any conduct or behavior issues. If the high school suspended you for a day, then it's your counselor's job to report it. There's at least one box on every counselor recommendation form that asks if the counselor has any reservations or concerns about your conduct or character. In most cases (96%+), the answer is no, the counselor has no reservations. When a counselor does have reservations about your character, they usually don't put the details in writing; they check off "yes" without providing details, leave the question blank, or write "contact me" over the box. Most counselors prefer not to put negative comments in writing for fear of providing evidence for a lawsuit. On occasion, parents of applicants who have been rejected sue (the college, the high school, the counselor), and inevitably the recommendations are key pieces of evidence. For this reason, counselors will typically either not say anything negative or only communicate negative observations verbally.

Despite this reluctance to communicate a negative character evaluation, it is the counselor's responsibility to inform the admissions office of conduct problems an applicant has had; if an admissions office discovers that a high school has attempted to conceal an honor code violation, the admissions office will usually hold the high school responsible and generally stop trusting the school's counselors. Then the admissions office will inform other colleges of the high school's attempt to conceal an honor code violation, and the high school (or a specific counselor) may be, in effect, blacklisted; every applicant that comes from that school will be viewed suspiciously and reviewed rigorously in an attempt to discover concealed problems.

In most cases, innocuous conduct problems involving alcohol are usually dismissed by colleges. But problems involving breaking the honor code or other academic violations are usually grounds for rejecting a student, even an academic superstar. I know of many students who have 1400+on the SAT, straight-As, multiple APs with 5s, but who were rejected because of conduct involving academic violations (which usually means cheating, plagiarizing, selling old tests and so forth). If you've done any of these, you should ask your counselor how it would be reported before you apply to college. Most top colleges will automatically reject applicants who have been punished for serious violations of a school's honor code.

The best counselor recommendations are brief, give a precise context for your courses, and honestly report any violations of the honor code. Counselors should be very diligent in expanding on a student's rank and grades. A student may have a seemingly low rank or mediocre grades because she's taking the hardest classes offered by the school (and all at once). If this is the case, the counselor must make this very clear. The difference between a college viewing your B average in a positive light or a negative light will probably depend on your counselor's recommendation.

The Teacher Rec. Top colleges require a second (and sometimes third) recommendation. Colleges tend to prefer, and students usually assume, that this recommendation come from a teacher. This is generally true, but if the recommendation form doesn't say "teacher," then don't assume it must be a high school teacher. The second recommendation form is meant to give the admissions committee an idea of who you are as a person, what your strengths and weaknesses are, what your personality is like and, perhaps most importantly, if you are truly interested in learning. Colleges do not want a recommendation from a teacher that reiterates your performance in class—they already know how you did in your classes because they see the grade on your transcript. This is important to remember because if you ask a teacher to write your recommendation and this teacher only knows that you sat in the back of his chemistry class, then usually the recommendation will just be an expanded version of the grade you received in that class. This is a wasted recommendation. A good recommendation will expand on your interests in chemistry specifically and learning in general, your ability to cooperate with other students, your tremendous contribution to class discussions, and your interest in helping other students to learn. The recommendation should also touch on your interest in doing extra credit work, willingness to accomplish more than the minimum required, and interest in making the class an enjoyable learning experience for all.

If you choose a teacher to write your second recommendation, follow these tips:

- Choose a teacher in whose class you worked very hard, participated constructively in class discussions, completed all the work on time, attempted the extra-credit assignments, and showed an honest interest in the subject; it does not need to be a class in which you earned an A+(though it shouldn't be a class in which you earned a C either).

- Choose the class/teacher as early as possible, and then start to work very hard in that class; the sooner you decide on a class/teacher, the sooner you can start to turn in highly impressive work.

- Preferably choose a teacher with whom you have taken more than one class.

- Choose a teacher you've had either this year or last; don't choose someone who taught you three years ago.

- Preferably choose a teacher of a subject in which you have an interest, perhaps the subject in which you intend on majoring college. Depending on the specifics of your application, it may seem odd if you put "chemistry" as your intended major, you've taken chemistry and AP chemistry at your school, you scored a 780 on the SAT II Chemistry test, won several county chemistry awards, and then have your history teacher write your recommendation. The college will rightfully wonder "why not the chemistry teacher?" You may have a perfectly good reason for this, but just make sure that reason is somehow obvious to the admissions officers.

The best teacher recommendations are concise and discuss your academic qualities. Teacher recommendations should not primarily discuss a student's personal qualities. Admissions officers are mostly interested in knowing whether or not the applicant is truly interested in learning, how the applicant reacted to stressful academic situations, and whether the applicant was a constructive and productive member of the academic community. If your teacher recommendation answers these three questions in a positive way (and in 100 words or fewer), then you have a great recommendation in your hands.

A great teacher recommendation does not necessarily say "this is my best student in ten years." You may be surprised to learn that top colleges receive many recommendations that say such things, so these "best student" recommendations aren't particularly special or informative.

If the recommendation form does not specifically ask for a teacher's recommendation, then you need not assume that a teacher's recommendation is required (or even necessarily beneficial). Once again, the college wants to hear from someone who knows you well, so your pastor, music instructor, coach, or community service advisor may be a better choice than a teacher. Some colleges make it clear that they want a non-academic evaluation of you by requesting a personal reference. Either way, you should choose someone who knows you well and will be able to elaborate on your qualities as a person.

Hey! Read this: One very important note about teacher recommendations: about 70% of a teacher recommendation will be derived from your class participation (the other 30% from your tests and papers). There will be specific boxes to check and questions to answer about your class participation, and many of the other questions on the teacher recommendation form are directly related to your class participation. If you don't participate much in class, you must start doing so now. The best student will get a mediocre recommendation if she doesn't speak up in class. If you're shy, then take a debate or speech class, or join a club that requires public speaking (Model United Nations, for example). Admissions officers consider this "class participation" rating as crucial, so make sure the teacher who recommends you will say that you participate often and intelligently.

Recs and Test Scores. Finally, a college will typically compare a teacher recommendation to your score on a SAT II or AP in the same subject. If your Spanish teacher says you're the greatest student ever, the college will look to see if you have a Spanish SAT II score. If you do, that score better be above a 700. If your Spanish teacher claims you're her best student in twenty years, but your Spanish SAT II score is a 540, then the college will likely disregard the entire recommendation and perhaps reconsider the value of your transcript. Although your recommendation doesn't need to come from a teacher in whose class you earned an A, it should be a subject you performed well in, particularly on standardized tests. The bottom line: if you're getting a recommendation from a physics teacher (for example), only submit your SAT II physics score if it is high. If it is low, don't send it, or the college may disregard the teacher recommendation and your physics grade.

In all cases you should speak with your counselor about your teacher recommendation(s). If your counselor has been at the school for a few years, then he will know which teachers write good recommendations and which don't and will probably steer you clear of the later. Just be aware that your counselor will probably be very subtle and diplomatic if he's trying to keep you away from a bad recommendation writer. If you've chosen Mrs. Crabapple to write your recommendation, your counselor may know that Mrs. Crabapple writes awful recommendations. But he won't say, "Mrs. Crabapple is an illiterate buffoon who couldn't write a complete sentence if her soul depended on it." Instead, your counselor will say, "Perhaps there's another teacher—Ms. Henley?—who knows you better." This is a hint: do not ask Mrs. Crabapple for a recommendation because there's something wrong with her. The bottom line: always get your counselor's approval before you ask your teachers for recommendations.

Peer Recs (and other feel-good detritus). A few colleges, most notably Dartmouth, ask for a peer recommendation. This is a recommendation from a friend. Peer recommendations are used to get to know the personal side of an applicant; however, peer recommendations are mostly ignored. In most cases, the only peer recommendation that influences an admissions decision is an extremely bad recommendation. One in a thousand peer recommendations will read like this: "John asked me to write this because he thinks I'm his friend, but he's too arrogant to realize he has no friends. He's mean to everyone and cheats on his tests." I'm not kidding—sometimes admissions officers receive such peer recommendations, and those are the only ones that carry weight. (In the case above, the admissions office would call the high school counselor or principal and discuss the accusation to see if it's valid.)

One More is Too Much! Some students send in many more recommendations than requested; this will surely annoy the admissions office. Neither the quantity of recommendations nor the position of the person making the recommendation is of importance—only the content of the recommendation is of interest to the admissions office. Should you try to get the state senator or a CEO of a major corporation to write a recommendation? What about the Pope or your uncle, who is an alumnus who contributes money? The answer is: if the person knows you well, then ask for a recommendation; if the person doesn't know you well (or at all), then don't bother. And only send in more recommendations than the application requires if the additional recommendation adds substantial weight to your application. Under no circumstance should you send in more than one additional recommendation.

Usually, the best reason to send an additional recommendation is if you have an extraordinary talent. For example, if the college asks for only two recommendations—one from your counselor and one from a teacher—then you might want to send a third recommendation from your oboe instructor if you are a wonderful and dedicated student of the oboe. (If this case, you should probably send a tape of an oboe performance along with your additional recommendation; keep in mind, though, that both the recommendation and the tape will probably be reviewed by the college's Professor of Oboe, so you should only go this route if you are confident that you are an exceptional oboist.)

Random letters of recommendation from politicians, alumni, and other college contributors often only serve to irritate admissions offices. Years ago, most top colleges asked for recommendations from people outside of your school, often from local alumni. During these years, alumni often wielded a great deal of influence in the admissions department. If an alumnus really liked you, then you had a very good chance of being admitted. Obviously, the wealthiest and most influential families usually had the best connections, so now these sorts of recommendations have been largely excluded from the admissions process because they are viewed as unfairly excluding less privileged students.

Today, most admissions deans are under tremendous pressure from every direction to admit certain students; each sports team, academic and fine arts department, contributor, and alumni group—not to mention the development office—provides a list of applicants it wants admitted. And the admissions department plays a polite but sometimes contentious game of politics, trying to offend no one while still maintaining its independence. It is usually not wise to apply additional pressure to this volatile mix of interests because admissions offices are as likely to respond negatively as they are likely to welcome your lobbying efforts.

The Scoop. Do good or bad recommendations really help? The truth is that most recommendations are the same and most are good. A bad recommendation can sink an otherwise good application, so you must be sure that the person making the recommendation will write a positive report of you. You may think it surprising that a few recommendations are bad considering the care and thought that students must put into choosing the people who will write their recommendations, but a "bad" recommendation is not necessarily one that doesn't recommend the student. Because nearly all recommendations are good, a "bad" recommendation may be one that exhibits the slightest hesitation or doubt. If you ask a teacher to write a recommendation, and she is the least bit hesitant, you should probably find someone else to write the recommendation. In addition, top admissions offices will deny admission based on recommendations that hint at social or personality issues; I know of a highly qualified candidate who was denied admission to an Ivy because the recommendation seemed to paint a picture of someone who is "dark." This may seem trivial, but recommendations and essays are the only two tools that admissions officers have to meet the "real" you, and since most recommendations are great, these specks of doubt are magnified. Most top colleges have more qualified applicants than they have spots in the freshmen class, so they are always looking for reasons to deny admission.

As noted, most recommendations are simply good; they are neither bad nor great. Therefore, a great recommendation does help, and sometimes a great recommendation will put you over the top. How do you get a great recommendation?

Some of the components of a great recommendation you can control, and some you cannot. First, give the person who is recommending you a good deal of time; you should give him or her the recommendation form by early September if you're applying early decision/action and by late October if you're applying regular admission. Those who ask for a recommendation after Thanksgiving are decreasing their chances of getting great recommendations because the period between Thanksgiving and Christmas is the busy season for recommendations; each popular teacher probably has dozens of recommendations to write in the four weeks between Thanksgiving and Christmas. Second, since the person recommending you needs to be articulate, choose a teacher who communicates well. Your chemistry teacher may love you, but if he is inarticulate, his recommendation may be a dud. And as noted above, choose someone who knows you well, someone who will be able to describe those ineffable qualities about you that make you so much more wonderful than the other 14,500 students applying to Princeton.

One thing about recommendations that you can't control, aside from the obvious, is the quality of the person's writing. Perhaps 50% of a great recommendation depends on the student, and 50% depends on the communication abilities of the person writing the recommendation. Therefore, many students ask English or history teachers to write their recommendations; they assume these teachers will be better writers. This assumption, of course, is not always true. However, it's a good idea to ask the teacher helping you edit your application essays to write your recommendation. This strategy will give the teacher a better idea of who you are and will give you a better idea of the teacher's writing skills. After working on the application essay for a week or two, decide if you wish to ask the teacher for a recommendation.

The Bottom Line. The people who write your recommendations—your counselor and a teacher or two—must be able to write about the qualities that make you unique; you must give them something to write about by making them aware of what makes you unique. The sooner you start to charm your counselor and teachers by showing them what a diligent, hard-working student and wonderful human being you are, the better your recommendations will be.

Solid Gold. Now I will give you an example of the golden recommendation, one that brings tears to the eyes of every admissions officer and will make them forget about your low SAT scores. One student of mine decided to implement a recycling program for her high school. In tenth grade, she worked with the principal, the vice principal in charge of the physical plant, and a janitor to implement this program. By the fall of her senior year, the program had been operating successfully for about sixteen months. She regularly met with the principal, vice-principal and the janitor; she bought Christmas presents for all three, and they grew close as they worked together over the months on this substantial project. So when it came time to get recommendations, she got one from her counselor, one from her Chemistry teacher, and a special third one. Who did she ask for that third recommendation? The principal? The vice-principal? Of course not. She got a recommendation from the janitor, who was an uneducated, older Hispanic man who spoke little English. Technically, his recommendation was awful (some of the sentences didn't exactly make sense). But the janitor conveyed how the student cared about him and his family, asked how he was doing, and made him feel important and involved in the school community. Of course, this recommendation struck every multicultural save-the-world nerve in every admission officer's body. Despite a 1320 on the SAT, she was admitted to three Ivy League colleges. This is a golden recommendation—and it wasn't from a CEO or a Senator.

Chapter 21

Essays

"I'm writing my essay on the Amnesty chapter I started at my high school. I learned a lot about hate and stuff."

I get asked this question all the time: *do the application essays really count? are they really read? does anyone really care about them?* At top colleges, the answer is yes to all of the above. However, essays are similar to recommendations: about 80% of all essays are neither great nor bad, and don't help or hurt an application. Admissions officers spend all of two minutes reading these essays; they skim them for a few main points, make a note or two, and move on. About 10% of all essays are so wonderful that they significantly boost an overall application; a mediocre student may be admitted because of one of these essays. And about 10% of all essays are so bad that they may actually sink an otherwise admitted applicant. While a bad essay can sink an application and a great essay can push it over the top, most essays neither help nor hurt.

Strategically speaking, if your grades and test scores are above average for top colleges, then you should aim to write a good, solid essay. Such an essay will probably land you in that 80% of essays that are mediocre, but your grades, test scores, and extracurriculars will push you over the top. (Above average grades and test scores for top colleges are usually 1450+on the SAT, above 720 on three SAT IIs, and almost all As in difficult classes.) However, if your grades, test scores and extracurriculars are average or worse, you should do everything you can to place your essay in the top 10%. So take a risk, be a little daring, and put in a lot of effort. However, it should be worth the extra effort when you consider that most of those applicants in the middle 80% will be rejected. If your grades and test scores put you in the middle, you need to do something to put yourself over the top. The essay is the place to do it.

A Good Essay. The essay is one of the few things that you have control over in the final weeks leading up to the application deadlines. It's imperative that you work on the essay for several weeks and get professional feedback from a teacher, a counselor, or anyone else who knows what to look for in a good admissions essay. The best piece of advice I can give you is that most students think the first draft of their admissions essay is great when, in fact, it's often not very good. Never work on an essay for less than one week; you need time to build the perspective necessary to judge and edit your essay. A poorly or hastily written essay can sink an otherwise good application. Once again: the key ingredient in your essay is time.

When to start…You can get essay topics from previous years via the Internet anytime you want. The essay question for your admission year may be different, but essay questions often do not change from year to year. In addition, simply practicing writing a great, 500-word essay will help you hone your writing skills.

If you're still a junior (or younger), then go online and download a few essay questions so you can start thinking about them. Most colleges mail and post online their current applications in late July, so at that point you can go online and get the essay questions you will need to answer. Before you start actually working on the essay questions, you need to decide what your top 2-3 colleges are, and start with those. Forget about the other college essay questions until you've completely finished the questions from your top 2-3 colleges. In most cases, you can modify the essays you wrote for your top 2-3 colleges for all the other colleges. Just make sure you modify the essay for each college so you address the nuances of their questions. Most college essay questions vary slightly, so you should vary your essay. The key is that your essay should vary with each application. Admissions officers are quite attune to standardized essays that applicants paste onto every application. It doesn't help your chances of being admitted if an admissions officer thinks you've pasted the same essay onto twenty-five applications.

What if the college asks about an important experience in your life, and you've written a great essay about your favorite book? Of course, you write an essay on an important experience, but can you submit an additional essay on your favorite book? The answer is the same here as it is with recommendations. By submitting more than the application asks, you are running the risk of annoying the admissions office. Do you want to do this?

On the other hand, an extraordinary essay will help you; in fact, it may put you over the top. I had a student submit an additional essay to Harvard, and after he was admitted, I asked the admissions office what put him over the top; they said his second essay, which truly was extraordinary. In most cases, submitting a second essay is in bad form and not to be done. In the rare case where you have an extraordinary essay that does not answer the essay question, you may submit it along with an essay that does answer the essay question. However, you must be certain that your essay is extraordinary. It's my opinion that only about 1% of all applicants to top colleges are capable of writing an essay good enough to be submitted as an additional essay. (Yes, I am trying to discourage you.)

How to Start? First, read the essay questions, and take notes. If you start this process in your junior year, you should take a notebook with you on any trips, community service activities et cetera, and take notes. These notes will come in handy when you need specific names or dates later. After you have a good idea about what you're going to write about, start writing. Please understand that whatever you first write will probably be bad; good writing isn't written; it's rewritten. Your initial goal is just to get your ideas on paper. Most college essays are about 500 words, but do not hesitate to write much more. It's easier to trim a 700-word essay than it is to make a 120-word essay magically grow. Just get all your thoughts on paper—don't worry about length, sentence structure, quality, or anything else at first.

A good essay starts from a personal experience and then expands that experience to some important aspect about you or something you've learned. Finally, the essay should mention something about the college to which you're applying. Good essays do not wax poetic on philosophical issues or discuss vague concepts. An essay that asks, "What experience has significantly affected your life and why?" is really asking, "Tell us more about you." If the question asks about your favorite book, the admissions office really wants to know about you; a question about your idol is really about you. Get the idea? Find an important experience in your life, relate it to the specific question, expand it to a more general life lesson, and finish off by linking it to the college.

A Bad Essay. Are there essay topics you should avoid? In general, avoid writing about anything that you could imagine many other students writing about such as Thoreau, *The Great Gatsby*, John Steinbeck, breaking your arm. (You may use a quote, but don't write about the book—write about you!) If you are going to bring up a book, then try to use something a little out of the ordinary, something that isn't read by two million high school students each year. Unless you have had an extraordinary experience, do not write an essay about Outward Bound, Amnesty International, Habitat for Humanity, NOLS, SADD, Sierra Club, or any sports team. Top colleges get thousands of Outward Bound/Amnesty essays each year; they are trite and predictable. Most of them fall into the "I went through a traumatic experience and came out a better person" category. The "How I Took A Risk" essay starts with a description of the risks and the weather ("I didn't know if I would be successful" and "It was ten degrees outside and all I had was a hibachi" or "It was a dark and stormy night and I didn't have an umbrella."), describes the struggle, and ends with some lesson learned ("Persistence is the key" or "What doesn't kill you makes you stronger" or "Success is a matter of effort" or "Risk-taking is worth the reward"). Usually, the application reader never gets to the end of these kinds of essays because the reader is sound asleep. If you write an essay like this, you will be one of 2,000-3,000 applicants with the same essay. (I am not exaggerating this figure; Princeton probably gets 2,800 of these essays, Penn gets about 3,400, and Harvard over 4,000.) Do not write an essay like this unless your experience was truly unique. The "Outward Bound" essay is good if you attended high school in Nepal while training to be an Olympic runner. When you conclude "Risk-taking is worth the reward," the admissions officer will believe it. But if you're doing something that 10,000 other high school students are doing (Amnesty, Habitat, SADD), then you can't exactly call it a risk, can you?

The "How I Saved Humankind" essay is similar. While most Outward Bound essays are of the "risk" genre, most of the Habitat essays are the "Save Humankind" genre. In this essay, you take on the persona of Gandhi or Jimmy Carter and talk about the significant contribution you made to the world. The essay starts with the writer going to a forsaken part of the world (the Dominican Republic or Newark, New Jersey), then moves on to being shocked at how bad the conditions are ("I didn't know people lived like this"), struggling to cope with a strange new world ("I can't believe people eat this stuff"), and ending with some revelation about how people are the same and deserve a better world. If you think political speeches are bad, you should read a few of these essays. They are formulaic and cloying, and each top college gets a few thousand of these every year.

Together, the "How I Took a Risk" and "How I Saved Humankind" essays comprise 40%-60% of all the essays a top college receives. The final large essay genre is the "Tribute" essay. This essay is a tribute to a person, usually dead, who made a difference in your life. In many cases, the dead person is a grandparent, and the difference is something about being successful or being a good person or putting family first. Unless your grandparents are truly extraordinary, don't write about them. (Most grandparents are the same.) A dead parent is worth writing about, but the essay better be good! Tribute essays often account for 15%-30% of the essays a college receives (depending on what the essay question is). Together, the Risk, Saved Humankind, and Tribute essays make up 50%-80% of the essays a college receives. If you write one of these, you are risking being lumped into the 80% mediocre pile. (Perhaps you could write about how you are taking a risk by writing about taking a risk—perhaps not.) I suggest avoiding these three essay genres unless your experiences are truly unique.

Good and Readable. The key to talking about you is to make yourself unique. A personal, meaningful story is (almost) always unique and compelling, so start with you, not with a book or movie. Most importantly, do not write about your transcript or anything on your transcript. Colleges already know about your classes and your great grades; the essay is your opportunity to give them something new. Your essay should offer new information. Your transcript isn't new and Amnesty isn't new, so don't write about them. You would probably be surprised at what makes a truly unique essay; the topic is focused usually on just one thing, and that thing is often surprisingly mundane at first glance. A well-written essay on your love of African violets will probably be better than an essay on Outward Bound or Amnesty.

As noted earlier, admissions officers are not the world's most sophisticated readers, so you should not be subtle in your style or intricate in your logic. Be forthright, state things clearly, and make your point. If you want to say something, say it. If you leave your point to nuance, then the admissions reader may not get your point at all. And do not say things that could be construed negatively. If you say, "I'm a quiet person," the admissions reader may take this to mean that you don't contribute to your class or community. If you say "I spend six hours each night doing my homework," the reader may think you're a boring person. You should try to be sure that everything you say can only be taken one way so that there's no potential for a negative impression.

Colleges are looking for a few important character traits in the essay: honesty, integrity, maturity, and initiative. You probably can't demonstrate all of these in a single 500-word essay; your job is to showcase one of them. Here's a brief description of each of these qualities.

Honesty—Colleges aren't so much looking for the "I don't steal" kind of honesty. They are looking for the "I have strengths AND weaknesses" kind of honesty. Do not write an essay that attempts to show why you may soon be canonized; write an honest essay that illustrates both the good and bad side of whatever topic you choose. Colleges know that you aren't perfect; colleges know that you have significant gaps in your knowledge—if you knew everything, then why would you need to attend college? So don't write the "I am an angel" essay.

Integrity—Much like honesty, integrity is one of those ineffable qualities colleges seek in every applicant. How is this conveyed in an essay? One way applicants can appear to lack integrity is by being vague, evasive, or obscure. Do not mention that you were suspended without addressing why; do not mention "the night the police picked me up" without expanding on it. If you are trying to explain something bad that appears elsewhere on your application (on your transcript or counselor recommendation), do not be vague, even if you are mentioning the unfavorable incident in passing. Your essay should be clear in every context, but this is particularly true if you are discussing your weaknesses. This does not mean you need to present yourself prostrate to the admissions committee nor should you needlessly embarrass yourself (unless you have a reason for doing so). Integrity often comes through when you discuss something that is a weakness, and you discuss it in a very clear, objective manner.

Maturity—The obvious advice here is don't discuss your doll collection, your parents, your love of lollipops or anything else that smacks of immaturity. Of course, there are good reasons to discuss any of those subjects, but you should make sure you have a good reason. Remember, colleges are inviting you to live in their community of scholars, and they know you will be, in most cases, living by yourself for the first time in your life. They want to know that you can handle it, and if you write about your parents and the toy collection in your bedroom, you may give the admissions committee the impression that you aren't ready to leave home. The less obvious advice is don't use slang, poor grammar, or ridiculously poor word choice. You must sound reasonably intelligent and mature; most colleges assume that you can sound intelligent if you so choose, so if you choose not to sound too intelligent on your application essay, they will assume you lack the maturity to understand the gravity of the situation. Finally, choose your topic carefully. You do not need to write about a particularly "mature" topic, but neither should you write about an immature topic. Topics that convey immaturity (and lack of good judgment) include your love of parties, how you live for school vacations, your first sexual experience, or how you like to smoke because it annoys your parents. Believe it or not, good applicants have submitted application essays on all these topics and were denied admission every time, usually because their essay screamed of immaturity or lack of good judgment. Top colleges expect you to be interested in reading books, attending classes, working hard, and conducting yourself in a reasonable and mature manner.

Initiative—Colleges expect students to be active participants in their communities. About 50% of the activities on a college campus that occur outside of the classroom are managed by students—publications, clubs, events, government. Colleges are fond of applicants who exhibit leadership abilities by starting clubs or solving problems. If there's an activity you like but your high school doesn't have a club for it, start the club (e.g. photography club). If there's a problem at your school but no evident solution, create the solution (e.g. recycling). While colleges would appreciate your leadership position in an existing club, they will truly admire your initiative in starting your own club. So be inventive: do something that demonstrates your interests, enlist others to help you, get funding and make a difference. Then, of course, write a great essay about it.

After you have your rough draft, sit on it for a week. Re-read it a few times; you will probably add a few things you forgot. After a week of reflection, start editing it. Think about its structure: what does the first paragraph talk about? The second? What's the conclusion? How much do you need to cut? And most importantly, what does it say about you that nothing else in your application says?

You should find someone who can help you edit your essay, and you should find a few good application essays that were successful in the past (your counselor will have a few). Just be careful not to take anyone else's ideas. You may find that after you've rewritten the essay a few times, you don't care for it. This is okay. Write another essay. It's okay to write a few rough drafts on a few different topics, and choose the one you like the most. Remember, you're looking for something that's original and helps the admissions officer understand who you are. Hopefully, if you've followed the other advice in this book, you will have various experiences from which to draw including experiences from travel, community service, sports, and extracurricular activities (from yearbook to youth groups). Once again, try to avoid discussing purely academic subjects.

Once your essay is "done," you should allow 2-3 weeks pass to let it ripen. During this time, tinker with it, perfecting every sentence and word. Your essay must not have any grammatical, spelling, or punctuation errors. Do not use gargantuan, cumbersome words unless you really use them in your other writing. Your essay should sound like you; admissions officers are leery of essays that sound too good, as if a professional wrote them. And finally, do not submit an essay that's substantially longer than the allotted space. (I suggest not submitting an essay that's longer than the allotted space, even by a single word, but sometimes you have an extra sentence or two that simply cannot be deleted.) If you are allotted one page, do not decrease the font size and the margins in order to fit 900 words on the page. You aren't fooling anyone and will probably annoy the very people you're attempting to impress. And this trick does not work in reverse either. If you only have 200 words, increasing the font and spacing does not fool anyone.

In most cases, you may either type your essay onto the space provided on the form, or you may attach your essay to the essay page. While typing the essay onto the form is a bit nicer, admissions officers tend not to care as long as you follow their directions regarding attaching essays (some colleges will ask you to staple the essay to a very specific place, while other colleges will strictly forbid stapling). And, of course, you must type your essay. If you don't, you will not only be denied admission, but you will also be held in scorn for decades.

What if a college asks whether or not someone helped you write/edit your essay? (For example, Duke's recent application asked this sort of question.) These questions may seem silly; don't all students have someone—parent, teacher, friend, counselor—read their essay and advise them? Wouldn't it be stupid not to have someone proofread your essay? Of course, 99% of all applicants to top colleges have at least one person, if not several people, help them write their essays. So what's up with this question?

As noted above, colleges detest private college counselors. This question isn't about whether your teacher, parent, or friend helped you. It's all about whether a private counselor helped you. Colleges think the use of private counselors is unfair, but they haven't the guts to say it, so they trick you by asking if anyone helped you. Of course someone helped you! Almost all applicants get some help on their essays. Colleges are only interested if you hired a private counselor.

Any college who asks you this question puts you in an unfair predicament. If you are using a private counselor (which, if you can afford it, you should), then the college will hold it against you. A good counselor would never write your essay for you; she would provide the assistance that a great high school counselor would provide if he had the time. So do you tell the college the truth and take the punishment?

My first recommendation is: don't apply to any college that has the disingenuous audacity to ask such a duplicitous question. It's none of their business. It's ridiculous that colleges think it wrong that a student hire a private counselor but have no problem with students hiring private tutors or attending private (prep) schools. Colleges should not judge the means by which you were educated; they should only judge the quality of your education, which they do by judging the quality of your application. By signing your application, you are confirming that everything contained in the application is true and is your work. That should be enough for them, and if they don't trust you, then you shouldn't trust them.

But what if you really want to apply to a college that asks such a question? If you used a private counselor, then you will be shooting yourself in the foot if you write that on your application. However, it's not believable if you write that you used no one; as I said, everyone uses someone. So what do you write if you used a private counselor? I suggest writing that you used a family friend; don't use the words "private counselor." Write that a friend of your parents read the essay and offered a few pointers. Let me be clear: this is not the truth, but I don't think you have a choice. If you're not comfortable with this, then you shouldn't apply to that college. Most of the other students who are applying to that college and who used private counselors will lie; by telling the truth, colleges will peg your application as "artificially exceptional." A college that asks such a question is teaching a very unfortunate "real world" lesson: sometimes withholding the truth is justified when you're confronted with a detestable situation.

Of course, the great irony is that colleges are looking for honesty in their essays and yet are forcing thousands of teenagers into a position of dishonesty by this very question. Such a question requires students to choose between honesty and maturity: the honest approach simply states that you did use a private counselor, whereas the mature approach exhibits a dash of *real politic* and waffles.

Chapter 22

Interviews

> "My interview sucked. All my interviewer talked about was how to make sesame seed cookies. I'm not applying there now."

The interview is dying; fewer and fewer colleges are performing admissions interviews (though oddly, more and more graduate and professional schools are requiring interviews). There are two types of interview: the "informational" interview and the admissions interview. An informational interview is not designed to judge or test you in any way; it exists only to answer your questions and to convey a positive image of the college. I refer to these as "sales calls" because the interviewer's primary objective is to convince you to apply. Most interviews conducted by less competitive colleges as well as most alumni interviews are sales calls. (It should be noted that most alumni won't "hard sell" you, but many admissions officers will.) If the interview is not required or if the interview may contain more than one student, then chances are it's a sales call. (Yes, many "interviews" will be conducted with a small group of students instead of one.)

The other kind of interview is the admissions or evaluative interview, where your performance may actually weigh on the admission office's decision. (Many specialized colleges, particularly religious colleges, request or require evaluative interviews for obvious reasons.) Similar to recommendations and essays, most interviews are neither great nor bad; they are okay. But it's easy to give a great interview if you prepare because your competition probably gives lousy interviews (most high school students do not interview well). By the way, this situation is where your rhetoric or debate skills will come in handy (if you took my advice and participated in rhetoric or debate). You should prepare for an interview by having a professional ask you tough interview questions; any good college counselor will be able to prepare you for an interview. I've included a list of interview questions below. The interview is completely under your control, so you should practice as much as possible. Practicing the interview in a strange place (your mother's office) with an unfamiliar person (your father's partner) is very valuable. It doesn't help much to practice in your living room with your sister or mother asking questions; you will not feel the tense strangeness of an actual interview. If you cannot practice in a strange place, then re-arrange your living room furniture so it looks a bit like an office, and ask a neighbor or other family friend to ask you questions. Do this (at least) twice; ideally, you should practice interviewing a month prior to your first interview, a few days before your first interview, and a few days after your first interview—by doing this, you'll be great for your second and third interviews.

Bring copies of your transcripts, test scores, and anything else of relevance to your interview. Also, know your class rank. (Saying "my school doesn't rank" is not an acceptable answer to the question "what is your class rank?" Your school may not rank, but the interviewer will want a good guess as to where you stand in your class.) It's also okay to bring along anything else of significance; for example, if you are applying as an art student, you should bring your portfolio.

Some admissions officers will tell you that all interviews are weighted equally regardless of whether they are conducted by an admissions officer, alumnus, professor, coach, or current college student. This statement is not true. The only interview that an admissions office fully trusts is one done by the admissions office. They assume, and rightfully so, that almost everyone else has an agenda— the alumnus wants more applicants admitted from his home town, the professor wants more applicants admitted who will major in his field, the coach is simply interested in filling that one position on his team, and so forth. In addition, the admissions officer who interviews you may be the same person who votes on accepting or rejecting you. In most cases, none of the other interviewers will cast an official vote. So admissions office interviews are, by far, the most influential.

In fact, at many colleges, the admissions official will give your interview a score that will be used together with your academic and extracurricular score (often on the same 1-5 or 1-9 scale). Admissions offices typically do not permit other interviewers to give you a score; all other interviewers are limited to providing a narrative description of the interview. Obviously, being interviewed by the admissions office can hurt you if you give a bad interview, but it will certainly help you if the interview goes well.

If a college offers neither an admissions nor an alumnus interview, then you should try to get an interview with a faculty member or a coach. A good interview with anyone at the college is much better than nothing. Of course, you need to impress the person, but having someone—anyone—act as your advocate at the college is a huge plus. If you're an athlete and you may play at the college, then simply contact the admissions office and inform them; they will provide you with the contact numbers for the appropriate coaches. If you aren't an athlete or do not wish to play at college, then ask the admissions office if you may speak with the chair of the academic department in which you're interested in majoring. In both cases, you should make arrangements to speak to the interviewer in person. Keep in mind that coaches and professors are busy people; while they enjoy speaking with prospective students, they don't want to be pestered with a thousand annoying questions. Remember your goal: to get this person to recommend that the admissions office admit you. Do everything in your power to come across as the ideal candidate for the college.

Some crazed parents believe they should do everything within their power to get their son or daughter an interview with the dean of admissions. This is a very bad idea. Unless you are expertly coached, you should not interview with the dean. First of all, by "pulling strings" to get interviewed by the dean, you are sure to annoy the dean. (Now you've personally annoyed the most powerful person in the admissions office.) Secondly, because most applicants give poor interviews, the last thing you want to do is to give a poor interview to the top person in the admissions office; it's a sure-fire way to sink your application. As an aside, most parents think their son or daughter is wonderful and will give a great interview; parents are very poor judges of their children. Never assume you will give a good interview unless you are coached. I know of a few instances where parents pulled a few strings with board members and had their son/daughter interviewed by the dean. In every case, the dean was annoyed by the parents and unimpressed by the applicant. (One dean said, "I can't believe the parents wanted me to interview their son. He was positively awful. His grades and test scores are good, but I can't get that awful interview out of my mind.") In every case, the applicants were rejected.

In other cases, parents pulled strings to have their son/daughter interviewed by colleges that do not offer interviews. Of course, this also irritates the admissions office, but—more importantly—it falls prey to the same fallacy as the above example: do not assume an interview will help you unless you've been coached. Most high school juniors and seniors give awful interviews. You may end up hurting your application by getting an interview, particularly if you've already irritated the admissions office. The bottom line: request interviews if they are offered and prepare for them; do not request a special interview and do not give an interview unprepared.

When should you ask for an interview? Most students interview at the most logical time: in the fall of their senior year. However, many colleges start offering interviews in the late spring. I recommend doing late spring interviews for two reasons: first, interviewing early will exhibit your eagerness to attend that college, and second, the spring interviews are less booked, so you will be able to choose a more convenient time and day. As with everything else in the admissions process, doing something early is much better because you'll beat the rush and you'll appear more interested than everyone else.

Preparing for an Admissions Interview. You, the student, should call the college or the alumni association to arrange for the interview. In many cases, if you are a legatee, then you should arrange for an alumni interview through the alumni council. If you are not a legatee, then you need to arrange for an interview through the admissions office. In some cases, interviews are only given to legatees.

Regardless of the specifics, if the college offers an interview, you should accept it. If you prepare, you will give an above-average interview (because, as noted above, most high school students do not interview well). If you have the option, you should choose an interview with an admissions officer rather than with an alumnus; a good impression with an admissions officer will help you more than a good impression with an alumnus. And finally, if you are doing interviews at several colleges, arrange them from least-favorite/safety college to top-choice college. Your first interview should be at a safety college or a college in which you aren't too interested; that way, you can practice your interviewing skills without risking too much. Always do your last interview at your top-choice college so you will be polished and experienced. If you are scheduled for an interview at your top-choice college early (like in September), then try to arrange one or two other interviews before it for practice. It's usually a bad idea to walk into an interview at your top-choice college without any experience.

Local/Alumni Interviews. Often, your only option is to do a local interview, typically conducted by an alumnus. The college will provide you with a name or phone number, and you call the alumnus to arrange for the interview. (Sometimes the college does the opposite; they provide your name and phone number to the alumnus, and he or she calls you.) You should call, politely explain that you're applying to the college in question, and that the college provided the alumnus's name and phone number. Here are a few tips regarding your conversation:

- refer to the alumnus as Mr. or Ms.
- never assume their age & don't act like a teenager (the alumnus may be 23 or 83)
- don't use slang (no "cool" or "like")
- don't use repetitive language or repetitive answers
- use good grammar; poor grammar is jarring to an educated person; you must know the difference between adjectives and adverbs, the subjective/objective, and passive/active voice. If the interviewer asks "how are you doing?" you must answer "well." If you say "good" you will sound less than fantastic.

- be flexible; if they say that Tuesday at 7pm is good, then it should be good for you as well unless you have life-saving surgery that evening.

- remember that this alumnus graduated from this college and loves the college so much that she volunteers her time to talk to dullards like you; she's already chosen this college and invested her time, money, and energy at the college, so she LOVES this college; do not, under any circumstances (even if invited to) disparage the college in any way. (If you're asked, "So what do you think this college's worst feature is" then your answer should be something like "It's too hard to get into!" That answer is actually a compliment.)

If you're doing a local or alumni interview, you will often meet at the interviewer's house or place of work. Sometimes they will interview you at a local coffee shop or library. It's their choice, so be flexible. If you aren't sure of how to get to the location of the interview, consult your parents and a map (don't ask the interviewer), and by all means, leave very early for the interview. You should not be late.

Admissions Office Interviews. If you can, you should try to have an interview at the admissions office. Feel free to try to arrange this along with your college tour. Keep in mind, though, that interviews and college tours do not necessarily run on the same schedule; a college may give tours year-round and only give interviews August through December. You will need to contact the college to find out whether or not doing both in one trip is possible; if you live a great distance from the college and are not likely to visit it twice, then try to arrange a tour and interview during a single visit.

If the interview is not a sales call, then your interviewer will probably take notes that will be included in your admissions file. Most interviewers are looking for these characteristics: maturity, honesty, initiative, and energy. Yes, these are the same characteristics that admissions offices are looking for in a good essay. (Interviewers will also notice your appearance, communication skills, and attitude.) Colleges value these characteristics very highly, and your transcript doesn't generally exhibit evidence of these qualities. Here's a summary of how you can exhibit these qualities:

Maturity—Maturity is how you dress, how you behave, if you are polite. You should dress "semi-formal," which means slacks and a tie, or a dress or skirt; you may wear a sport jacket or a sweater. No one expects you to show up in a tuxedo, and no one expects you to show up in a sweat suit. I know of too many students who went to their interview in their soccer or lacrosse uniform "because I didn't have time to change." This attitude is unacceptable. You must find the time to be presentable. (In fact, I know of one legatee applicant to an Ivy who went to his interview at the admission office in his soccer uniform because he "didn't have time to change." He was rejected, in part, because of his complete lack of respect—despite the fact that his father was one of the more generous alumni.)

You should refer to your interviewer as "Mr." or "Ms." and while you need not be too quiet, you should usually wait to speak until you're spoken to; do not start blabbing on about how great Cornell is, or how great you are, or how great your grandfather is (who attended Cornell) unless you're asked—and it's unlikely that any interviewer will ask you a question about how great you are. When you arrive, shake hands—don't be too timid—introduce yourself, and ask your interviewer how he or she is and how their day is going. Appear to be interested in their answer (you may not care, but you should not show it).

Obviously, you shouldn't put your feet up on the desk, chew gum, swear, use slang, keep looking at your watch, or stare out the window. Pretend you're at one of your parents' dinner parties, and you've been told to be on your best behavior. Speaking of parents, they may drive you to the interview (at the admissions office or alumnus' house), but they should not accompany you into the interview. Repeat: parents, DO NOT accompany your child to the actual interview. If your parents drive you and the interviewer notices them, you should introduce your parents (say, "I'd like you to meet my parents, Mr. and Mrs. X; mom and dad, this is Mr. Y, who is going to interview me"). Your parents should say hello, shake hands, and promptly excuse themselves; they should not wait to be excused. (Some interviewers will not ask parents to leave; they will simply permit them to stay and then be annoyed that they stayed.)

Honesty—Honesty is an aspect of maturity. Do not attempt to hide your weaknesses; in fact, you should be willing to bring up your weaknesses first. Don't begin or end the interview with a discussion of your limitations, but you should bring up your weaknesses near the beginning, briefly and freely discuss them, then move on to your strengths. You should not discuss personal problems; only discuss issues that appear on your application (no need to add weaknesses!).

Remember: you are not the greatest student ever; perhaps you found AP chemistry very difficult; perhaps you are awful at the piano; perhaps you played varsity soccer but rarely started a game. It's okay to discuss weaknesses: just keep the discussion short and candid.

Leadership/Initiative—How have you solved a problem? Initiated a solution? How will you bring this to the college? These questions concern admissions officers. After all, they are charged with the task of creating a small town that is largely operated by students volunteering their time and energy. For a college to be successful, it must have leaders. Think of answers to the above questions prior to going into the interview. If your interviewer doesn't ask these questions, then bring up the answers yourself.

Energy—High energy always makes a positive impressive. (I mean wholesome energy, not unnatural mania.) You should appear excited, interested, and enthused. If you appear disinterested, an interviewer may assume that the college is your safety or that you're arrogant; either way, it leaves a bad impression. Remember that in nearly every case, your interviewer either attended the college or is paid by the college (or both), so appearing disinterested will leave a very negative impression. Even if the college is your safety, you must appear enthused.

How does one appear enthused? First, be communicative. Do not answer questions with one-word responses. Do not wait to be asked to elaborate. Give an answer, provide details and support for your answer, and ask a question in response. Second, be interactive. Do not be afraid to ask questions of your interviewer or to ask your interviewer to clarify a question. Third, show positive facial expressions. Smile, look at your interviewer, and nod your head as he or she speaks (as if you're listening). If you frown and stare at the floor, you will make your interviewer uncomfortable.

Ask Questions About the School—Your interviewer may end your interview by asking if you have any questions. A few interviewers will start an interview by asking if you have any questions; I find this tactic a bit cruel, and I suspect that the interviewers who do this are inexperienced or lazy. (One bit of warning: if an interviewer looks at an application and concludes that the applicant has little or no chance of being admitted, the interviewer will often spend most of the interview discussing the college and/or current events. The interviewer won't be particularly interested in discussing you because you have very little chance of being admitted. If you think this is happening, feel free to ask the interviewer if you have a chance of being admitted. If the interviewer's reply is not positive, ask what you can do to improve your chances of being admitted.)

You should know as much about the college as possible and always have a few questions prepared. If necessary, you may write the questions on a notepad and refer to the pad. Even if you don't have any questions—and if you've really done your homework, chances are you won't—you should always ask one or two good questions.

What kind of questions are good questions? Generally speaking, the kind that shows that you've done a bit of research and that you're genuinely interested in the college. Do not ask, "So how many students attend this college?" This will show that you haven't done any research. So you must ask questions for which answers are not readily available. While you should not be negative or derisive, you should not shy away from asking tough questions. You are considering buying a product that costs $50,000-$160,000 from this college; you have a right to ask tough questions.

For example:

I'm interested in _____; how is that department? What are that depart-ment's strengths?

Do teaching assistants (TA's) teach many courses? Which courses do they usually teach?

What do you think is this college's greatest weakness?

What kind of student is most successful here?

What is the crime rate on campus?

Do many students stay on-campus or in town during the summer?

Do many students live on-campus their junior or senior year?

You may think of other questions to ask while doing your research on the col-lege. Just be sure that your questions are intelligent and aren't easily answered by a quick look in any college guide. Interviewers appreciate intelligent questions and are annoyed by questions that waste their time. Some of the above questions, for example, may be bad questions for some colleges; if the college publishes in their view book the percent of students who live on-campus for each of their years at the college, then asking a question that pertains to that would be asinine. Use your good judgment, and ask good questions.

If an admissions officer interviews you, then, at the end of the interview, you may ask about your chances of being admitted. While the admissions officer can-not give you a definite answer, they can gauge your chances of being admitted given the current year's and/or prior year's applicants. Usually, they won't give you a direct response but rather one of three coded responses. If they think there's a 75%+chance of you being admitted, they will encourage you to apply early deci-sion or early action. If they think your chances of being admitted are 50%-75%, they will encourage you to apply but tell you to also keep your options open. If they believe you chances of being admitted are below 50%, then they will simply encourage you to apply elsewhere. In a few rare cases, the admissions officer may be quite blunt. A few outstanding students will receive immediate offers of admission, while a few particularly poor students will simply be discouraged from applying. (Usually, the "instant offers" are given to outstanding recruited athletes or artists.) If you are completely unsure of your chances of being admitted, then you should ask the interviewer. There's no point in going forward if the inter-viewer is discouraging.

After the interview, you should thank your interviewer and ask for a card (or something with their name and title on it). Do not rely on your memory or com-mon spellings; these days, there are many ways to spell "Smith" and "Jones." You should immediately write a thank-you note. So that you can be sure to spell the interviewer's name and title correctly, you should get something with his name spelled on it. (You may have already received a letter from the college with the interviewer's name spelled on it; however, it's always nice to ask for a business card on your way out—you may have lost the letter.)

A final word about interviewers: most interviewers are nice, professional people who are not "out to get you." They are truly interested in discovering the real you, but they aren't going to pull it out of you. They will give you the platform to express yourself, but it's up to you to take advantage of the opportunity. In a sense, this is a performance, and you're the performer. Some interviewers do little tricks that may seem cruel; for example, they may invite you into the interview room, ask you to have a seat, and then do nothing. They will wait until you say something. Of course, you're sitting there waiting for the interviewer to say something, which results in an uncomfortable five-minute silence. There's no constructive reason an interviewer would give you the silent treatment, and I can only assume that those who start the interview with the silent treatment are bored or sadistic (or both). Regardless, the interview is a stage. If your interviewer sits silently and waits for you to speak, then open up your mouth and start! (A good ice-breaker to ask the interviewer would be, "So did your parents drive you here?" Get it? It's a joke—many interviewers start by asking the student this question, so if the student starts by asking the interviewer this question, the student comes across as relaxed, conversational, and witty.)

And keep in mind that there's usually a kook in every admissions office, and that kook may interview you. I know it's difficult, but you shouldn't let a poor interviewer tarnish your perception of a college. One of the worst interviewers I've ever heard of is an admissions officer at Yale (I think he's still there). He uses his interviews to delineate his political positions and rarely discusses Yale or the applicant. I recently knew a student who interviewed with him and left Yale so disgusted by the way this officer conducted the interview that the student refused to apply to Yale. (The applicant applied and was accepted early to Princeton.) I know it's difficult to separate an interviewer from the rest of the college, but nearly every admissions office employs some kook, and these people usually don't reflect the college as a whole.

INTERVIEW SUMMARY

- Talk about your strong points as early as possible; don't dwell on meaningless stuff (such as your car ride up to the college). If your interviewer asks if there's anything he forgot to ask, do not hesitate to bring up your strengths.
- Do not be afraid to discuss your weaknesses, but make the discussion short. Do not begin or end an interview by discussing your weaknesses. Do not discuss any weakness that is not on your application to that college.

- Your goal during the interview is to illustrate why you're unique. What makes you special and a good fit for the college's community?
- No school is your safety! Never give the impression that you are bored or arrogant.
- Introduce your parents if you came with them. (Introduce them formally, when appropriate, but make sure they know to stay out of the interview.)
- Get a business card if necessary so you can write a thank-you note.
- Memorize your interviewer's name before you go in. Your interviewer may prod you to see if you know his name (some interviewers do this as a sort of cruel game because they know that many students are shoved into interviews by their parents and don't even know the interviewer's name.)
- Use good grammar. Don't use slang. Don't be repetitive.

Sample Questions. Here is a set of sample questions that your interviewer may ask you; have your parents or a family friend ask you these questions. Do not have one of your friends ask you these questions; your mock interviewer should be an adult, preferably one who makes you feel slightly uncomfortable (your mean aunt or uncle?). This list of questions is not comprehensive, and most interviewers are just normal people trying to get to know you. They will ask various questions, but most of their questions are simply prompts for you to talk about yourself. While you shouldn't babble endlessly, you shouldn't feel the need to restrict your answers to short, precise responses. In a sense, every question your interviewer asks is: "So what's so unique about you?"

I've put a few comments under each question to help guide you in answering them.

1. **So did you drive or fly up here?** Icebreaker. Here's you chance to show your energy—don't answer this question with just one word!

2. **How was your drive?** Don't say "good" and then clam-up. Mention something about the drive—perhaps the scenery, the stops you made, the museums you visited.

3. **Did your parents come?** If the answer is "yes" and your parents are in the immediate vicinity, invite the interviewer to meet your parents.

4. **So how's school going?** This is a maturity question: don't say, "school sucks." Your answer should be some variation of "it's going great, but it's difficult this year—I'm juggling a lot of responsibilities and difficult classes such as AP Physics."

5. **How is the football/soccer/baseball team doing this year?** Another icebreaker—make sure you answer in at least one or two full sentences.

6. **What's the most important thing you've learned at high school?** Another maturity question—you're answer shouldn't be "how to pick up chicks." Your answer should be something about responsibility, diversity, goal-setting and hard-work.

7. **Tell me about yourself. (Grades, class rank, test scores, activities, social/ethnic activities, sports, community service, et cetera.)** You should bring up your weaknesses, but don't make excuses. Briefly state your weaknesses and then move on to your strengths. You should ask the interviewer if they've seen your transcript so that you don't bore them with information they already know. If your interviewer has not seen your transcript, then briefly cover the courses you've taken and your grades. If your interviewer has seen your transcript, then just discuss your weaknesses and strengths and move on to non-transcript items such as community service and other non-academic activities.

8. **What's your greatest failure?** Do not bring up anything that isn't on your application—don't bring up "I tried to kill my little sister two years ago and didn't succeed." Either discuss a poor grade, low test scores, a sport, or your desire to have done more community service, and your discussion should be mature and lack emotion. (Don't say, "Holy cow! I wish I got an A in Latin!!" while you pound your fist on the interviewer's desk.)

9. **What's your greatest success?** If you have any sort of disability, bring it up here. If you are a minority or are any ethnicity apart from Anglo-Saxon, discuss it here. You can also discuss a weakness here; for example, "My greatest weakness was that B in AP Chemistry, but my greatest success was that it wasn't a C! I had to work extremely hard to get that B."

10. **What's the worst part of being in high school?** A classic maturity question. Bad answer: living with my parents. Good answer: most of my courses are prescribed for me and take up most of my time so I don't have much time to explore areas of interest outside of the required work for each course." Interviewer's response, "Like what?" Your response, "We read Twain's *Huck Finn* for English last year, and I really wanted to read a biography and a few more of his novels, but I didn't have the time during the school year. However, I did squeeze in *A Connecticut Yankee in King Arthur's Court* over the summer."

11. **Who's your favorite author?** Picking any airport-paperback author is not a good idea. Try to pick someone dead (or, at least, very old) or a minority. Bad answer: John Grisham. Good answer: Charles Dickens, Balzac, Jane Austen…you get the picture.

12. **Who's your favorite teacher and why?** Bad answer: Mrs. Holliway because she liked me. Good answer: Mrs. Holliway because she pushed me to work harder.

13. What do you think about the situation in Iraq? A top college—particularly an IR school—will want to know if you keep up with daily events. Tip: buy *Newsweek* or *U.S. News* the day before your interview, and read it cover to cover.

14. Name someone you think is successful. Why? It's okay to pick your mother or father; it's not the person that counts, it's the reason. Your reason should be mature. Bad answer: my father because he's rich. Good answer: my father because he overcame a lot of obstacles in life.

15. What are you going to bring to this community? You better bring something! Do you have any unique hobbies? A unique perspective? A unique background? Energy? Insight? Have an answer before you walk into the interviewer's office. Bad answer: I'm going to bring my killer stereo. Good answer: I'm going to bring my passion for community service.

16. Where do you imagine yourself in ten years? It's okay to say, "I don't know." In fact, it's not so great to have an extremely specific idea of where you're going to be—planning too far ahead in life isn't realistic or mature.

17. What do you want to do with your life? Once again, it's okay to say, "I don't know." But don't blurt it out sarcastically. Instead, think for a moment, and say "I don't know" pensively, as if it's the greatest thought you've ever had. Then add, "But I hope to be productive and happy. Ultimately, I guess, I hope I'm just a good person and good at whatever I decide to do." Okay, maybe that's a little sappy, but you get the picture.

18. What school do your parents want you to attend? Another maturity question; do you or your parents want to you attend this college? Bad answer: this one. Good answer: they are helping me make the best choice, but it's really up to me—they aren't pushing me in any direction. Colleges get a little nervous if your parents are pushing you.

19. What worries you most about attending college? Don't mention parties or your parents. Mention acclimating to college life and the rigorous academics. Or you can say something like, "taking advantage of everything here—there are so many things I want to accomplish!"

20. What attracts you to this college? Once again, don't mention parties or parents. And don't blab on about the "great academics"—everyone says that. Mention the community, the feeling the college gives you ("it just feels right"), the way that the academics, the community, and the extracurriculars all come together. Also, if you want to be a stud, mention a specific department that attracts you or a specific professor, publication, or other academic activity.

21. What is the worst thing about this college? Bad answer: almost anything. Good answer: I don't know; I was going to ask you that! (You may say, "It's expensive, but all colleges are." That's an actual criticism that won't hurt anyone's feelings, and it will give an opportunity for your interviewer to spew some financial aid spiel at you.)

22. What is the best thing about this college? Same question as "what attracts you to this college."

23. Any questions for me? Yes. You always have a few questions (such as "What's the worst thing about this college?").

One final note: Remember that most high school students are awful at interviews because they are unresponsive, uncommunicative and not energetic. It's easy to fix those things, so do it, and your interview should be great.

Chapter 23

Standardized Tests

"Four hours on one Saturday morning and
my life could be ruined. What the hell is that?"

What are standardized tests? Standardized tests are tests that allow people from different backgrounds to be compared using a single set of standards. The tests you are probably most familiar with are the PSAT, SAT, SAT II, ACT, and AP tests. You probably have also taken tests in school that are given by the state in order to certify your school. A standardized test may be content-based (such as a driver's license test that simply measures your knowledge of laws), aptitude-based (such as an I.Q. test that measures how you think rather than what you know), or some mixture of the two. There are over a thousand standardized tests in the USA.

The Road to Hell is Paved with Theories. In theory, a standardized test allows any test-taker to be compared to any other test-taker—from across the country, from twenty years ago, from a completely different socio-economic and/or cultural background. You probably assume that all test-takers take the same test (at least all test takers taking the same test on the same day). None of these assumptions is true. In most cases, standardized tests often reveal a test-taker's background more than his intelligence or what he knows about a specific subject. And rarely do any two randomly compared test takers take the same test. For example, there are between fifteen and fifty different versions of the SAT given each year; there are other tests, such as the GRE, for which no two versions are the same (there are literally thousands of versions).

So if you randomly selected two people who took the SAT, for example, chances are they did not take the same test and that the test reveals more about their socio-economic background than their academic skills. Clearly, standard-ized tests are far from being an "equalizing measuring stick" and more often reaf-firm disadvantages than mitigate them. Then why are they used?

159

The standardized test was created in the 10th century by the *Song* dynasty of China. Every year, teenagers took the *jin-shi* test to become a civil servant. Only about 50 students aced the test, and *Song* literature is filed with tales of male test-takers failing because of wine and women. (Oddly, *Song* literature does not blame television for low test scores.)

The French! (Again.) The modern version of the aptitude test (e.g. the SAT) was developed about 100 years ago by two Frenchmen, Alfred Binet and Theodore Simon (hence the famous Binet-Simon IQ test). These early IQ tests were created to illustrate that white, northern Europeans were intellectually superior. The test-makers assumed that wealthy, white Northern Europeans were intellectually superior, but a method was needed to find the poor white wealthy Europeans who were also intellectually superior. These early IQ tests were designed to achieve this goal.

Ah, bigotry. The SAT was developed from these early IQ tests and has its direct roots in IQ tests used for the Army. The man who developed the SAT, Carl Brigham, was an enthusiastic racist and eugenicist, and tests like the SAT were used in the 1920s-1940s to retard the social mobility of immigrant groups (primarily Southern Europeans and Jews). Despite the similarities between today's SAT and the SAT of the 1940s, ETS and the College Board will deny that the SAT is an IQ test. However, the SAT is remarkably similar in many ways to IQ tests and, surprisingly, the two tests correlate very highly. If you took the SAT twice, your second SAT score would correlate to your first SAT score to the same degree as an IQ test would correlate to your first SAT score (which means that the variance between two SAT scores is the same as the variance between an SAT score and an IQ test).

ETS and College Board claim that the SAT is designed to predict your grades for your first year of college. The problem is that SAT scores are only about 17% predictive, which means that it only measures about 17% of factors that determine how well you will perform in your first year of college. ETS and College Board admit that your high school grades are much better predictors. Then why do colleges use the SAT?

Tests & Transcripts. Colleges use standardized tests for one reason: they do not trust transcripts. As you can gather from reading the section on transcripts, grades, and rankings, colleges have a good deal of trouble making sense of what you do in school. Originally, rankings helped; if you were ranked #5 in a class of 300, then that seemed to mean something. However, some public schools began to finagle rankings so average students could be ranked in the top quintile. As long as high schools are determined to make even the bad students look good, colleges will rely heavily on standardized tests. And with the booming number of public schools, the growing prevalence of charter schools and home-schooling, and the increasingly mobile population, standardized tests are the one apparent constant that provides a uniform foundation for assessing all high school students.

Colleges view standardized tests differently, but one thing is true of all of them: they are considered more valid than your grades and recommendations. If your SAT II physics score is a 530, but your physics grade is an A, the SAT II score will be considered valid, and colleges will assume that your physics teacher grades easily. Regardless of what teachers claim or believe, they are or should be teaching to these tests. It will not matter what grade a student earns if he scores poorly on the standardized test for the subject. And overall, if you have above-average grades (an A average, for example) but below average SAT scores (a 950, for example), colleges will assume that you are a below-average student who either worked very hard or who attends a very easy high school (or both). They will not assume that something is wrong with the test.

Colleges generally treat the SAT like an IQ test. College admissions officers, despite what they might say, believe that the SAT broadly measures intelligence (which acknowledges the SAT's history as an IQ test). If your counselor says you are extremely intelligent but your SAT score is a 910, the admissions office will assume the SAT is correct and, in fact, you are not very intelligent. If your biology teacher says you are the school's best biology student but your biology SAT II score is a lame 560, then the admissions office will assume the score is correct and your biology teacher is mistaken.

This has one very practical result: do not submit a low SAT II or AP score for any class in which you've earned a good grade or are getting a recommendation from the teacher. In other words, if you have an A in biology and/or are getting a recommendation from your biology teacher, a 520 on the SAT II biology would probably negate the good grade and the recommendation.

Of course, standardized tests such as the SAT have proven to be highly biased and very coach-able, which makes doubtful the claim that it should be the nation's academic measuring stick. If $2500 and four months of hard work can raise your SAT score by 250 points, then it's odd that colleges think test scores are of greater validity than grades. But until colleges can trust and quickly compare transcripts, they will continue to rely on standardized tests.

Why? Invariably and in contradiction to what most colleges claim, admissions officers equate test scores with intelligence. If your test scores are low, they will assume you're not very smart. If you have low or average test scores and high grades, admissions officers are more likely to assume that you're hardworking but not very smart. Conversely, if your test scores are high and your grades are low, admissions officers are more likely to assume that you are smart but bored in class. I've witnessed this scenario many times: admissions officers look at an applicant with a 1450 on the SAT and B-/C+grades and say, "smart kid, I bet he was bored silly in his classes." But rarely (if ever) have I witnessed an admissions officer look at a 1000 on the SAT and A/A+grades and say, "smart kid, I bet she just doesn't test well." Instead, they assume the applicant is a hard worker of average (or below average) intelligence.

These prejudices run contrary to everything we know about standardized tests and significantly hurt those who consistently score lower (women and minorities). Men consistently score higher on the SAT than women; does this mean that men are more intelligent than women? Of course not, but this is what admissions officers tend to assume. Apply the logic that SAT scores roughly measures intelligence across the board, and the conclusions are revolting: men are more intelligent than women, whites are more intelligent than blacks, Asians are more intelligent than Hispanics, northerners are more intelligent than southerners, and so forth. While these conclusions are repugnant to common sense, they are the logical conclusion to the assumptions that most admissions officers have about standardized tests.

Similarly, ETS and the College Board claim that the SAT helps predict college grades. On average, men score 40-60 points higher than women on the SAT, but women usually earn higher grades in college freshmen classes. So women score lower on the SAT, but earn higher grades in college. Clearly, the SAT is not predicting college grades. Standardized tests should be abolished, but this can't happen until colleges trust high school transcripts.

Colleges respond to these charges by saying that they take an applicant's socioeconomic background into consideration. First, if this is a valid statement, then it means that the SAT more reflects one's socio-economic background than one's aptitude. The obvious question is: why do we need a test that measures one's socio-economic background?

Second, the claim that colleges take into consideration one's socio-economic background is only partly true. A wealthy Hispanic will get more "consideration" than a poor Jew or Asian. In fact, a wealthy Hispanic—one who does not even speak Spanish—will get more "consideration" than the poor white applicant. The white applicant will be required to come close or equal to the college's average SAT scores, whereas the Hispanic, disadvantaged or not, will be considered even if he scores 100+points below the average. I've seen cases where a Hispanic student who does not speak Spanish (English was her first language), whose parents are wealthy doctors, was admitted to top colleges with SAT scores 150-200 points below their averages. No white or Asian non-recruited student is given that kind of consideration, regardless of how poor they may be. The bottom line: standardized tests more often reinforce prejudice than level the playing field and are often used to create new prejudices. It's a sad tangle of conflicting priorities usually left to be sorted by people who aren't very intelligent. Unfortunately, it's a game you must play; there's nothing you can do about it now.

There are about 200 colleges that do not require standardized test scores. Of these 200, only about five are good colleges, and most of them make SATs optional. These colleges know that 95%+of their applicants take the SAT, and they know that those who get high scores will report them. The obvious conclusion is that those who do not report SAT scores are those who scored low. It's unfortunate but true: if you apply to a "SAT optional" college and withhold your scores, the college will assume you have low scores (which would be the only reason to withhold them). If colleges were earnest about abolishing the SAT, they wouldn't make them optional; they would refuse to consider them.

Who? The people who make the PSAT, SAT, AP tests and about 500 other tests are the College Board and ETS. Technically, the College Board owns the SAT, and they contract ETS to manage the SAT program. The people you primarily deal with are ETS (those are the people in New Jersey). Ostensibly, ETS is a non-profit educational company that makes bubble tests; the College Board has a for-profit side that sells test-prep.

These people are neither educational experts nor statistically competent psychometricians. If you read ETS's May 1995 report on scoring and scaling the SAT, you'd realize (as so many did) that ETS is filled with nabobs and rubes whose statistical acumen wouldn't earn them a 2 on their own AP Statistics test. ETS "recentered" their test to artificially boost everyone's score by about 100 points. They had two possible explanations: 1, the test was bogus and they had to artificially insert some credibility into it, or 2, they had been mis-scoring the SAT for decades and only now realized it. In truth, both explanations are true. But ETS chose to sell the second one. (More on this later.)

The disingenuous attitude of the College Board and ETS is ponderous—so much so, that many refer to them as the tobacco companies of education: they dissemble on important issues; they run all their own research and pronounce themselves good and their methods valid; they don't wish to release information critical of themselves; they demonize those who criticize their products. For decades, the College Board claimed that the SAT was uncoachable and went so far as to fire employees who discovered that it was coachable (e.g. Lewis Pike). But now the College Board offers test-prep (and they make a lot money doing it.) The College Board now claims that SAT scores are rising and they credit "students taking more difficult classes in high schools." Of course, they didn't mention that they added 100 or so points to everyone's scores a few years ago. ETS loses hundreds of students' tests, and they do not compensate the students for their time or energy. ETS automatically assumes a student cheats if he raises his score by 300 or more points. I could go on, but it would only bore you. Take my word for it: the College Board and ETS are not your friends.

No serious scholar would suggest that the SAT predicts how well you will do in college; there is no study that shows a statistically significant correlation between the SAT and high school or college grades. No intelligent college professor really thinks that the SAT reveals how smart or how motivated you are. So why does ETS keep inflicting the SAT on students? The answer is money. ETS likes money. You have it. They want it. Simple as that.

The PSAT. Most juniors take the PSAT in October; some sophomores also take it in October. Most students aren't quite sure what to make of the PSAT, so here's the scoop.

PSAT vs. SAT. There are two primary differences between the PSAT and the SAT. First, the PSAT is shorter by about an hour. Since many students can't sit still for three hours for the PSAT, sitting still for an additional hour for the SAT is awful. After sitting in one place for three hours for the SAT, many high school students just go berserk, which causes them to perform poorly on the last hour of the SAT. Because of this, many students (about 30%) actually score higher on the PSAT than on the SAT. The longer test (SAT) is actually more difficult for them. The second difference is that the PSAT has the Writing Skills Section (WSC). This section is the freak show of standardized testing. It tests your ability to make subject-verbal agreements and actually does not test your writing.

For what does the PSAT count? Nothing, really. A few scholarships and National Merit, but nothing worth fretting over. Some people think National Merit is a big deal, but consider that less than 10% of those admitted to Ivy League colleges are National Merit—this means that over 90% of those admitted to the Ivies were NOT National Merit. And the Ivies reject National Merit winners all the time, so if they don't care, why should you? (And no, the Ivies don't give you any money for being National Merit.)

One warning: some high schools put your PSAT score on your official high school transcript (the one they send to colleges) instead of putting it on your working transcript. Ask your high school counselor whether or not the school puts your PSAT score on the official transcript. If your school does this, tell your counselor to have the score removed. Colleges have no business seeing your PSAT score. Colleges do not ask for PSAT scores, and they are in no way considered in the admissions process.

Why the PSAT? If you ask ETS why students should take the PSAT, they will spew forth something about good practice and National Merit. The PSAT is not good practice for the SAT because it's not the same test—the PSAT is shorter and contains that inane Writing Skills section! The real reason ETS wants you to take the PSAT is because it's marketing for the SAT. If you take the PSAT in October, which standardized test are you going to take in the spring? The ACT? Probably not. You're going to take the test that you have some familiarity with (because you think you will get a better score on it than on the ACT or some other test). You've probably heard how drug dealers will give you a sample of drugs for free just to get you hooked, and then you will come back for more and pay for it. That's what the PSAT is: a little sample to get you hooked, then you come back for more later and you pay for it. Therefore, the PSAT is the crack cocaine of the testing world.

The other reason that ETS wants you to take the PSAT is so they can collect information about you and sell it to colleges. All of the information (name, address, race, religion, grades, et cetera) you give when you take the PSAT is sold to colleges. These colleges use this information to mail you brochures (usually in late February of your junior year). ETS owns the largest, most detailed mailing list of college-bound high school students in the world, and they get all of their information from the PSAT.

Should I take the PSAT? If you want to…but don't go out of your way. Colleges don't see your PSAT score and no one cares about your PSAT score, so it doesn't really matter. You should keep in mind that the PSAT is given by your school; the SAT is given directly by ETS and their proctoring henchmen. So you need to sign up for the PSAT with your school. Some schools charge a fee to take the PSAT; if your school charges a fee to take the PSAT, don't waste your money.

One Warning. Do not take the PSAT in your junior year unprepared. The fine people at ETS regularly monitor score improvements (from PSAT to SAT, and between SATs), and are very skeptical of large improvements. ETS assumes that any student who improves 250 points or more has cheated, and usually they will nullify your scores. (Yes, they will perform a perfunctory investigation that's surprisingly reminiscent of Stalin's circus trials.) Many students who have shown large score improvements have had their scores nullified by ETS, despite the fact that there's no proof that the students have cheated. Yes, you can sue ETS—as many do—but by the time the suit is resolved years later, you will already be in college and no longer care about or need your SAT scores. So if you take any ETS test unprepared, you may bomb it and subsequently lock yourself into that lower score range because ETS simply will not permit you to score considerably higher. It is not uncommon for students who score a 900 on a first test to prepare and improve by 350-400 points; and it's not uncommon for them to get a note from ETS stating that their test is being "reviewed." They usually receive another note two or three months later stating that their scores are null and void. In conclusion: prepare for every ETS test.

The SAT. Before I get into the details of the SAT and SAT II, I should mention a few preliminary notes. First, the SAT and SAT II are often as important as your grades and, combined, are often more important than your grades. This is true despite what college officials say. Second, colleges rely heavily on SATs for two reasons, one of which is explored above: they do not trust high school transcripts. The efforts by high schools to tweak the system and artificially boost grades or rankings often cause colleges to decrease their reliance on high school transcripts. The second reason colleges rely so heavily on SAT scores is that these test scores give them a very cost-efficient way to process applications. Imagine sitting in a college admissions office and receiving 15,000 applications in two months, and you and a few others must decide who gets admitted and who gets rejected. How do you do it?

Most admissions readers spend about 5-10 minutes on the typical application. They primarily look at your grades and SAT score. Why don't they spend more time? Because you only paid $40 to apply. If they charged you $250 to apply, then maybe they'd throw out the SAT and carefully read your essays, interview you and spend an hour thinking about you, but $40 isn't enough. So colleges are in a bind: either raise their application fees to $200 and actually read the essays, interview you, call those who recommended you, or keep the application fees low and use the SAT. Of course, they would still need some standardized method of comparing students since they still wouldn't fully trust high school transcripts.

Obviously, most colleges choose to keep the application fees low and use the SAT. Why? Because if they quadrupled their application fees, you would be annoyed at the colleges. But now you just hate the SAT, and colleges would rather you hate the SAT than the college.

So ETS likes the SAT because it makes them a tremendous amount of cash, and the colleges like the SAT because it allows them to keep their admission fee low (which presumably keeps you happy) and because they don't trust transcripts. Did you notice how much of this actually has to do with education? Yeah, exactly none of it.

No one in his right mind would ever suggest that the SAT measures anything other than how well you take the test. It doesn't measure how well you did in high school or will do in college. It doesn't measure how smart you are or how much you know. If anyone suggests that the SAT tests anything worth knowing, you should tell him to seek medical attention.

That's the bad news. The good news is that the SAT is "standardized," which means that supposedly everyone's scores are completely comparable. Now we know that's silly, but that's ETS's story, and they're sticking to it. So "standardized" means "same stupid test every year." The fundamental way that this test is made doesn't change. So if you can figure out how the test is made, then you can raise your score because ETS can't change the test. ETS is not going to tell you all their dirty little secrets, so using their books, software, or web site for learning tips and techniques is like asking the IRS for tax advice. But you should—must—prepare for this test. Good preparation can easily raise your score by 100 to 150 points, which is worth a lot in terms of most indexing formulae and can make up for poor grades. (As an aside, no SAT or SAT II scores can make up for awful grades. A great SAT score can make up for a 3.4 if the college requires a 3.7. But if you have a 2.1 GPA, great SAT scores won't help you get admitted to a top college. A 2.1 GPA and a 1500 SAT score will lead colleges to conclude that you're smart but very lazy and not too many colleges are looking for smart-but-lazy students.)

Given that the SAT (and PSAT) is "standardized," you may wonder about all the changes you hear about: antonyms are gone, calculators are permitted, a "grid-in" section was added, and the PSAT now has a "writing" section. Even the name of the test changed from "Scholastic Aptitude Test" to "Scholastic Assessment Test" to "SAT" (which stands for nothing, therefore more accurately describing what it tests). The changes to the test, like the changes to the name, are all cosmetic. When you prepare for the test, you will find that the SAT is largely the same beast your older brothers and parents tackled years ago.

Preparing for the SAT usually takes 8-10 weeks, and any preparation is better than none. It's reasonable to expect a 100-150 point increase with preparation, although many students improve their scores by 200 or more points. Usually, private tutoring is more effective than classes. Most prep courses and books teach similar techniques, so the difference between courses and tutors isn't the techniques; it's the teachers. In most cases, the more rigorous the hiring standards and the higher the pay, the better the teachers.

What is this SAT thing, anyway? Slouching out of Princeton, New Jersey seven times each year, the SAT is the 700-pound gorilla of the standardized testing world. No one likes it, but no one can seem to kill it. It throws its weight around the college admissions world and usually gets its way. Some day, some brave soul will free us from this beast, but until then, we endure.

The SAT has a murky past as a pseudo-IQ Army test. Princeton University was the first to decide that it needed a standardized IQ test (probably because it regretted admitting F. Scott Fitzgerald a few years earlier—he dropped out before graduating). What followed was decades of pain and suffering for millions of innocent high school students.

Good Scores, Bad Scores. Today, it's not uncommon for Harvard to receive 350-400 applicants with perfect SAT scores (1600) each year; it's also not uncommon for Harvard to reject about 150 of these applicants each year. Nationally, 500-600 students get a perfect score each year.

For top colleges, truly impressive scores are always over 1450, usually over 1500. A 1450 or less is simply not impressive or unusual. In fact, a 1400 would be below average at many top colleges. Equal scores or lop-sided scores with a high verbal are good; a lop-sided score with a high math is not good. SAT scores do not necessarily correlate to scores on other tests in the same subject; some students score a 650 on the SAT math (not very good) and still score a 5 on the AP calculus test, which is great. To stand out on the SAT, you need a combined score of 1500 or higher or a verbal score of 750 or higher. A score of 760 verbal and 680 math, though it adds up to a typical 1440, would be considered very impressive because of the high verbal score, which is much more difficult to achieve than a high math score. (On average, about 21% of test-takers score above a 600 on math, but only about 8% score above 600 on verbal.)

The "poor test taker" excuse won't get you very far in the admissions process if you are a non-recruited applicant. If you can't respond to pressure-packed timed-tests, then most colleges will assume that you won't perform well at college. Most top colleges are pressure-packed, and most colleges have 2-4 hour tests (just like the SAT). If you perform poorly on the SAT, then most colleges will assume that you will perform poorly at college. Once again, despite what colleges say, they put tremendous value on standardized testing.

SAT I v. SAT II. Many years ago (when Ricky Martin was still in Menudo), there was only one "SAT." But ETS decided to increase revenue, so they created two SATs: the SAT I Reasoning Test and the SAT II Subject Tests.

The "SAT I Reasoning Test" is just the same old SAT with a shiny new name. This is the test that everyone has to take to get into college. (By the way, I haven't found any "reasoning" on this test—if you find any, let me know. I've been looking for it.)

The "SAT II Subject Tests" are the old "Achievement Tests" that everyone previously ignored. The SAT IIs are 1-hour tests on a variety of subjects. Most competitive colleges require Writing, Math, and one other subject of your choice (usually a language, history or science).

Writing and Math SAT II? Yes, new tests, same old stuff. The SAT II Writing is the PSAT Writing Skills Component (WSC). The SAT II Math IC is the SAT I Math. (So they are selling the same tests twice to every student!) If you want to improve your SAT II Writing and Math scores, prepare for the PSAT and SAT I.

As noted, most competitive colleges require three SAT IIs: a math, writing, and a third one of your choice. You can take more than three SAT IIs, but most colleges only use your top three scores. However, submitting more than three high SAT II scores will help show the breadth of your academic achievement.

There's no such thing as a "good" score on a SAT II because the scoring curves vary significantly. For example, a good score on the SAT II Math IIC is a 760 or higher, whereas a good score on the SAT II Literature is a 670 or higher. A general rule of thumb is this: submit any score above a 700 to a top college, and submit any score above a 600 to a mid-level college. Any score below as 600 isn't worth submitting unless you are required to do so.

A few students claim that SAT IIs are much easier to prepare for than the SAT I, since the SAT I (and PSAT) tests "reasoning." This is not true. If the SAT is a reasoning test and the SAT IIs are content (or knowledge-based) tests, then one would expect to find significant differences between the two. In fact, the math section of the SAT and the SAT II Math IC are almost identical, and scoring trends between the two tests are consistent. Your math SAT I score and your math SAT II score are consistently related to each other. Similarly, you would think that the SAT II science tests would be clearly content-based, but they aren't. The Physics SAT II isn't much of a content test—even ETS states that the SAT II Physics tests "conceptual physics." What is "conceptual physics"? Mostly, it's all the physics you didn't learn in high school. (High school physics tends to be applied physics involving calculations and problem-solving.) So even the SAT IIs aren't truly content tests.

If a college doesn't require SAT IIs, you should still take Writing, Math, and a third one. You should only send the scores to yourself; you can then choose which scores, if any, to report to the colleges. While all of your SAT scores get reported to colleges regardless of your specific request, SAT IIs taken on or before June 2002 have a "score choice" option.

In order to take advantage of Score Choice, you need to select "Score Choice," and your scores will be only reported to you. Then you may choose to send any scores you wish to colleges. Because of Score Choice, you should take SAT IIs even if you aren't sure what you will score. If your score is low, you can keep it to yourself. There is no Score Choice option for tests taken after June 2002.

You should never walk into the SAT II unprepared; these tests are difficult— some students think they are more difficult than the APs. I don't think they are, but it's worth noting that very few students find the SAT IIs easy. You should buy the College Board publication *Real SAT IIs* and take several practice tests to gauge your scoring range. There's no point in taking the real test if you scored a 450 on the practice test.

If you're applying to a competitive college that doesn't require SAT IIs, such as NYU, it's to your advantage to submit good scores. Competitive colleges that don't require the SAT II usually assume that you have SAT II scores because, they infer, you probably applied to other competitive colleges that do require SAT II scores. Therefore, if you don't submit SAT II scores, they will probably assume it's because your scores are low. So even if a competitive college doesn't require SAT II scores, you should still prepare for and take two or three subject tests and sub- mit them if the scores are above 600.

If you're applying to a top college that requires SAT II scores, then you will need to take three subject tests and, in most cases, need scores of 700 or higher. You should take the SAT IIs no later than June of your junior year, leaving

October of your senior year open to take more SAT IIs if you need higher scores. Keep in mind that if you take tests your senior year, you may not be able to apply early decision or early action.

Because SAT IIs are not easy, you should carefully choose which tests to take. Most students take the SAT IIs at the end of their junior year in June; however, if you are taking AP European history in 10th grade, you should take the SAT II in world history in June of your sophomore year. Many students take U.S. history or literature, thinking these tests will be easy. They are surprised when they open their test booklets to find that both these SAT IIs are actually quite difficult. The literature SAT II, for example, tests your critical reading skills on poetry. If you haven't studied much poetry, this test will be very difficult for you.

As far as the choice between Math IC and IIC, nearly all students take Math IC. The Math IIC test is only expected from students applying to top technical colleges (M.I.T. or Stanford) and students applying as engineering or physics majors. All others, including those that are applying to top liberal arts colleges, should take the Math IC. There are two reasons for this: first, the curve on the IIC is very difficult because most of the students taking it are "math geeks," so a good score is the high 700s; second, most non-tech schools aren't as interested in which tests you take as they are in what your score is, so if you can score a 670 on the IIC, you can probably score a 750 on the IC, and that 750 will help you more—go for the higher number, not the harder test.

The ACT. The ACT is the only legitimate rival to the SAT. It is a very different test that is perhaps more fair than the SAT but less coachable. Most colleges claim that they don't give preference for either test; this assertion is not true. Colleges on the coasts prefer the SAT; these colleges' admissions criteria, indices, and formulae are all geared for SAT scores. If you submit an ACT score, they will translate it to a SAT score before using it. Colleges in the Midwest often prefer the ACT. You should try to accommodate the colleges to which you are applying by giving them the test scores they prefer. But also remember that the SAT responds much better to preparation than the ACT does.

If you are considering taking the ACT, you should specifically check with the colleges to which you are applying; several simply do not want ACT scores and may take issue with you submitting them. Some colleges, including some Ivies, specifically state that they accept ACT scores only if all the other colleges to which you are applying prefer ACT scores (meaning you're applying to Princeton and a bunch of colleges in the Midwest). This scenario is highly unlikely unless you live in the Midwest. To further illustrate the situation, of the 17,665 students who applied to U. Penn for admission in 1999, only 188 (about 1%) applied using ACT scores. So while there's no strict prohibition against using ACT scores, it's not recommended if you're applying to colleges on either coast.

The Advanced Placement (AP) Tests. AP courses and tests were designed for one reason: to give top high school students the opportunity to earn college credits while still in high school. Today, AP tests are also used in the admissions process, and taking AP courses is much more a matter of improving your college application than actually earning college credits. The College Board offers AP tests in 32 subjects; each test costs $77 to take. High schools offer yearlong courses to prepare for these tests; these courses follow a standardized syllabus. Most private high schools offer 12-22 AP courses, and most public high schools offer 6-18 AP courses. AP tests are scored on a scale from 1 to 5, 5 being the top score.

The College Board claims that thousands of colleges ("including the most selective") will give college credits for an AP score of 3; this claim is blatantly inaccurate. Only about half of those "thousands" of colleges will give college credits for a 3. Colleges that will not give any credit for an AP score of 3 include Cornell, James Madison, Penn State, Stanford, Tulane, Chapel Hill, UVA and Yale. For example, Yale will only give credit for a 5 on the English literature AP test. A few critics have even accused the College Board of falsely stating that a score of 3 will earn college credit in order to encourage more students to take the test; approximately 300,000 students each year score a 3 on an AP test, and these students generate $20 million in revenue for the College Board.

In the past, AP courses were somewhat rare, offered by only the best high schools. But today, AP courses are so prevalent that they have replaced honors or advanced courses as the top level of high school academic achievement. A few decades ago, top students were expected to take honors classes, but today, top students are expected to take AP classes while many average (and slightly above average) students are in honors classes. We've arrived at the point that AP classes are expected of top students, regardless of whether or not they will actually earn advanced credit in college. If you intend to apply to a top college, then you need (at least) three AP classes. If you score a 4 or 5 on three or more AP tests, then you are designated an AP Scholar by the College Board (sort of like a frequent flyer program, I suppose). Colleges love AP Scholars.

AP classes are still not offered at all high schools, and many high schools only offer a few of the most common AP classes (U.S. history and biology). Therefore, colleges don't officially use AP scores for admissions purposes because they can't require AP scores of all students. Instead, AP scores tend to be one of the many "floating factors" in the admissions process along with geography and the essay. The importance of your AP scores in the admissions process will depend on which AP courses you take, what scores you earn, what your GPA is, what your intended major is, and what other applicants scored on the same AP tests.

For example, an AP U.S. history score of 4 will do little for your application at Princeton. They see hundreds of 4's on the U.S. history test. Your 4 may be impressive if you come from a bad school system, such as Chicago's, or if you come from a remote part of the country, such as upper Idaho—in a typical year, Princeton receives few applicants from upper Idaho, and ever fewer (if any) have decent AP scores. But if you're a typical suburban northeastern applicant, your 4 doesn't have much weight.

If, on the other hand, you take AP Latin or Physics and score a 5, then your AP score will carry weight. The Latin and physics tests are not as popular as the history test (because Latin is "scholarly," and physics is simply difficult), and a 5 on these two tests would stand out. For this reason, AP scores are floating factors. Your counselor should be able to assist you in determining the weight of your AP scores.

Many colleges give credits for AP classes; others do not. Even most of the nation's top colleges (Harvard, Dartmouth) give credit for AP classes, so you should never assume that a college is too good to give credits for AP classes. Most colleges that do give credits distribute them based on score and class. For example, a 4 on AP biology may not earn you college credits, whereas a 5 on AP Calculus BC may earn the credits of two classes (as it does at Dartmouth and Stanford). At most top colleges, only scores of 4 and 5 will earn you credit. Whether or not a college gives credits for AP courses is the last reason you should consider taking AP classes; good AP course grades, an extra-weighted GPA, and high AP test scores impress every college to some degree, even if they don't give credits for AP classes. And if you do receive credits for AP courses, you should consider taking those classes in college anyway unless you need the credits for financial reasons. While I'm sure your high school AP courses are wonderful, your high school teacher probably does not have the breadth and depth of knowledge that a college professor has, the books you will read in college will probably be more substantially more sophisticated, and your classmates will probably be more motivated and better informed. Despite all the hoopla, high school AP courses are not equivalent to courses offered at top colleges. So use AP courses to improve your chances of being admitted to a top college, but don't assume that those AP courses are being taken in lieu of college courses.

Great AP scores are the single best way to over-ride a poor high school GPA and/or SAT scores. If your high school GPA (9th-11th) is a 3.4 and your SAT score is a 1300, you probably have little chance of being admitted to a top college (assuming you aren't recruited). However, if you take AP history and AP chemistry in 11th grade and earn 5s on both AP tests, then your chance of being admitted significantly improves. A 3.4 GPA and a 1300 on the SAT conveys that perhaps you aren't a serious student, but a slew of perfect AP scores on hard tests goes a long way toward erasing a mediocre GPA and below-average SAT score (1300 would be below-average for a top college). If your overall GPA suffers because of poor freshmen or sophomore year grades, or if you are a "poor test-taker" and your PSAT/SAT scores are below-average, then you need to get yourself into as many AP classes a possible (preferably two or more prior to your senior year), and you need to perform remarkably well on the AP tests.

Ideally, you should try to take one AP class in your sophomore year and at least one in your junior year. In most cases, these classes are European and U.S. history. A few high schools have prohibitions against sophomores taking AP classes, which should engender justified complaints from parents. Most teachers admit student to their AP classes based on prior grades, and often admission is very limited. Therefore, your chances of taking an AP class in 10th or 11th grade will depend on your 9th (and maybe 8th) grade performance, so you can never start getting good grades too early.

Usually, you should plan to follow an AP exam in May with an SAT II in June in the same subject—unless, of course, you think you're going to score a 1 or 2 on the AP. Use the month between the two tests to prepare for the vagaries of applying your AP knowledge to a standardized test. (Keep in mind that while the APs and SAT IIs are different in many ways, they are written by the same people at ETS/College Board.) If, for whatever reason, you need to choose between the AP and the SAT II, choose the SAT II since the SAT II is more often factored directly into the admissions process. However—and I know I've said this before—you should remember that if you're applying to a top college, AP courses and AP test scores will be expected of you even though they aren't officially required; only those applying from schools which do not offer AP classes are exempt.

What can you do if your high school does not offer AP classes? How can you show admissions officers that you're ready for college-level work? I have two suggestions. First, take many SAT II Subject tests, even if the college doesn't require them and even though most colleges will only officially consider your top three scores. By submitting four or five good SAT II scores, you are illustrating the breath and depth of your knowledge on standardized tests. I suggest taking writing, a math, a history or literature, a foreign language, and a science.

Second, explore the possibility of taking classes at your local community college or junior college. Many high schools can arrange for students to take classes during the school year and over the summer at the local community or junior college. By taking one or two classes and earning good grades, you will demonstrate your readiness for college-level classes. Make sure your counselor knows you're doing this (so she will write about it in the counselor recommendation), and make sure you take serious classes (no Basket Weaving 101) that are easy enough for you to earn good grades; don't take a class that's so difficult that you cannot possibly earn anything above a C. Finally, be sure that these college classes are transferred to your high school transcript; in most cases, you don't want to submit a college transcript, even a community college transcript, if you're applying as a freshman. This may cause the college to think you're a transfer applicant, and confusion will ensue. Your counselor should be able to work out the details so these college classes are reported via the high school as high school credited classes (that you took at a college).

International Baccalaureate (IB). IB is an honors program offered at some American high schools (about 350) and many high schools throughout the world. The program and the resulting diploma are recognized at many of the top universities in the world. Essentially, the IB program is a large collection of AP courses that culminate in a special high school diploma. (It would be similar to taking ten AP classes, scoring a 4 or higher on each AP test, and receiving a special diploma acknowledging this feat.) The IB program gives tests in each subject (similar to AP tests) that are scored on a 1-7 scale (7 being the best). The purpose of the IB program is not to earn individual scores but an IB diploma. Most colleges give credit for individual scores of 5 or higher or for the diploma.

The IB program is very impressive—far more impressive than having a few AP scores. In fact, an IB diploma will earn you sophomore standing at Harvard (so an applicant with an IB diploma can earn a bachelor degree from Harvard in just three years). However, the IB program is much more limited in this country than the AP program is; if your high school or district has an IB program, I strongly recommend applying to it and working hard once you're in it. For more information about the IB program, contact them at 212-696-4464.

Chapter 24

Putting the Application Together

"I think my application will look a lot more personal if I handwrite it.
I like using purple pen. It shows my personality."

Eventually the time will come to put the application package together and mail it. You are probably a little worried that perhaps a word is misspelled or a page is missing; this is good, you should be a little worried. Students who aren't worried often misspell words and leave out pages!

What's a Typewriter? First we must address the rather nasty business of completing the forms. Obviously, you need an old-fashioned typewriter to complete the forms, but who has a typewriter? In most cases, only lawyers still use typewriters (all those legal forms, I suppose), but your counselor should be able to recommend a local typist who is expert at completing college forms. The typist will charge a fee and will usually need two weeks notice; remember that he's probably inundated with applications between Thanksgiving and Christmas, so get your application in before Thanksgiving. And yes—if it's not obvious by now—you must have your applications typed.

Be sure to read the directions for every application thoroughly; a few admissions offices prefer papers be stapled in a particular order, while others detest staples all together and want you to use paper clips. In general, admissions offices prefer to receive the fewest number of envelopes possible, so try to have your counselor mail everything in one envelope (with the exception of your test scores, which must arrive directly from the testing company). The best scenario is for your counselor and teacher recommendations, transcript, and entire application (including essay) to be mailed in one large envelope by your counselor (of course, you should address and stamp it). See the section on dealing with your counselor for more details.

Like the Plague. Under no circumstances should you use the Apply software, the Common Application, or any newfangled online application (unless the college requires it). Your counselor will probably tell you that colleges treat the common application as if it were their own application; counselors may tell you this out of ignorance or sloth. The Common Application significantly decreases the amount of work the counselor must do, so it's in the counselor's best interest to encourage the use of the Common Application. However, it's not in your best interest. Despite what college representatives might tell you when they visit your high school, they do not treat the Common Application as an equal to their own application (nor should they). Colleges are in a bind: they wish to accept the Common Application so they don't miss out on any great applicants, but in order to accept it, they must "agree" to treat it as they treat their own application. So while they give preference to their own application, they must continue to attest publicly to the Common Application's equality. Only insiders know that colleges truly prefer their own application, which is why your counselor may—out of ignorance—tell you to use the Common Application.

The only colleges that prefer the Common Application are those that only accept the Common Application (such as Boston College). Colleges prefer their own application for many reasons. They assume that if you use their own application, then you took the time and effort to call them, review the view book, and fill out the application (instead of getting a Common Application from your counselor's office and photocopying it for two dozen colleges). In addition, the essay question on the Common Application is not usually the same as the essay(s) colleges ask on their own applications, and they prefer that you answer their own questions. Most top colleges will require more than one essay (or short answer), whereas the Common Application asks only for one essay. Inevitably, you will be leaving the college with some unanswered questions about you if you use the Common Application.

In addition to asking different (and fewer) essay questions, the Common Application also does not ask about AP or IB scores. Obviously, AP scores are very important for top colleges, and yet the Common Application offers no place to report them. The original idea was the offer a solution to this perceived problem: underprivileged students and students from rural, under-developed schools do not have easy access to applications and don't have the money to call colleges to request applications. The prevailing mentality at most admissions offices triggered the creation of a single, widely distributed application. (Remember, this is the same mentality that may hold it against you if your father is a doctor and your mother is a lawyer.) The Common Application was not designed to be used by middle- and upper class students to apply to top colleges.

Finally, the Common Application asks for information in a different order than the college's own application does, which means that application readers will be slightly disoriented when they review a Common Application. Further, because information is not in the same place, the reader may become a little annoyed. Once again, if you're very socio-economically disadvantaged, the reader will give you the benefit of the doubt. If you live in a middle- or upper-class area, if your parents are college-educated, or if you live near the college, then the reader will assume that an applicant who uses the Common Application is lazy or not very interested in the college. I've heard a great number of admissions officers complain about the College Application, and the vast majority of them would strongly prefer to ban it for all but the poorest of applicants. In the privacy of their offices, admissions officers think the Common Application is an annoyance.

It is all the rage these days for counselors to require that their students type up and insert a resume into every application, even if the resume simply repeats information on the application. This is a mistake. Most top colleges are not interested in a resume (or anything in addition to the application) unless it adds significant information. Everything a college wants to know about you they ask on the application. And they only give you a limited number of lines on the application to list your activities because they want to you to choose those activities which are most important to you; under no circumstances do they want a complete list of everything you've ever done. If you do include a resume, make it short and direct. Some admissions representatives speak kindly about resumes but, similar to the Common Application, they deride this "resume craze" and find it annoying. Unless a college (such as Villanova) specifically asks for a resume (or activities list), do not include it. The problem arises when your ill-informed counselor requires you to insert a resume into every application. You do not want to annoy your counselor and should decide on a case-by-case basis whether or not you should follow his advice.

You should have an independent person look over your application before you seal the envelope; go over the checklist of necessary items (usually one is provided by the college); be sure everything is presentable (no coffee stains or torn pages). Your application package is a sales tool much as the college's view book is—the college mailed you a lovely, professionally produced brochure that obviously required a lot of time and thought to create, so you should reply with a similarly high-quality sales tool.

When it absolutely needs to get there in two weeks. A few people FedEx everything, and many worry endlessly over whether or not something has been received. First, if you mail something between late October and mid-January, chances are it will take the admissions office about two weeks to open and file it. So don't mail something on Monday and call on Wednesday to see if it was received—chances are, even if it was received, the admissions office might not know about it. Interestingly, most admissions offices have no idea if you've mailed something in by the deadline. If the deadline is January 15, then chances are everything mailed on the 13th through the 17th will sit in a big pile and probably won't be opened until the 25th. Once the mailroom gets to this pile of mail, they open everything and stamp it with a date. Then they file it. So mailing anything next-day is usually a waste of money. I have never heard of a college rejecting an application because it was a day or two late. And you should not mail anything "return receipt"—this annoys the mailroom people who must deal with thousands of pieces of mail per day. Your requested return receipt only serves to annoy them.

The moral of the story? If you must call to know if the admissions office has received something, you should give them two weeks. And you should try to mail everything in early—although a college usually won't know if you mail something in a little late, they do stamp everything with a date which the application readers see, so the earlier the date, the better.

What Happens. Once everything is received, a regional reader looks at your file and makes initial notes. Then a second reader will read your file (at most colleges and in most cases—this is discussed in the chapter "How Colleges Actually Admit Students"). Often, weeks go by between these two readings. So if something truly important happens to you after you've mailed in your application, feel free to inform the college (or have your counselor inform the college) because, in most cases, your application will be read again in full before any final decisions are made. Type a letter regarding your achievement, and mail the letter to each college to which you're applying. Be sure to put your name at the top of each page and explain in the first paragraph that you have already applied and would like to submit an additional piece of information. Such achievements may include winning a major competition or being named to an important position in your community. Submitting information such as this after you have completed and mailed the application is okay as long as the information is substantial. At most colleges, you safely have until the end of February to truly complete your application. Of course, you should give the college everything they ask for by the application deadline, but you usually do have until the end of February to add significant supplemental information.

A final note about mailing application items: most colleges will review your application even if it's not complete. Generally speaking, if the actual application and your transcripts are in, a college will review your application. Sometimes official test scores or a recommendation comes in late; in most cases, it's okay if a few items are late. No college is interested in rejecting a student because a recommendation came in three weeks late. If you are rejected from a college, rest assured that it wasn't because your teacher mailed in the recommendation on January 17th when the deadline was January 15th. In fact, the teacher probably could have mailed the recommendation on March 1st, and it wouldn't have mattered. If you were rejected (and everything was mailed in by, say, early March), then you were rejected because your application wasn't strong enough, not because something was late.

Chapter 25

The Application Cycle

"So I'm cruising through the summer between my junior and senior years and my mom is like *holy crap you have to apply to college right now!* I told her I have lots of time. At least a week or two."

Here's an overview of the application cycle with both the recommended timetable and the typical timetable. Obviously, it's best to start thinking about college as early as possible, preferably in the eighth or ninth grade. The sooner you set goals, the more likely your high school performance will be exemplary. Students who all-of-a-sudden realize that they are going to college in the 11th grade are often the same students who have terrible grades. Planning ahead will ensure that you attend the college of your choice instead of attending the only college that would accept you.

Junior Year

August. You should enter your junior year with as many honors and AP classes as possible. Usually, you need to register for such classes in the second half of your sophomore year. You will also need extracurricular activities and community service to report to colleges. Decide early what you're going to do to fulfill these needs. Typically, you should have at least 30-40 hours of community service by the end of the academic year.

September. One year from now, you will need to ask one or two teachers to write recommendations for you (as well as your counselor). Decide which teachers you will ask, and work very hard in their classes. Usually, it's best to choose two teachers even though in most cases you will only need one; this leaves you with a backup. Do all the assigned work, participate in class, complete extra-credit assignments, and remember at all times that colleges will be reading what this teacher has to say about your academic ability. Also remember that your counselor will write a recommendation too. So be nice to her; be helpful; attend all of her college planning sessions (or anything she offers). You must appear interested in college, mature, well informed, and motivated. Such characteristics will translate into a good (or great) recommendation. (Of course, you need good grades too). And as noted earlier, do everything within your power to make your counselor love you! This person will write the all-important counselor recommendations, so his opinion of you is very important. If he doesn't think very highly of you, your applications will suffer tremendously.

October. Take the PSAT. Remember: it's an ETS sales tool and is used to gather information that is then sold to colleges. Do not worry about it (and if you don't want ETS to sell your information, decline their college search service). However, it's recommended that you prepare a little for the PSAT for two reasons: 1, ETS has a habit of being suspicious, so you never want to bomb an ETS test or they might suspect you of cheating if you vastly improve your score on a subsequent test; and 2, if you're prepared for the PSAT, then you won't let standardized testing become a barrier to success—some students are a bit traumatized by the PSAT and become convinced that standardized tests are a barrier to their success.

November-January. Prepare for the SAT. Register for and take the SAT in January if possible. (The January SAT is the most preferable SAT to take if it's your first time. It's early enough so you have time to receive your scores and thoroughly prepare again for May or June, and fewer students take it, so it's not quite the circus that the March/April and May SATs are.)

December. Gather your PSAT scores, transcripts, and other relevant information, and make a list of twenty or so colleges in which you're interested and to which you have a chance of being admitted. Your "You in 12th Grade" exercises should help you to quickly pinpoint possible colleges to which to apply. Start to research your college list.

December-January. Call or write to the colleges on your list to obtain view books, course catalogues, financial aid information, information on specific departments and majors, and any other relevant information. You should receive all of this information by late February.

March/April. Take the SAT. Do not wait until May to take the SAT for the first time (no matter what your counselor tells you). If you wait until May, you will not get your scores back in time to further prepare until your senior year. You need the printed report in order to know your weaknesses (the scores-by-phone are useless as they don't provide details) and if you don't prepare, you are highly likely to receive the same score the second time you take the test.

April. Narrow your college list to 10-12 colleges. Visit them (tour, interview, visit classes, stay overnight) and continue to research them. Plan on doing something exciting this summer: a great community service project, studying abroad, learning to fly fish in Patagonia (for example).

May. Take the AP tests.

June. Take the SAT IIs. You should take writing, a math (IC in most cases), and a third SAT II of your choice. The third SAT II you take should be in a course you have just completed and have received an A in—remember, SAT IIs are fairly difficult. Buy *Real SAT IIs,* and practice before taking them.

July. You should have your junior year final grades by now, as well as SAT, SAT II, and AP scores, so you can narrow your college list to 5-8 finalists and prepare to visit them in September. Be realistic. Request applications and view books from the colleges on your final college list. Make copies of the applications, and begin to complete them—you will not have much time once school starts. (You should receive all the applications by early August.) Write the college essays.

Senior Year

August. Work on application essays, and consider who will write your recommendations; if you chose two teachers a year ago, you will now need to select who will write your recommendation (if you only need one). Decide on an early decision and/or early action college, if any. Prepare for the Oct./Nov. SATs and SAT IIs if necessary.

September. Visit colleges as necessary. Cut 1-3 colleges from your list so you have 1-2 top choices, 2-3 middle choices, and 2 safety choices. If you're applying early decision or early action, you should give your recommendation forms to the appropriate people by early September and request your test scores be sent to the appropriate early decision/early action college.

October. Take the SAT or SAT IIs, if necessary. Send in early decision/early action applications (filing dates are usually Oct. 15, Nov. 1 or Nov. 15); check with your counselor to be sure that your recommendations and transcripts are being mailed in a timely manner, and if you're applying for financial aid, the appropriate forms must also be completed and mailed at this time.

November. Take the SAT or SAT IIs, if necessary. For regular decision colleges, give all of your recommendation forms to the appropriate people; be sure that all your test scores (SAT, SAT II, AP, ACT) are being reported to all the colleges on your final list; complete the essay and the application forms. Your goal is to mail out everything before Thanksgiving.

December-January. If you're applying for financial aid, complete the forms as soon as possible after January 1 since much financial aid is awarded on a first-come, first-served basis. Do not wait until February. Continue to get great grades. Your senior year grades do count! You will need to provide your counselor with a mid-year report form for each college, which will report your grades for the first semester. Colleges consider slipping grades in their admissions decisions.

January. Early Decision reply-by dates are in January. You must formally accept and mail a deposit to your early decision college if you are accepted. And you must notify all other colleges that you are withdrawing your applications.

March-April. Wait patiently, and remind yourself that you did your best, if you did. If you didn't do your best, keep that in mind when you get to college. You will repeat this entire process if you apply to graduate or professional school, and your college grades will—once again—be very important. At that point, though, your high school grades will be long forgotten.

May. Reply to the college you wish to attend with a deposit. Most colleges have a May 1 reply-by date—don't miss it. All colleges are sitting on long lists of deferred students, and once the reply-by dates pass, the colleges will offer your seat to someone on that list.

May-June. End your senior year well; get good scores on any APs you're taking, and maintain good grades. AP scores and grades may be very relevant in determining which classes you're permitted to take in your freshman year at college. And colleges will revoke an offer of admission if your senior year grades are terrible—don't let this happen to you.

Chapter 26

Early Decision & Early Action

"My college counselor told me I had to apply early decision somewhere or I wouldn't get into college."

The confusion between early decision and early action stems from the assumption that they are related; despite similar names, they are not related. Early Decision is a serious, binding choice that you must weigh with utmost sobriety. Early Action, on the other hand, does not require significant forethought.

Early Decision. Early Decision is an admissions process whereby you submit your application "early," usually by November 1, and the admissions office will admit, deny, or defer you early, usually by December 15. Some colleges use earlier dates (such as October 15 and December 1) or later dates (such as December 1 and January 1). The catch is: if the college accepts you, you must matriculate at that college. Because of the binding nature of early decision, you must be sure that the college to which you are applying is your first choice.

As an aside, I put the word "early" above in quotes because you may submit your application before November 1 as a regular decision candidate, which means that you will be informed of the admissions offices decision in March or April (usually) and an offer of admission is not binding. In order to be considered an early decision candidate, you must apply prior to the deadlines and mark your application for early decision. Most colleges also require you sign a form (e.g. a moral contract) that requires you to attend the college if you are admitted. But if you do not wish to apply early decision to a college, you still may submit an application before November 1, and such an early submission is beneficial if the college's admissions process is rolling.

Is early decision good or bad? There is no single answer that applies to every student, but you should know that some colleges have strong feelings about early decision. Many colleges like early decision for selfish reasons: they prefer to evaluate students with the knowledge that an offer of admission is binding. Colleges wish to avoid competition with other colleges—with both admissions and financial aid. If a college accepts you as an early decision candidate, which occurs around December 15, then you are required to withdraw your applications from all other colleges. This means you will never know if you would have been accepted to other colleges or how much financial aid, including grants and scholarships, they would have offered you.

Early decision requires that you accept the college before it accepts you. If you apply early decision and you renege by not attending the college, then the college will probably become self-righteous and inform the other colleges to which you applied in an effort to have all your acceptances revoked. (Yes, this happens.) How does a college find out where you applied? They call your counselor. Colleges and counselors usually side with one another, so if you renege on an early decision acceptance, you may not be able to attend college in this country. It should be noted that early decision is not an actual contract; it is not a legally binding agreement.

Perhaps more importantly, it requires that you start the application process in August so that everything is completed by mid-October. This means that you need to make your college decision in August, while regular decision applicants make their college decision eight months later in April. Those additional eight months can translate into a more informed decision. Students would probably be better served if early decision did not exist. You would have more time to make the important decision of choosing a college; you would be able to weigh acceptances and financial aid offers, and you would have many more months of experience and consideration.

Harvard, to its credit, recognizes all of this and therefore does not offer early decision. In fact, Harvard cites its lack of an early decision option as the primary reason it has the country's highest 4-year graduation rate, which is about 97% (which means 97% of Harvard students graduate within four years of initially matriculating). Harvard believes that early decision sometimes coerces students into making bad decisions. Sometimes a student will change her mind in the course of her senior year, and yet she is required to attend her early decision college if accepted. A dissatisfied student will attend the college for one year, as required, and then transfer out. (By the way, if you are accepted to a college as an early decision applicant and you change your mind, this is the thing to do: attend the college and midway through your first year, apply to transfer out.)

Easier? There is another side to early decision. Most colleges like it and wish to encourage it, so they admit early decision applicants at a much higher rate. This is true at most colleges. For example, Penn's admission rate for early decision applicants is about 40%, whereas its admission rate for regular applicants is about 20%. Princeton's early decision admission rate is about 40%, whereas its regular admissions rate about 9%. (The actual rates for regular admission are actually worse; see "Your Real Chances of Getting In" below.)

Most early decision acceptance rates for colleges are usually (at least) twice their regular decision rate. For example, Yale filled 43% of available seats for the Class of 2007 with Early Decision applicants, and those applicants were admitted at a 22% rate (about 560 admitted out of 2,600 early decision applicants). While regular decision applicants to Yale for the Class of 2007 were admitted at a 9.6% rate (1,458 out of 15,120 total applicants). Early decision admission rates for Cornell, Dartmouth, and MIT are all between 25% and 45%. Perhaps more important is the number of students who are admitted early decision relative to the total number of students admitted. In the recent past, like Yale, Princeton fills up almost half of its freshmen class with early decision applicants. That means that almost half of the available seats were gone by the time regular decision and most recruited students mailed in their applications. Colleges such as Stanford, Dartmouth, MIT, Penn, Columbia, Amherst, and Williams fill 30%-40% of their freshmen class with early decision candidates. A small number of top colleges, most notably Cornell, do not confer significant advantage on early decision applicants, and a few others, most notably Yale, do not fill a significant portion of the freshmen class with early decision candidates.

That early decision admission rates are, in most cases, twice as high as regular decision admission rates is particularly remarkable because many special admits (e.g. recruited applicants) are regular admission, which means that regular decision admission rates for normal, non-recruited students are very low. There are two explanations for why early decision admission rates are so extremely high. The first one is given by the colleges: early decision applicants are self-selecting. This reason is true to an extent. Who is more likely to start the application process in July or August of their senior year, the top student or the average student? Obviously, it's the best, most obsessive and well-organized students who are worrying about and working on college admissions during the summer between their junior and senior years. The average and below-average students don't start thinking about applying to college until October or November of their senior year. So the option to apply early decision usually attracts the above-average students.

This explanation is reasonable and explains much of the increase in the admission rate for early applicants. But admissions offices' eagerness to admit students early—after all, they are eager to admit students early or they wouldn't offer early decision—also helps explain why early decision admissions rates are so very high. I know many students who are admitted early decision to a college when students with the same credentials are denied regular admission to the same colleges. Colleges are eager to admit early decision students for many reasons. First, they like to admit as many binding applicants (i.e. early decision applicants) as possible because it makes the registrar's and housing office's jobs a little easier. Admissions offices, together with the registrar and housing office, can better plan for and control the incoming class if there are a high number of early decision students.

Second, early decision students are the wealthiest pool of applicants. Colleges like to admit early decision applicants because they tend to require less financial aid and typically consume little of a college's grant money. Early decision applicants tend to be wealthier than regular decision applicants because early decision applicants disproportionately come from expensive prep schools, use private counselors, or come from public schools in wealthy suburbs.

Third, admissions offices that admit a high number of early decision students can (as if by magic) appear more selective. Imagine if a college, such as Princeton, normally receives 15,000 applications for 2,000 freshmen seats. To fill those freshmen seats, Princeton must admit 3,000 students, 2,000 of whom will choose to attend Princeton while the other 1,000 will choose Harvard, Yale, or some other college to which they were admitted (meaning Princeton has a 67% yield). So Princeton must accept 20% (3,000 out of 15,000) of the total applicants to fill 2,000 seats. How can you magically make Princeton more selective? The next year, admit 1,000 early decision students! How does this make Princeton more selective? Let's say out of 15,000 total applications, 2,300 of them applied early decision, and Princeton admits 1,000; these students are required to attend Princeton and now only 1,000 seats remain available. Now the other 12,700 applicants apply regular decision. In order to fill the remaining 1,000 seats, Princeton must admit 1,500 students. So in total, Princeton has admitted 2,500 students (1,000 early decision and 1,500 regular decision) out of the same number of applicants (15,000). Now, Princeton's acceptance rate is closer to 16%. So any college can magically shave off four (or more) percentage points by simply admitting more early decision applicants (even with the same number of total applicants). While I used Princeton as a conjectural example, you would be surprised how many colleges boost their selectivity by simply admitting more (sometimes substandard) early decision students. When your competitors are becoming more selective and the president of the college wants you to lower the admissions rate from 30% to 25%, the easiest way to do it is to admit more early decision students.

So is early decision a good idea? If you are a person who changes his mind often, the answer is no. Do you buy a sweater only to decide a week later that you dislike it? Do you make commitments—to go to dinner, a movie, to play a sport or baby-sit—and sometimes regret doing so? If you waiver in your decisions, even in the slightest, then applying early decision is probably not a good idea.

However, if you are consistently satisfied with your decisions when you make them, and rarely—if ever—regret a commitment, then applying early decision to your first choice college, in most cases, greatly improves your chances of being admitted. Once again, you must be very confident that your early decision college is alone at the top of your college list, with absolutely no competition. If this is the case, then applying early decision will usually greatly benefit you.

Most top colleges accept early decision applicants at a rate of 35% to 50%. Of those not accepted, a great number of them are deferred. If you are deferred, then the college may offer you admission in the spring; however, you are no longer bound to attend the college and are free to apply anywhere you choose. If you are deferred, you must aggressively pursue other choices. The chances of a deferred candidate being admitted in the spring are about nil. A top college may defer 1,000 early applicants in December and accept 0-75 of them in late May to early June. (Yes, there are years when a top college will accept none of the students it defers. This happens when the percentage of accepted students who enroll is higher than usual.) Colleges defer early admission candidates for many reasons; legatees are usually deferred instead of rejected (only to be rejected later). Applicants who have famous/powerful people recommending them are usually initially deferred instead of rejected. For political reasons, colleges defer many applicants who they should (and intend to) reject. For example, a college will defer a valedictorian if they accepted a student ranked lower in this class. They do this so the valedictorian's parents won't be angry. Rarely will a college outright reject an early decision student ranked significantly higher than another early decision student from the same school who was accepted.

In a very few cases, colleges defer students who they may later accept, depending on the strength of the regular decision applicant pool. But as the admission rate of the regular applicant pool is so low, meaning the college only accepts the very best of the regular pool, being accepted after being deferred, regardless of how qualified you are, is rare. Don't expect it. If you are deferred, then I suggest either you or your counselor call the college and ask what your chances are of being accepted. It's best for you <u>and</u> your counselor to call because an admissions officer will be more candid with your counselor, but if only your counselor calls, then it might suggest that you don't care very much. As always, your parents should not call. Most admissions offices will discuss a deferred applicant's chances of being admitted. Usually, you should speak to the officer in charge of your region; this person can also give you advice for improving your application.

Whenever you talk to an admissions officer, you should keep in mind that they almost always speak in generalities. They rarely speak of specifics from your file because, among other things, it opens a can of legal worms. An admissions officer won't say "Well your SAT score was 1360, and the other two students who applied from your school scored a 1420 and 1430." But they may say, "our average SAT score thus far is 1390 and average GPA is 3.8." An admissions officer who says that is telling you that your SAT scores and GPA are low. Whatever statistics the officers rattle off, they are telling you that you are low by comparison. Perhaps even more discouraging is if an admissions officer says, "Our average SAT is 1390 and our average GPA is 3.8," and you realize that your SAT score is 1390 and your GPA is 3.8. This would seem good, but the average student at a top college is rejected. If the officer gives you "average" statistics, and you're below or equal to them, then the officer is telling you that you will probably be rejected. If the officer gives any definite glimpse of hope, then you have a chance. For example, the officer might say, "we'd like to see your senior year grades." Now you have a chance—of course, your grades must be great (and hopefully you didn't drop any AP courses!). In either case, whatever the officer mentions—SAT scores or grades—you only stand a chance if they improve dramatically. If the admissions officer only mentions test scores, then you should ask if it's worth it to retake them.

If you are deferred, you should contact the college, discuss your chances, and immediately write a note to the person with whom you had the conversation. Your brief letter should simply state that the college is still your first choice, and that you will do everything you can to improve your application. You should mail this letter by late-February. If your grades have improved, be sure to have your high school counselor mail an updated copy of your transcript. You may also have more test scores sent if you've taken more tests and the scores are much higher. Finally, if you've won any new awards or honors, be sure to send something to the college (in writing) that gives the details of your award. In conclusion, if you are deferred, you should do something to improve your chances of being admitted since your chances are incredibly low of being accepted once you've been deferred.

You may have a teacher send an additional recommendation if the recommendation will add new information. Do not send another recommendation if it will look like the other recommendations you have already sent. And do not send any information that isn't new or substantial. You will only annoy an admissions office if you send them a large number of letters and other material. Do not mail four more recommendations. Do not mail them a 3-page essay (unless it was published somewhere after you originally mailed in your application). Do not call the office more than 2-3 times. Do not have your parents call. Anything you send to additionally support your application should be mailed by the second week of March.

If you are accepted early decision, then you must withdraw all of your other applications (if any), and reply to the college (usually with a deposit) by the reply-by date. At that point, your college search is over as you are bound to attend your early decision college. If you are accepted early decision, you should not wait more than 2-3 weeks to notify the other colleges to which you applied. Top colleges share very little information, but the one thing they do share is early decision (and often early action) acceptances. They do this so they can know if you applied to more than one college early. If you did, they may do any number of things ranging from nothing to revoking the offer of admission. Regardless, you should inform the other colleges quickly if you've been accepted to your early decision college. If you are rejected, c'est la vie. Your counselor may call the college to ask why you were rejected, but do not call them in anger (and restrain your parents). Nothing is gained from being angry with a college. Aggressively pursue the other colleges on your list. You should take a moment to consider why you were rejected and apply that knowledge to your other applications. In most cases, you will have 2-4 weeks to submit your regular admission applications because most deadlines are January 1-15.

Early Action. Unlike Early Decision, Early Action is non-binding. In most cases, Early Action uses the same deadlines used for Early Decision: apply by November 1, and receive a decision by December 15. However, you are not required to accept the college's decision if you are admitted, and in most cases, you are not required to respond at all until the spring. (See "Reply-By Dates" below.)

Early Action has the obvious substantial benefit of being non-binding. This means you may apply to an early-action college in mid-October, and then apply to several other colleges at your leisure. Come March and April, you may compare the offers and financial aid awards of all the colleges to which you were accepted and choose accordingly. Unlike with Early Decision, Early Action allows to you wait to hear from all the colleges in which you're interested. As noted elsewhere, some colleges believe that Early Decision requires some students to make premature decisions, subsequently resulting in unhappy collegiate experiences— Harvard and Brown are notable among the colleges that only offer Early Action. In fact, Harvard credits its nation-high graduation rate of 97% to its policy of only offering Early Action.

It may seem that Early Action is superior to Early Decision, and obviously it is in some ways. However, unlike Early Decision, Early Action does not provide any particular benefit to the college; an early action applicant is no more assured than a regular decision applicant to enroll. Because of this, Early Action applicants are not, in most cases, admitted at a higher rate than regular decision applicants. Early Action gives neither the college nor the applicant a significant advantage.

Should You Apply Decision or Early Action? The answer is: if you are completely confident in your first choice, you're not likely to change your mind, and everything is in order, then apply early decision or early action, whichever the college offers.

(Most colleges offer one or the other, but if a college offers both, then remember that Early Decision offers you a better chance of being admitted.)

In most cases, students who are able to successfully apply early started the admissions process by the end of their junior year, including visiting all the colleges, and being satisfied with their SAT, SAT II, and AP scores. If you apply early, the college will only consider your 9th-11th grade work. If your 11th grade credentials—including SAT and SAT II scores—are likely to get you admitted, then applying early decision will probably greatly improve your chances of being admitted.

Can You Apply Both Early Decision and Early Action? Some high school counselors will not permit you to apply early decision to one college and early action to another. Obviously, early action colleges would prefer that you not apply early decision to another college. However, because early action involves no obligation, there is nothing to stop you from applying early action to one college and early decision to another. In most cases, I highly recommend it. By applying early decision to your first choice and early action to your second choice, you will know whether or not you've been admitted to either one of your top two choices by mid-December. If you've been admitted to your top (early decision) choice, then you must attend that college. If you've been admitted to your second (early action) choice, then you can either not bother to apply to any other college, or you may wish to apply to your #3 and #4 choices, wait for their decisions in April, and make your final decision in May. In fact, you may apply early action to a dozen colleges if you wish. Then you will know which colleges have accepted you by mid-December. If your 9th-11th grade record and test scores are strong enough, I suggest applying early action to as many of your colleges that offer it and applying early decision to your top choice. This will improve your chances of getting admitted, force you to work on your applications over the summer (which means you can focus on your grades during the school year), and will allow you to make your decisions and college plans by December.

If your high school counselor will not allow you to apply early decision and early action, you should have your parents speak to the principal. There is no reason—legal, moral or otherwise—that you should be prohibited from applying early decision to one college and early action to another (or early action to several colleges) unless the college specifically prohibits this strategy. You should balance the fact that your counselor must write your recommendation, with the knowledge that you are in charge of your education and your counselor should not limit your chances of being admitted to the college of your choice.

If you have applied early decision to one college and early action to another, and you are accepted to your early decision college, then you must handle your early action college a bit carefully. Some colleges get a bit greedy with their early action candidates: though they don't want to offer early decision, they do want their early action candidates to treat the process a bit like early decision. If you're offered early decision admission to one college, then you must notify your early action college that you're withdrawing your application. You should notify them in writing and simply state that you must withdraw your application. Be sure to date and sign your letter and include your home address.

If you inform your early action college that you must withdraw your application because you were accepted early decision at another college, the early action college might call your counselor and complain; even worse, the early action college might call your early decision college and complain. It's unethical for colleges to do this, but some do. (They can behave like spoiled brats when they lose a desired applicant.) The best way to handle the situation is to simply inform the early action college that you need to withdraw at this time and not mention any other colleges or early decision. It's also a good idea to wait a few weeks to notify your early action college so your letter doesn't correspond so directly to the early decision notification date (usually December 15). And finally, you may throw in a line like "I may apply to your college again if I am able to." Such a statement isn't untrue and may mollify them. Keep in mind that, as noted above, most top colleges report to each other who has been accepted early decision and, in some cases, early action. So do not tell them an outright lie; they may be looking at an early decision acceptance list with your name on it from another college.

Some colleges clearly state that applying to multiple early action colleges is okay; most colleges say nothing in the hopes that you only apply early to one college. Harvard, on the other hand, clearly states that an applicant may not apply early action to Harvard and apply to any other school—you must wait until you hear from Harvard. Yale is also using this "prohibited early action" system for Class of 2008 applicants. Princeton uses vague, intimidating language that conflates early action and early decision and requires that you promise to apply early only to Princeton. Essentially, Princeton does not want you to apply early decision to Princeton and early action to Brown. Princeton's statement on early decision, which they require you to sign, is so muddled and disingenuous that one wonders if it is the result of an overreaching admissions office or simply poor writing. Regardless, if you apply to a college which requires you to sign a statement that says you cannot apply early to any other college, then you cannot apply early to any other colleges no matter what the generally accepted or logically obvious meaning of "early action." You can be sure that Princeton checks Harvard's and Brown's early action list, and if it finds any of its applicants that it admitted early decision, things get ugly. My general suggestion in such instances as Princeton's is this: don't apply to the college. If their idea of an admissions policy is to intimidate teenagers, then you should look for another early decision college.

I suspect that Harvard's recent decision to require applicants who apply early action to forgo applying to any other school (early or otherwise) until they hear from Harvard is a response to Princeton's petulance. The bottom line is that early action doesn't preclude one from applying simultaneously to other colleges, but top colleges can make their own rules. So when it comes to applying to Princeton or Harvard, it's their playground and they get to make the rules.

Rolling Early Decision. This works the same way as early decision, except that the dates are "rolling." This means that you may apply anytime up until the deadline (usually between mid-January and late-February), and the college will notify you of their decision quickly, typically in four weeks. If the college accepts you, you must attend. Brandeis is a notable college that offers rolling early decision.

Early Decision and Early Action Warning. The one great caveat to applying early is: if you are rejected early, most colleges will not permit you to apply again until the following year. If you apply early and are rejected, then you cannot apply to that college again until the following autumn. Some colleges, such as Cornell, are getting more aggressive in rejecting more early applicants (instead of deferring them). So if your early decision/action college is your top choice, and you think your senior year grades and test scores will greatly improve your chances of being admitted, then you probably should apply regular decision.

Reply-By Dates. The "Reply-By" date for any college is the deadline by which you need to inform a college of your intention to enroll; usually, you accept in writing and send a substantial deposit. In most cases the reply-by date is May 1. However, some colleges require earlier notification, often in March or April; often, these colleges will have offered you admission in December or early January. It's not unusual for a college to publish a reply-by date of May 1 but for them to pressure the admitted student to reply much earlier. They may pressure you by stating in their admission letter that "although the formal reply-by date is May 1, we urge you to notify us by March 15 if you intend to accept our office of admission in order to secure good housing." There is no law or regulation forbidding colleges from doing this, and they do this to better manage their enrollment and housing; of course, this often results in students being pressured to accept an offer of admission from one college prior to knowing whether or not they've been admitted to another college.

You should keep a few things in mind if a college pressures you to reply earlier than their published reply-by date. First, if they have offered you admission and their published reply-by date is May 1, then you have until May 1 to reply. The college cannot renege an offer of admission because you didn't respond by the earlier, unpublished reply-by date. Colleges are free to pressure you to reply by an earlier date than the published date, and you are free to ignore the pressure. Once again, colleges cannot renege on an offer of admission unless something substantial changes with your credentials (i.e. you bomb your senior year grades; you're arrested for armed robbery; you plagiarized your admission essay).

Second, if a college is pressuring you to reply and you still haven't received a response to your application from other colleges, then you should talk to your high school counselor. Sometimes, if a college is pressuring you to respond by early or mid-March, you probably haven't heard from a few colleges and don't know if you will be accepted to rejected. Clearly, you do not want to accept an offer of admission from one college without knowing if other colleges are going to accept or reject you. In most cases, your counselor can (and should) fax the offer letter and financial aid award (if any) to the colleges that have yet to respond, and those colleges will—if they are inclined to offer admission—respond early to you. In a sense, you can use one college's pressure to reply early to pressure all the other colleges to respond early to your application.

If you are being pressured to reply early to an offer of admission, take the admission letter and financial aid award letter (if any) to your counselor. If you have yet to hear from all the colleges to which you applied, your counselor should fax the admission and financial aid award letters to those colleges so that they will respond to your application early. Your counselor may also contact the college that is pressuring you to inform them that you have yet to hear from all the colleges to which you've applied. And in every case, you aren't required to respond to an offer of admission prior to the college's official reply-by date. Don't let the pressure get to you.

Chapter 27

Your Real Chances of Getting In

"So Princeton is like 14% acceptance rate, right?
How come everyone I know gets rejected?"

Here are the recent admissions statistics from a top college. This will give you a good idea of your actual chances of being admitted to a top college.

The college received about 14,000 total applications, of which 2,000 were Early Decision applications. Of the 2,000 students total the college admitted, 600 of them were Early Decision. So 600 of the 2,000 Early Decision applicants (or 30%) were admitted. That left 1,400 regular decision spaces open. (Most of the 1,400 Early Decision applicants who were not accepted were deferred, and about 100 of those 1,400 deferred applicants were accepted in the spring.)

Of the 1,400 regular decision openings, about 400 were reserved for recruited athletes, 300 for legatees, 200 for recruited minorities, and 100 for foreign students. That left 400 openings for non-recruited, non-legacy regular decision applicants. (In most cases, the legatee admission rate for top colleges is 40%-60%. Even Harvard and Princeton, who have composite admissions rates of less than 14%, admit about 40% of all legatee applicants. For Penn, early decision legatee applicants are admitted at a 65%-70% rate, while regular decision legatee applicants are admitted at a 40% rate. Keep in mind that early decision legatee applicants are almost never rejected outright; they are deferred.)

So if you applied regular decision, were not recruited, were not a legacy, and were a US citizen, then your chance of being admitted was not 14% (which was the reported admissions rate) but rather the much lower 3% (400 out of 14,000). If you wish to be very precise, then you should remove the 2,000 early decision applicants and about 1,000 other special applicants, making your chances of being admitted 3.6% (400 out of 11,000). This college reports an overall admissions rate of 14%, but one cannot find a group of actual applicants admitted at this rate. Instead, you will find Early Decision applicants admitted at a rate of 30%, legatees admitted at a rate of 40%, recruited athletes admitted at a rate of 70%, and non-recruited, non-legacy US applicants admitted at a rate of 3.6%.

Of course, even that 3.6% isn't completely accurate. If this college is, for example, in New Jersey, and you're from New Jersey, then your chances of being admitted are even lower than someone from, say, Utah. So if you're a non-recruited, non-legatee regular decision applicant from New Jersey, your chances of being admitted are probably 1 in 50 (2%); if you're from the Northeast, then it's about 1 in 40 (2.5%); if you're from the Dakotas, it's probably about 1 in 15 (6.5%), and if you're from a foreign country and reasonably qualified, it's probably about 1 in 6 (17%). Crazy, isn't it? (For some tips on this, look at the section on geography in the Strategy chapter.)

The admissions rates for most top colleges follow this example. The overall admissions rates that are reported in college guides are not very useful. The actual admissions rate for recruited students (athletes, minorities, and so forth) and for Early Decision students is substantially higher than the reported rate, while the actual rate for non-recruited regular admissions students is much lower. If a college has an overall admissions rate of 25%, then its Early Decision admission rate is usually 40%-50%, and its non-recruited regular admissions rate is about 10%.

What are your chances of being admitted? It depends. If you're Early Decision or recruited, your chances are probably closer to 50% than you think. If you're a non-recruited regular decision applicant, then your chances are close to or less than 10%.

Chapter 28

How Top Colleges Actually Admit Students

"College admissions at Columbia? I'm pretty sure
an abacus and Ouiji board are involved."

Now let's look at the actual admissions process. Admissions offices usually divide applicants into two broad categories: non-recruited and recruited/special applicants. Non-recruited applicants are further divided into early decision/action and regular decision. See the chapter on early decision/action for more details. Recruited applicants are generally athletes and/or minorities, and special applicants are legatees, celebrities, and major contributors.

I discuss each category below. It's important to know the differences and exactly where you fit in. I strongly recommend that you read this entire chapter even if you don't fit a particular category; everyone should read the last section ("Everyone Else") to get a feel for the general process that all applications undergo to some degree.

Admissions rates to top colleges are, on average, as follows: celebrities 95%, top recruited athletes 90%, regular recruited athletes 70%, minorities 50%, legacy 44%, early decision 40%, major contributors 35%, regular decision 8%. These admissions rates would typically combine for an overall reported admission rate of 20-25%.

In determining these averages, I left early action out because so few top colleges offer it, thereby making an average somewhat misleading. In most cases, early action admission rates are not considerably higher than regular decision rates. If the overall admission rate for a college is 25%, then the early action admission rate is probably 28%-31%. There are also "special talent" applicants, as discussed below. There is no overall admissions rate for these applicants; if your special talent helps you to be admitted depends on your talent, the college's needs, and the other applicants. If you're a good oboe player, the college's only other oboe player is a graduating senior, and the college doesn't have any other oboists applying, then your chances of being admitted are probably better than 90%. (I've seen this situation happen at an Ivy—the only oboist to apply was accepted despite her test scores and grades because the college's only other oboist was graduating.)

A college may get one or two celebrity applicants each year (at most), so one can dismiss the celebrity category as an aberration. The best way to ensure your admission to a top college is to be a top athlete; the second best way is to be a minority. Despite the fact that many people think that admission to a top college is all about money and connections (legacy status), neither one of these is as good as being a great athlete or a minority. Combined, money and connections are about as helpful as simply having a decent academic record and applying early decision—which anyone can do.

Non-recruited, non-special regular decision applicants are usually admitted at the lowest rate of all the application sub-groups. If you're non-recruited and non-special (i.e. not a minority, legatee, or major contributor), then applying early decision is your best bet.

What follows is a description of each sub-group, ranging from most desirable to least desirable. You should think of your chances of being admitted to college in terms of how "desirable" you are. Why would a college want you? Pure academic achievement doesn't rank very high at top colleges; if you think of it in terms of supply and demand, there's a big supply of high academic achievement in this country and not a big demand by top colleges for pure academic achievers. As a result, the admissions rate at top colleges for pure academic achievers is less than 15% and typically less that 5%.

Celebrity. Celebrities are highly desirable for the same reason that a championship sports team is desirable: lots of free publicity. A well-known celebrity can bring a college millions of dollars in free publicity. Most top colleges get (at most) one or two celebrity applicants each year, and to be in this category, you or your parents need to be of national renown. Your name should be recognized in every U.S. household. Most celebrity applicants are only tangentially handled by admissions departments. These applicants are often reviewed directly by the dean and president. Rarely do they need to meet any academic requirements. If you're the daughter of a famous actor or son of the president, you will be quickly and easily admitted everywhere. When I heard that the Olsen twins had applied to the University of Dayton, I suspected a hoax—why would such famous and wealthy actresses apply to a third-tier school when Brown would be happy to have them? Moreover, the Olsen twins are juniors, so they won't be applying until next year.

That's right boys: you can start tracking the Olsen college applications in the winter of 2003-04, but look for them to attend something more prestigious than U. Dayton. (The Olsens-go-to-college email was a hoax started by a sophomore at Emory.)

The child of a senator will get special treatment but won't receive the same "auto-admit" treatment that a national figure would. If you attend a top college, chances are you will hear of a few famous people on campus; rest assured that these people were admitted because of their name not their grades. If you are a celebrity, your first call should be to the college's development (i.e. fundraising & marketing) office. Once you tell them your name, they should start falling all over you—if they don't, then you aren't a celebrity. If they do fall all over you, then they will successfully guide you through the celebrity version of the admissions process (which will likely involve more photo ops than standardized tests).

Athletes. Most top colleges (including and especially the Ivies) admit gifted athletes who would not otherwise have been admitted based solely on their academic records. Each year, athletic departments scout high school teams for the athletes they need; they then court the athletes and send the admissions office a list of highly desirable students. The admissions office then must go through the unseemly task of sorting out this list; not all the athletes on the list will be admitted. Athletic directors try to recruit reasonably literate students, but sometimes the applicants fall so far below the college's standards that the admissions office has no choice but to say no. Most of the athletes will fall below the colleges' academic standards but will show enough evidence that suggests that they will be able to handle the college's course work. (Remember that the courses at most top colleges aren't actually more difficult than the courses at less competitive colleges.) If it appears that the athlete can do the work and he will contribute significantly to the team, then he will be admitted. This is how the star quarterback of your high school football team gets admitted to Dartmouth with a 1190 on his SATs, whereas you get rejected with a 1400. Recruited athletes to top colleges, including Princeton, typically enjoy a 65%-75% admission rate. If you're one of the top 2-3 recruits for a particular sport, then you have an 80%-90% chance of being admitted. Large team sports, such as football, virtually guarantee admission for the top recruits. The top ten recruits for Penn's football team have about 95%+chance of being accepted. The sports that have the lowest standards of admission for recruited athletes are ice hockey, football, and basketball.

Why are athletes so coveted at top colleges? Top colleges, particularly the Ivies, Stanford, and Duke, compete in a large number of varsity sports with a small number of students. The average Ivy League college competes in 35 varsity sports, whereas U. Michigan typically competes in only 21-22 varsity sports. At U. Michigan, less that 2% of the student body competes in varsity sports but more than 25% of Princeton students play varsity sports. Athletes are coveted and are such a high percentage of the student population at top colleges because these colleges are very serious about sports and have much smaller student bodies than the sprawling public universities. This explains why as much as 20% of the entering class at many top colleges consists of recruited athletes. In addition, many top colleges compete for the same top athletes, even in sports you've (probably) never thought about—squash, for example. Colleges use the national squash rankings to locate the most desirable players, so every top college with a good squash program (such as Harvard) has its eye on the same top twenty graduating seniors. Of these twenty squash players, maybe ten of them are "viable" (meaning they have the minimum academic record to get accepted to college and play college sports). Of those ten, there are maybe three who excel on the squash court and in the classroom. Several colleges (Harvard, Trinity, Princeton) will compete vigorously for those three players.

Is this unfair? It is as unfair as any other non-academic criteria for admission. However, the theory is that popular sports teams generate substantial revenue and free publicity for the college, which in turn increase the college's national stature, make admissions more competitive, and cause alumni to give more money (just ask Georgetown). A great football or basketball team can do more overnight for a college than two decades of traditional public relations and marketing. Colleges also claim that since athletic recruiting often targets minorities, recruited athletes often add diversity to the campus. Of course, colleges have been criticized for recruiting so heavily. A former president of NYU took Princeton to task for recruiting so heavily, and many professors are vocal that such recruiting lowers the university academic standards. (In fact, Princeton's president has admitted that recruited athletes are not of the same academic caliber as non-recruited students.) Despite such criticism, athletic recruiting is not diminishing.

The "recruiting increases donations and diversity" arguments have been debunked. Two recent, comprehensive studies determined that successful sports teams rarely make money for a college and that athletic recruiting has no impact on a college's socioeconomic or racial diversity. (The NCAA recently reported that its 970+member colleges had $3 billion in sports-related revenue and spent $4.1 billion, meaning that on average, a NCAA college looses money on its sports programs.) In addition, the studies contradict the notion that successful sports teams increase alumni giving. For every college that raises tremendous sums through its sports teams (Penn State), there's another college that raises even more without the benefit of nationally recognized sports teams (Swarthmore). For every team that recruits many minority athletes (football, basketball), there's another team that recruits primarily white athletes (swimming, hockey, fencing). For every team that recruits less-wealthy athletes (football), there's another team that tends to recruits wealthier athletes (crew). In the end, these studies suggest, a college ends up in the same place it started.

But this fact remains: most colleges recruit athletes and being recruited can be a huge advantage. If you think you have recruitable athletic skills, you should first ask your coach's opinion. The college's athletic director will want a recommendation from your coach, and your coach probably has had at least a few athletes play in college, so he knows what it takes. If your coach agrees that you have collegiate-level skills, then you need to discuss what division you could play in. There's a world of difference between Division I and Division III and between conferences. If your coach agrees that you could play in college, and you think you have a good idea of what division you could play in, you need to figure out if you want to play sports in college. If a college recruits you to play sports and you accept, then you have a responsibility to play sports. In many cases, it's a deal with the devil: they've admitted you despite your academics, so you must play sports even if you don't want to. This decision is a big one because for most Division I athletes, playing sports is a full-time job. Getting an education is a side-hobby. (Most Division I athletes, despite what you might hear, do not receive an education in college.)

After you have those three questions answered, you should then directly approach the coaches and athletic directors at the colleges in which you're interested. The coaches will gladly speak to you during the off-season; in fact, that's what their off-season is for—speaking to and recruiting good athletes. If the coach is interested, you must visit the college and meet with the coach. Often, the coach will ask you to work out with the team. You must also decide if you like the coach; this person is possibly going to spend more time with you in college than anyone else! If you dislike the coach, your life will be miserable. If the coach likes you and wants to recruit you, then you will have a formidable friend in the admissions process. Usually, all you need to improve is your numbers (GPA/rank, SAT, and SAT II scores). Nearly all recruited athletes are admitted by-the-numbers, so as long as your numbers are reasonably decent, you will probably be admitted. Your coach will help you complete the necessary NCAA forms and inform you about NCAA requirements. At most colleges, if a recruited athlete is rejected, usually one of three things caused it: very low grades/rank, very low S scores, or very low SAT II scores (for colleges, such as the Ivies, that them). The bottom line: get recruited if you can and if you want to pla college and get your numbers up!

If you are a recruited athlete, then you must qualify to pla guidelines. Your high school coach can give you the details. S additional regulations or indices that they use to qualify pla Ivy Group (a.k.a. Ivy League) uses an academic index to cases though, the minimum requirement for any single player is quite low; the more stringent requirements are those that apply to the team as a whole. For example, a college may require that a team have an average SAT score of 1250, but any individual player may have an SAT score as low as 1050. So for every player recruited who has a 1050, the coach will recruit another player with a 1450. Chances are that the 1450 player won't ever play; he's on the team just to pull up the SAT average. What does this mean to the recruited player? Nothing. If you think you can be recruited, talk to your high school coach and contact the college's coach. If you're highly desirable, the coach will usually be able to find a way to enable you to play.

Top recruits must often go through the trying process of dealing with aggressive coaches. A coach at one college may assure you that you will be recruited, while a coach at another college may promise you a private dorm room, and the coach at the third college may tell you that you're number one on his recruiting list. A few things you should keep in mind: except for the top coaches in the top money sports in the country (Bowden, Paterno), coaches cannot make promises about admissions, dorms, or anything else. The only promises a coach can make are in regards to his team (and even then, those promises are non-binding). Some coaches make promises to lure recruits; in nearly every case, those promises are not (and cannot be) kept. At top colleges, coaches never make admissions decisions and cannot make any admissions-related promises. If a coach tells you that you are his number one recruit, you should keep two facts in mind: you may be his number one this week, but recruiting lists usually change each week and being "number one" still doesn't guarantee admission. Often, a coach will make promises before checking with the admissions office. After the coach has piqued your interest, he will run your numbers past the admissions office. The officer responsible for the recruits for that team may inform the coach that you will not be admitted because your numbers are too low, at which point the coach will look for another number one recruit. If you are a top recruit, you should be interested in the colleges that are pursuing you but remain non-committal until you've thoroughly investigated each one. Do not let coaches pressure you into committing to a college.

As far as top colleges go, the athletic recruit that has the best chance of being admitted is the poor minority from a bad school who has uneducated parents. If such a candidate is also a great athlete, he may be admitted with sub-1100 scores n the SAT and a C average. The recruits who have the most difficult time being 'mitted are (usually white) athletes from prep schools whose parents are lthy. Admissions offices simply hold him to a higher standard. The other item te is that not all sports and not all colleges have the same academic require- A college that has a top-rated team will do (almost) anything to maintain its high ranking, so that college isn't likely to let a top recruit get away. For example, Princeton will usually be much more aggressive in recruiting basketball and lacrosse players because these are two of Princeton's premiere sports. Similarly, Harvard and Yale are generally more aggressive in recruiting athletes than Dartmouth. So just because a coach at one college says your scores are too low, this doesn't mean that all top colleges will reject you; if Dartmouth thinks your SAT scores are too low for you to be recruited, then try Brown. You should find a college that specializes in your sport and who aggressively recruits athletes in your sport. Your counselor and coach should be able to help you find the colleges that are most likely to recruit you for your sport.

What if you're not an athletic recruit? It's (almost) never too late to start. I know of hundreds of students who didn't start playing a sport until their sophomore or junior year in high school and were top recruits for top colleges. Since the best way to ensure being admitted to a top college is to be a top athletic recruit, then it's worth a shot.

Here are a few tips. First, investigate the colleges to which you're interested. There are a few top colleges that do not recruit athletes (usually very small liberal arts colleges); all of the Ivies recruit, as do most larger top colleges. Second, choose a sport that naturally fits your physical build. You're not going to overcome a significant physical barrier in a year or two. Third, investigate lesser-known sports. Colleges recruit for swimming, fencing, softball (women's), and squash. So if football or hockey isn't your thing, then keep looking. Chances are, there's something that fits your interests and skills. Fourth, train and play all year. Your high school season will probably only last 10-15 weeks, but in order to be a serious recruit, you must train and play 40+weeks per year. You should join the local club team, play at the gym, and practice with friends during the off-season. Run two miles a day, five days per week. Lift weights four days per week, fifty-two weeks per year. Attend semi-pro camps during the summer. Often, it's this year-round dedication that makes high school athletes stand out.

You do not need to be a superstar to be a recruited athlete. If your high school has one of the best soccer teams in the state, it's likely that the top 4-6 players will be recruited (not necessarily all to top colleges though). So you do not necessarily need to be the best athlete in the county or in your high school to be recruited. Small liberal arts colleges often cannot recruit the best players, so they go to the second tier. If you're willing to put in the time and effort, then you have a good shot at being recruited.

Minorities. When colleges talk about minorities as special admits, they are usually talking about everyone except white and Asian students, but they are particularly talking about black and Hispanic students. This is what colleges mean when they refer to "underrepresented minorities." I suppose colleges think they have enough Asian and Jewish students. Ironically, many top colleges such as Harvard and Princeton had quota-ceilings for Jews in the 1920-1940s. Today, many top colleges have similar quota-ceilings for Asians and whites. It's not uncommon to find a quota-ceiling for Asian-Americans at 20% or 25% and a quote ceiling for whites at 60% or 65%. These percentages represent the maximum number of students of each race a college wishes to admit for a particular year. A white quota-ceiling of 60% means the college can claim they are composed of 40% minorities; of course, this number is deceptive since most of these minorities are Asian-Americans, who the college doesn't consider a minority for admissions purposes.

If you are a black or Hispanic student with good grades and SAT scores, the admissions world will be different for you. Colleges such as Harvard and Stanford will write you personal letters and you won't even need to pick up the phone. You will get a personal letter and business card from an admissions officer who specializes in minority recruitment and will personally handle your application. If your scores and grades are decent (1250+on the SATs and a B+average), you will be recruited like a star athlete because of the color of your skin and/or your ethnicity. In fact, the only students who are regularly recruited solely for academic reasons are black and Hispanic students. In addition, you may win special recognition from the National Merit Scholarship Corporation if your PSAT score is above 1150 (math plus verbal) and you're a minority.

Is this fair? It's similar to colleges using legacy considerations: high legacy admissions rates aren't fair, but colleges spend so much money that they must give extra attention and consideration to alumni. Simply put: colleges must continue an unfair policy to make up for past and current mistakes. Racial preferences— the racial profiling of the academy—are unfair, but so was the way that many top colleges previously treated the non-white, non-Protestants of the world. Colleges routinely discriminated against blacks, Jews and Catholics. It was almost impossible to get into a place like Princeton prior to the late 1940s if you were anything other than a white, male Protestant. It makes sense that colleges offer reparations for past wrongs, and the debate will rage whether or not racial preference is the way to do it. Regardless, if you're black or Hispanic, you will be given special consideration. You might as well use it to your advantage. The primary way that colleges find out about your race is through the College Board's insidious little "College Search Service," through which the College Board sells your PSAT information to colleges. This information includes your name, address, race, religion, PSAT score range, grades, and intended major. Colleges buy lists of minority students with high PSAT scores and grades and mail to them. If you choose to participate in the "College Search Service," then you will know if you are attractive to colleges; you will start to receive mail in the spring of your junior year (about six months after you take the PSAT) and will continue to receive mail until the fall of your senior year (a year after you take the PSAT). If you scored high enough on the PSAT, your mail will be from top colleges.

Usually, the mailers will come from the minority recruiter who will include a special letter and e-mail address. Save this information. The minority recruiter's job is to recruit minorities, so they want you to apply and get accepted to the college. It's their job to get you to apply and to be admitted. Feel free to call or e-mail the minority recruiter with any questions you may have. They will be pleased to answer your questions. Often, these mailers also include a minority view book. This version of the view book has all pictures of blacks and Hispanics, has a listing of minority clubs, and every other sentence contains the word "diversity." In most cases, it will not be made clear that the view book is a special minority version. I've worked with dozens of minority students who don't even realize that this special view book isn't the view book that everyone else sees. Yes, colleges are pandering to you in the worst way by mailing to you a special view book. The assumption is that your primary interest in a college is to be around people of the same race. Instead of pursuing Martin Luther King's dream of judging people by the qualities of their character and not the color of their skin, colleges thrust marketing propaganda at you that seems wholly based on the color of people's skin. Colleges seem to think that all you're interested in is being around other blacks and Hispanics. It's remarkable in its crudity, but it's to your advantage to respond.

If a college is recruiting you because you are a minority, then make sure you contact the minority recruiter at the admissions office; visit that person, write a thank-you note to that person, and e-mail him or her with questions. The minority recruiter will become your biggest advocate. Write your essay about the trials and tribulations of being a minority (or a related topic) and make sure your numbers are as high as possible. As with other recruited applicants, many minority decisions are based on grades and test scores. Colleges are interested in minority applicants and are willing to admit anyone who seems capable of doing the work and is unique; however, they must nevertheless keep an eye on those pesky numbers that they report to college guides. Those numbers result in a college's rankings. No college, regardless of how caring they are, will sacrifice their ranking in *U.S. News* for a few minority students. (Some colleges actually do not include recruited minorities when computing their average GPA and SAT scores.)

What does it take to be a recruited minority from a top college? First, your SAT scores should be around 1200 or higher. Recently, if you scored higher than an 1150 on the PSAT, you would rank in the top 5% of all minorities who took the PSAT (which would make you about 1 of 10,000 top minorities). So an 1170 on the PSAT would get the attention of most top colleges in the country. (In sum, there will be about 50 highly competitive colleges with a total of 130,000 open seats pursuing those 10,000 top minorities.) If you come from a wealthy background and have highly educated parents, a top college (Harvard, Dartmouth) may want SAT scores around 1300; but if you come from a poor background, a bad high school, and have uneducated parents, an 1160 is often good enough. Either way, minority applicants get a 150-300 point break when it comes to SAT scores.

For grades, you will typically need a B average and you will need to have taken at least one or two very difficult classes (AP or high honors). You will need to show some leadership and enthusiasm in your schoolwork, a love of learning and desire to be educated, and an ability to succeed in a high-pressure environment. In most cases, a minority from a middle-class background with a 1250 on the SAT, a B average with 2-3 very difficult classes, and a few challenging extracurricular activities has a good chance of being admitted to most top colleges.

The bottom line: Whether the current system of minority recruiting is right or wrong is irrelevant to you; there's nothing you can do about it except use the system to your advantage. Other candidates will use anything they can to help them get admitted, and so should you.

Legacy. "Legacy" means that you are a relative of someone who graduated from the college/university. For most colleges, "legacy" means your parents or grandparents graduated from the college. Great uncles and sisters-in-law don't count. A few college guides tell you that grandparents don't count or graduates from professional schools don't count; this is not true. A few colleges don't count grandparents or graduates of professional schools, but many do. The specifics of the definition of "legacy" will vary by school; if you have a question, call the alumni office.

Colleges like legatees for two reasons. The mushy reason is that they believe (or say they believe) that it builds a better college community and sense of tradition when entire families attend the same college, particularly for generations. You might ask: but how can an entire family attend the same competitive college? Wouldn't that assume that everyone would get high SAT scores and great grades? That's true to some degree, but legacy considerations are an old tradition and, believe it or not, most top colleges (including the Ivies) were not very difficult to get admitted to a century ago. Almost any reasonably well-educated (and white Protestant) student in 1890 could get accepted to any Ivy League college. Colleges introduced legacy considerations to encourage families to become attached to one college. The second reason that legacy considerations exist is less mushy: alumni "families" (groups of relatives who attend the same college) tend to donate more money than individuals. And colleges need (or want, in most cases) lots of money. Therefore, colleges favor those students who may bring about greater donations.

In most cases, legatee applicants are considered separately from regular applicants (just as athletes, minorities, and special applicants are). Most colleges set aside a certain number of seats each year for legatee applicants. It's common for a college with 2000 freshmen seats to have 150-400 of them reserved for legatees. The rate of admission for legatees is typically two to three times that of regular students; so if a college has a regular admission rate of 14%, legatees are probably being admitted at a 30%-45% rate, whereas a college with a regular admission rate of 30% probably had a legacy admission rate of 60%-70%. Even Harvard and Princeton, who have composite admissions rates of less than 14%, admit about 40% of all legacy applicants. For Penn, early decision legacy applicants are admitted at a 65%-70% rate, while regular decision legacy applicants are admitted at about a 40% rate. Not all top colleges treat legacy applicants with the same enthusiasm; at Yale, admitted legatees make up a fairly large number—15% of the student population, whereas at Dartmouth, legatees only comprise about 7% of the student population.

Is this fair? Consider the economics of the situation. The average top private college spends between $45,000 and $65,000 a year per student, and yet only charges about $28,000 in tuition. Where does the money come from to cover the extra expense of about $25,000 per student? Mostly, the money comes from alumni donations. A top liberal arts college can raise $100 million per year from alumni but may only earn $80-$90 million from tuition. Therefore, alumni can actually account for a greater percentage of revenue than student tuition payments do. Since most good private colleges spend much more per student than they charge, colleges must pay for these excess expenses with alumni donations. However, a legatee with an 1150 on the SAT usually has no chance of being admitted to a top college, whereas a recruited athlete with the same score will be seriously considered for admission; athletes are given more consideration than legatees.

One of the myths about legacy admissions is that colleges often admit dumb applicants with influential parents. This is not true. In a recent study of more than 15,000 students at over two dozen top colleges (including Harvard, Stanford, Columbia and Duke), non-legacy students were more likely to have a GPA lower than 3.0 (B- to C-). This means that if you found a student at Harvard with a C- average (a 2.1, for example), they are more likely to be a non-legacy student. In addition, the study found that legacy students were more likely to have an A- average (a 3.8, for example) than non-legacy students. This study contradicts the notion that many (if not most) of the students at top colleges with very poor grades are the dumb students who were admitted because their parents were influential alumni.

If you ask, most private colleges will bluntly tell you these facts. They may actually be more conservative when stating expenses per student: they may tell you they spend $40,000 per student when they actually spend $50,000 per student (some colleges don't wish to admit now much they frivolously spend). The biggest criticism one could level is that colleges must unfairly admit the children of alumni because they need the money, and they need the money because their spending is out of control. No organization has less fiscal responsibility than the modern university (not even the federal government). Universities (and large colleges) spend millions on the most inane, boondoggle things, and then they massively increase their tuition (for the 30th year in a row) and fleece their alumni for more money. So if you complain that legacy admissions is unfair, colleges will reply that they spend $50,000 on you and are only charging you $25,000—which is true. Of course, if they had one fiscally responsible bone in their bodies, they wouldn't be spending $50,000 per student. The bottom line: there's nothing you can do about either situation.

Legacy & Early Decision. Early decision legacy applicants who are not admitted are almost never rejected outright; they are deferred first (in December) and rejected later (in April-June). Nearly every admission office gets a "wish list" from the development office (which is responsible for fundraising). The list contains the names of legacy applicants who are large or potentially large contributors. Some colleges, such as U. Richmond and Duke, seriously consider this list, and a few admissions decisions are made because of this list. Other colleges, such as Princeton (and most Ivies), largely ignore this list. Despite the Ivies' image of being an old boys club, they do not weigh one's contributions as much as you might think. The Ivies have so much money that the potential financial contribution of any single alumnus is not a major consideration. The Ivies do consider one's legacy status, but they consider it primarily for reasons of tradition and community, not for getting more money from your parents or grandparents.

Legacy & Interviews. In many cases, legatees can be interviewed by special alumni interviewers instead of the admissions office. A few decades ago these alumni interviewers had a great deal of influence; they no longer do. An alumni interview won't help you more than any other kind of interview. If you're a legatee and match the average criteria for an admitted applicant, then you will probably be admitted. Some admissions offices are more aggressive than others in admitting legatees. Princeton gets a little testy when it comes to alumni admissions (probably stems from their feelings of guilt for being a bastion of rich, white, Protestant men for so long), while the University of Richmond is more aggressive in admitting legatees.

If you are a legatee, you should take advantage of it. Your parents (or grandparents, depending on who graduated from the college) should donate some money, but they should not otherwise bother the school. The alumni association and development office will harass the admissions office for you. If your parents or grandparents wish to make it clear that you're applying, they should first do it through the alumni association. The application will ask if you are a legatee, so there is no need to pester the admissions office with this fact. Ask the alumni association what percentage of total students admitted were legatees and what the rate of admission was for legatees; you will probably be surprised to learn that, for example, the Ivies admit almost 40% of legacy applicants. Every little bit helps.

A number of alumni ask an obvious question: do top colleges really track how much money you give? The short answer is yes; the development and/or alumni office tracks every penny. They will then submit a list of "top legatees" to the admissions office. Depending on the college, this list may have ten names or a hundred names on it. Usually, the top two or three will be admitted regardless of their grades or test scores. The rest will be required to meet some minimum standard (sort of like the NCAA minimum for being admitted as a recruited athlete). How much do you need to donate in order to get on the list? Typically, $100,000 or more prior to applying with the promise (or, more diplomatically, the suggestion) that your parents will donate another $100,000 or more once you've been admitted. So the minimum price of admission to the list is typically $200,000 to $250,000. This amount will earn you access in most cases, but only to the bottom of the list. You won't be one of the automatic acceptances.

The price tag for a spot at the top of the list is typically $1 million or more prior to applying with the promise of $1 million or more after being accepted. A $2-$5 million donation will earn you one of the top spots, but you still must meet some basic qualifications. If you are a complete academic failure, your family will typically need to donate $10 million or more to the college prior to applying in order for you to be accepted. No top college that I know of will turn down that much money. (Although it should be noted that, as with everything in America, the better the college, the higher the price. A college that is one of the best 2-3 in the country may require a donation of $50 million or more in order to accept an applicant with a 2.4 GPA and a 970 on his SATs.) At most top colleges, the admissions office doesn't really handle the applicants at the top of the list; these applicants are often reviewed directly by the development/alumni office and the office of the president, and the president decides whether to accept or reject the applicant (he always waits for the check to clear). Bottom line: you should donate a little just so your name shows up on the alumni giving list, but you will need to donate $200,000 or more to really be noticed.

Why does it take so much to get a college's attention? Many top colleges and universities have endowments worth billions of dollars, and many of these alumni offices conduct multi-billion dollar fund-raising campaigns. Can you imagine attempting to raise $2 billion dollars through donations? When an alumni and development office regularly uses the word *billion*, a $20,000 donation simply doesn't mean much.

Special Talents. Special talents are remarkable skills that have been recognized by people other than yourself and your parents. Gifted musicians, composers, artists, actors, or anyone else who will enhance the reputation of the college can be given special consideration. If you think you have a special talent, you must have outside, objective recognition of your talent. Then you must get the sponsorship of a professor at the college to which you're applying. Nearly all colleges who are considering a special talent student will require the student to exhibit that talent for the head of the department most relevant to that talent. If you're a great oboist, then the head of the music department will evaluate your playing either in person or by tape. (Colleges much prefer to do these things in person.) Whether or not you're given special consideration will depend on the opinion of the head of the department. If they love you, chances are you will be admitted as long as your numbers are okay. If they don't love you, then you will probably be required to compete for admission with everyone else. Keep in mind that a special talent that isn't considered recruitable by one college may be recruitable at another, so keep trying if one college turns you down.

You should keep in mind that in most cases your talent will be evaluated by a professor and/or professional in your field. Your talent must be extraordinary to impress these people, which is why you must have objective recognition of your talent. Do not send extra material if you are simply a hobbyist; if your talent isn't extraordinary, you will only annoy the admissions officers and professors by making them deal with and evaluate your extra material.

The bottom line: if you have a special talent, get objective recognition and contact the admissions department so that the college's faculty may evaluate you. You must get a faculty member to support you in order for your special talent to significantly help your chances of admission. In all cases, ask the admissions department for the name and address of a professor who can assess your talents, and be sure to inform the professor that you are applying for admission and would appreciate his or her support.

Early Decision and Early Action. Read the chapter on early decision and early action for details on these two options.

Major Contributors. See the discussion on Legacy applicants above. A major contributor is anyone, legatee or not, who donates (or promises to donate) something of great value, always worth more than a million dollars, usually worth more than $10 million. If your parents are thinking of making a major contribution to a college to which you are applying, then they need to contact the development office. They should do this as soon as possible, preferably a year or two prior to the time you submit your application. Keep in mind that different colleges will value gifts differently. Although all colleges like cash, some will not highly value works of art because their museums are already stuffed with art and others will not value land because they already may be irritated by managing thousands of acres of donated land. If you're unsure how a college will value your contribution, start calling development offices and shop around.

Everyone Else (Regular Decision, Non-Recruited Applicants). By the mid- to late-1980s, an applicant usually had to fall into one of three categories to get admitted to a top college: accomplished leader/special talent, top athlete, or minority. Either you're a leader within your school or within an academic or extracurricular field, you're a great athlete on a good team, or you're an "under-represented" minority. Standard-issue white students (particularly male students) from suburbia stood little chance of being admitted to a top college, regardless of how successful their academic record was; those standard-issue applicants competed for the few remaining seats (often 7,000-12,000 applicants competing for 150 open seats!).

For many reasons, this situation has somewhat changed. As the previous chapter shows, times haven't changed that much—top colleges still reserve a large number of freshman seats for minorities, athletes, and superstars. The only way to avoid this problem is to apply to a college that doesn't recruit in all these areas; for example, Reed College in Oregon does not recruit athletes. Most colleges have now recognized the usefulness of standard-issue students. By the early 1990s, top colleges were filled with recruited superstars, athletes, and minorities; often these groups did not get along. They often broke into sects, balkanized and belligerent, and fought each other for institutional support or power. The standard-issue student helps mitigate the extremes and adds gradations between the balkanized camps.

"Everyone else" mostly applies to these standard-issue students, who make up the majority of the applicants but for the past 15-20 years often made up the minority of admitted students. Colleges are trying to get back to admitting more students from this segment of applicants so that campuses more accurately reflect society (12%-15% black, 6%-10% Hispanic, 3-5% Asian, 65%-75% white). The problem is that new fad: early decision. Now there's another significant barrier to the "standard-issue" student: you're at a significant disadvantage if you don't apply early decision, and an ever-increasing number of colleges are adding myriad early decision options and hard-selling these options. Applying early isn't so much an option anymore; it's a necessity.

Mailing It In. For each application, you're mailing the actual application (sometimes in two parts), your teacher and counselor mail recommendations, ETS mails test scores, and additional information . Often, a single application can generate 4-8 pieces of mail. So from October to mid-January (3.5 months), a typical admissions office will receive between 50,000 and 125,000 pieces of mail. Can you imagine sorting 50,000 pieces of mail in three months? That's over 800 pieces of mail per day (it's actually over 1,000 pieces of mail per day if you exclude holidays). And that's for a small college.

Mail is typically processed 1-2 weeks after it arrives. For example, early decision applications that are mailed by November 1 are usually read 2-4 weeks later. It takes the minimum wage "techs" 1-2 weeks to open, stamp, and sort the mail. Each piece of mail is stamped with a date, sorted by region (at most colleges), entered into a computer, and filed into the applicant's file. If the application deadline is January 15, most colleges have no idea if you mailed your application on January 12th or the 20th unless they look at the postmark—either way, the mail was probably opened, stamped, and filed on January 23rd. Colleges are not going to reject you because your application arrived a day late. They probably won't know and certainly don't care if it's a day late. Don't bother mailing it via overnight express mail, and don't call two days after you mailed it to see if the college received it (they probably don't know). Always give an admissions office two weeks (or more) to sort and file before you call to ask if they received it.

Once the majority of the application is received, it's read by the regional admissions officer. Many applications are read even if they are missing a teacher recommendation. I estimate that as many as 20% of all applications are not complete by the deadline. Colleges don't care—as long as they are complete by late February/early-March and as long as the actual application is in "on time." Now let's look at what a reader does to your application.

The Reader System. Most admissions offices work on the reader system: a reader is a person who simply reads your files, makes notes, and gives you a score. In most cases, this first reader is a regional reader. If you're from Greenwich, Connecticut, then the first person who reads your file will know your school, all the schools surrounding your school, and all the schools in your state. This person will know that A.P. U.S. history at Greenwich High School is very difficult. The regional reader's notes and scores will be added to your file.

In most cases, applicants receive two numerical scores: one for academic achievement (rank+SAT+SAT II) and one for extracurricular achievement. Some colleges add a third score for character traits. In most cases, the entire application is read by a total of 2-3 readers; these people look at your scores, they read your recommendations and essay, and they consider The Unique Factor. The process of reading your file takes about fifteen minutes; it's rare for a reader to spend more than twenty minutes reviewing an application. The readers also pull up information on your high school, prior students admitted from your high school, the desirability of your geography, and any outstanding circumstances (legacy, you only have one leg, and so forth). These readers recommend admission or rejection. Deferrals are usually reserved for political rejections—legatees who are being diplomatically rejected are deferred. In most cases, your application will then have a few numerical scores (academic, extracurricular, personality), a few notes (for legacy, uniqueness, desirability), and few votes for acceptance or rejection. Your application is then taken either to the dean of admissions or to a committee that formally ratifies the readers' votes. At colleges such as Brown and usually Princeton, all applicants go to committee for a vote. In most cases, the committee's decision will reflect the majority of the readers' votes. At some other colleges such as Dartmouth, the best and worst students do not go to committee; about 85% of all Dartmouth applicants are accepted or rejected by readers and never go to committee. If the regional reader (the first reader) thinks you are in the top 5% or bottom 5% of all applicants, he will immediately take your application to the dean. The dean will either accept/reject you on the spot or send your application to be read by more readers.

One may think that the "single-reader" system has more potential problems; in my experience, the students selected by both systems are typically the same. Both systems usually accept and reject the same students so the "single-reader" option usually accomplishes the same thing the committee option does but in less time. In the single-reader system after the top and bottom 5% are dealt with, the remaining 85%-90% are usually sent to a second reader and then to committee. Even in very divergent admissions systems, such as Dartmouth's and Brown's, the majority of the students accepted at both colleges are statistically equivalent.

In brief, that's how you are accepted or rejected from a top college. Notice, for example, how much your grades influence the decision—not much. Poor grades can get you rejected, but so can poor test scores. Everything must be reasonably high, but no single factor—certainly not grades—will get you admitted.

The Gatekeeper System. A variation on the "single-reader" system is the gatekeeper approach: first, a "regional" reader will read an application, rate the applicant on academic performance, degree of difficulty of high school courses, recommendations, presentation (of application, interview), and personal qualities (usually as exhibited by extracurricular activities). This reader will then write a narrative summary of the applicant. This reader will recommend the applicant to a second reader (happens about 75% of the time) or recommend the applicant be rejected (happens about 25% of the time). Rejected applicants are given to an assistant dean for confirmation; the dean accepts the first reader's recommendation 95% of the time. This system is designed to limit the use of cumbersome committees. The regional reader's goal is to weed out auto-rejects.

In most cases, the first reader is "regional" in that he specializes in the applicant's specific region and usually has detailed knowledge of the applicant's high school. This reader is also capable of comparing you to other applicants from your school and other schools nearby. In the gatekeeper system, this reader's job is to weed out the bottom 25% of the applicant pool and pass the rest onto a national reader. In every case, it's the regional reader's responsibility to point out any oddities about the student, the school, or the region. All the other readers and the dean depend on this first reader's specific knowledge of the high school and region. The second reader is "national" in that she reviews a mix of applications from across the country. In the gatekeeper system, this national reader will reject about 20% of the applications that she reads and will write a narrative summary of the 80% who remain. Those lucky 80% (about 60% of the original number) are now passed on to top-level admissions officers. These officers typically reject 10-20% of these, and the remaining applicants are sent off to committees. At this point, most of the remaining applicants—about 50% of the original number—look remarkably alike. Their grades, SAT and SAT II scores, AP scores, and basic achievements are almost the same. The committees' job will be to accept 20%-40% of these students (depending on how many applicants there are and how many seats remain available in the freshmen class). Who are the people on these committees? The composition of the committees varies with each college and many colleges vary year to year. In most cases, these committees consist of admissions officials. In many cases, these committees also consist of faculty members. If you're applying to be a history major, a member from the history department may review your application and make a recommendation to the committee. In some cases, the committees contain students. A senior majoring in history may review your application and make a recommendation along with a faculty member from the history department; if they agree on a decision, that decision will probably be confirmed by the committee. At Rice, applications are reviewed by student committees. At Duke's engineering school, the final committees consist entirely of faculty. The exact makeup of the committee is irrelevant; what is relevant is to get to the final 50%, you need the grades and scores to keep you from getting cut. To get accepted, you need something else to stand out from the remaining 50%—almost all of those remaining students' transcripts look the same.

A final note: most committees depend heavily on the regional reader's remarks and the summary of your file. They assume the regional reader knows you better than anyone else. Who is this person? Typically this regional reader is the admissions representative who visited your high school, who represented the college at college night, and who took your name and address at the college's open-night at the local hotel. While this person probably won't remember your name, it's worth pointing out that in most cases, this person's knowledge of and relationship to your school (the principal, counselors, and so forth) is vital to you being admitted. If the regional reader votes to reject you—particularly in committee—you will most likely be rejected.

Since most committees do not read your entire file, they cast votes based on the regional reader's comments and the summary of your file. This summary usually consists of your academic and extracurricular scores, interview score (if available), AP scores, and the comments that the reader made when reviewing your file. In other words, the committee votes on the big picture; they do not vote on (or even know about) the little things about you, so something must stand out.

The Details of Admissions Scores. The grading criteria for academic scores vary by school. Most schools use a 1-5 (or similar) scale. The Ivies also use an index for athletes. On the 1-5 scale, a score of 1 is best. For the Ivies, an academic score of 1 is usually a GPA of 4.0 (out of 4.0, or, in other words, an A average), five to six test scores over 700 (the SAT math and verbal sections each count as one test score, and the other three test scores are SAT IIs), and 21-23 high school "solids," which are academic courses taken from 9th grade to the present. Non-academic courses such as culinary arts, the so-called family sciences, health, nutrition, and typing are not counted. At least 14 of these solids should be honors, enriched or AP classes. A typical "academic 1" student has a GPA of 4.0, a SAT score of 1480, a 740 SAT II Writing, 780 SAT II Math IC, and a 750 SAT II Chemistry. This applicant's transcript will have 22 solid courses (freshman to senior), with 17 honors, enriched, or AP classes. This applicant took 1 AP class in the sophomore year, 3 AP classes in the junior year, and 5 in the senior year. The sophomore year AP class was European history; the AP Euro test score was a 4. The junior year AP courses were U.S. history and biology; this applicant scored a 5 the AP U.S. history and a 4 on the AP biology.

A few academic students will stand out; for example, students who score a 700 or higher on the Latin SAT II or who have a 4.3 GPA (A+) with several honors and AP classes will typically be an "academic 1" applicant and will draw the attention of admissions officers. In most cases, only 10%-15% of all students who apply to top colleges—including the Ivies—are academic 1s. About 50%-65% are academic 2s or 3s. In most cases, academic 2s will have the same test scores as 1s, but their GPAs will be a little lower (3.9 or 3.8). An academic three will have a 3.9 or 3.8 GPA but will have slighter lower test scores (instead of 5-6 700+scores, they will have 3 700+scores). All these students will make it to the second round.

In addition to an academic score, you will also receive an extracurricular score on the 1-5 scale. An extracurricular score of 1 would be given to someone who holds a patent, started a successful company, published a book, or is an accomplished artist, musician, or public speaker. (Believe it or not, top colleges receive dozens of applications that are extracurricular 1s; however, most of these applicants have academic scores of 3-5). An extracurricular 1 has accomplished something outstanding; she is very unique. An extracurricular 2 would typically have state or regional accomplishments (such as winning a regional championship) or have some other unusual activity (spent a year in Nepal). Most students are extracurricular threes. A 3 would have some achievements such as captain of the football team, class president, or 100 hours of community service per year. None of these are extraordinary. Most applicants to top colleges are extracurricular 3s—a leader with community service but no regional recognition or unique accomplishments. A 4 would have no leadership roles and less than 20 hours of community service per year, generally a person who is active but has no leadership roles. A 5 does no community service and has no leadership roles.

What you do is more important than your title or position. For example, being class president is almost meaningless unless you actually have some significant accomplishments. The class president may have simply won a popularity contest or may have actually done something significant. Being class president may earn you an extracurricular score of 2 to 4, depending on what you accomplished. Similarly, being newspaper editor is usually a very good thing—if you have some significant accomplishment to show for it. Being the editor of an annual or biannual lousy newspaper does not mean much and may land you an extracurricular score of four; but if you are actually a good writer, studied editing, and increased circulation from 100 to 800 or increased ad revenue from zero to $1000 per edition, then you may score as high as a two. The bottom line: you must have something more than a title to show for your accomplishments.

It's important to note that an academic score of 1 doesn't help you very much if your extracurricular score is a 5. In fact, it's more likely that an academic 5 will be admitted to a top college than an extracurricular 5. In other words, applicants with lousy academics are more likely to be admitted than applicants with lousy extracurriculars. This should be viewed as positive because almost anyone can excel at something; find something you're interested in, and dedicate yourself to it. Extracurricular success goes a long way in mitigating a B average. In most cases, the only applicants who are cut from this initial scoring round are those who have an extracurricular five together with anything less than an academic one. In most cases, the only students that will be admitted solely on their academics are the superstars (who apply with 4-8 perfect AP scores). If you're not an academic superstar—and 90% of all top college applicants aren't—then you can't be an extracurricular five and still be admitted to a top college.

How Readers View Scores & Other Parts of Your Application. After the academic and extracurricular scores are given, usually two or three readers will review your essays and recommendations. They will consider your two scores, your essays, and your recommendations along with any other outstanding factors in order to come to a conclusion about you. One note about admissions readers: they are often bored out of their minds. Can you imagine having to read a thousand applications? Yuck. They can read applications for hours and not see anything interesting or new: the same essays, the same recommendations, the same academic threes and extracurricular fours. The essays will be about breaking your ankle while playing football or learning how to be on your own at camp. The recommendations will say "a very good student" and "a very hard worker" and "often the best in the class." About 95% of all recommendations are the same, and many colleges will receive the exact same "very good student" recommendation for several applicants applying from the same high school. (In fact, even a "best student in 20 years" recommendation is common at top colleges.) The GPAs are all 3.6 to 3.8; the rankings are all top 15%; the test scores are all 640-710 range. Most of these applicants will not be admitted. It is tedious, soporific, thankless work. What can you do about this? Write or do something interesting! Usually what grabs a reader's attention is the unique, the outstanding. It's these unique and outstanding applications that get noticed and (often) positively reviewed. So once again, being admitted to a top college isn't a matter of doing some math and admitting by the numbers; it's a matter of standing out, of being different. You do not need to be the best at everything; you need to be unique. Your uniqueness is usually your best chance of getting admitted to a top college.

Reader Recommendations & the Dean. In systems that do not rely heavily on committees, the readers will make notes and a recommendation for the dean. If the recommendation is unanimous, then the dean will most often simply confirm it. The dean's real work comes when one or more readers have a strong opinion that differs from another reader's opinion. The dean will read the application and discuss it with the readers before making a final decision. Sometimes, the dean will assign additional readers to the essay. In non-committee-based admissions offices, it's typical for a dean to read 50% to 75% of the applications that a college receives—which is startling when you consider that most top colleges receive between 8,000 and 18,000 applications. Most of the time, the dean is simply confirming the readers' opinions, but sometimes the dean is required to deal with odd situations.

There are a few occasions when readers do not make recommendations; they simply pass along notes to the dean and ask the dean to make a decision. For example, what if your test scores are very high and your recommendations are very strong, but your grades are all over the place: many As, a few Bs, a few Cs? Then the reader may assume you're simply bored, not in the right classes, didn't have good counseling, and/or should have attended a more rigorous school. If you are bored and academically unchallenged in high school, you should address it somewhere on your application. (However, you should acknowledge that there's no good reason for getting bad grades; you made a mistake, and you're simply explaining how it happened.) Low-GPA candidates with 750+test scores and great recommendations are usually passed on to a dean for a decision. The dean will then rely on his intuition. In most cases, you must have an extracurricular score of 3 or better to be admitted if you have a spotty transcript.

Another instance in which readers will not make a decision is when everything is great—great recommendations, all A grades, 700+test scores across the board—but the essay is terrible. By "terrible," I do not necessarily mean that the essay is poorly written; in fact, most academic ones and twos are good writers. But the essay may be terrible in its function: you are charged with a certain task and writing for a certain audience. A terrible essay may be very bleak, cynical, or pessimistic. A terrible essay may be too personal, perhaps unseemly. A terrible essay may not address the topic at all. In a few cases, a terrible essay may actually be poorly (perhaps hastily) written. Deans know that parents sometimes push their children to apply to colleges, and the children sometimes purposely sabotage the application by writing a poor essay.

Warning Signs. Readers and deans are also on the lookout for fragile students—students who would probably break under the pressure of a top college. While these fragile students include the obvious, they also include students who have had behavior problems, drinking/drug problems, or other serious problems. Students who appear to be "grade-grubbers" are also considered to be fragile: if your ego and identity are tied up in getting good grades, then you may be crushed when you are required to bear the brunt of an Ivy League history class and suffer a C grade to boot. So do not insert a complaint on your application regarding "the A+I should have had." Only fragile students are so concerned with grades; top students know that grades are secondary to what was actually learned. This "fragile" profile also fits students who revel in accomplishments that are commonplace at a top college. A student who thinks too highly of being class president or winning a regional math competitive will likely be viewed as too fragile. Why? Because you're most likely to be completely average at a top college, so if you need accomplishments to feel good, then you probably won't feel good at a top college. The superstar of Lincoln High School will not be a superstar at Yale. Admissions officers are alert to students who may be crushed by this truism. Although admissions officers are alert to these students and usually reject them, they are also alert to students who have an inner-strength and maturity beyond their years. Mature, honest, focused students are particularly welcome in the stressful environments of top colleges. You should avoid exhibiting fragility, and you should make a point of illustrating your maturity and ability to handle pressure while maintaining a reasonable perspective. (Such maturity is often exhibited in community service and employment.)

In these "fragile" cases, a reader is likely to note these defects and pass the application along to the dean without a recommendation. And in most cases, a bleak or very cynical essay will result in a rejection letter. The dean will probably assume the terrible essay is written by a student who is maladjusted, mentally disturbed, or simply isn't interested in the college. Colleges do not wish to court unstable students; applicants who seem less than stable or uninterested are almost always rejected.

Summary of the Process. Your application will go through one of three systems. The first is a reader system that does not rely heavily on the reader; the regional reader may accept or reject up to 10% of applicants, but most applications will go to a committee. The second is a reader system that relies heavily on the regional reader, who may accept or reject up to 30% of all applicants. The third is a committee system, which uses readers for advice but leaves all decisions to committees. In nearly all cases, your application is given an academic and extracurricular score, is reviewed and notated by a regional reader, and is read by a few more people. (FYI: Stanford, unlike most colleges, tries to avoid blatant scoring systems.) Regardless of the system, most applications will be read by 1-2 more readers and then voted on in committee; particularly good and bad applications will often be sent directly to the dean for immediate acceptance or rejection. In all cases, the dean confirms the final decisions of readers or committees, the application is marked with an "A," "R," or "W" on the outside of the folder (Accept, Reject, Wait list/defer), then it is sent back to technicians who enter the decision into your file in the computer's database. When late April rolls around, the computer starts to print out letters based on the decision the techie entered.

Notification Dates & Likely Letters. Many colleges, including the Ivies, use a predetermined date as their official notification date (usually within the first two weeks of April). The Ivies are bound by agreement to notify all regular decision students on this date. But like most other agreements, there are ways around this one. In early February, most top colleges, including the Ivies, mail out their first batch of "likely letters." These letters are not official offers of admission, but they might as well be. Top colleges send out these likely letters to let applicants know that they will receive an offer of admission on the official notification date. These letters are mailed to influence an applicant prior to the official notification date. Most top colleges will mail likely letters from early February through early April to every candidate they have admitted. While these letters violate the spirit of the Ivy Group Agreement, there seems to be no stopping them. Top colleges will use every advantage they can to ensnare the top applicants.

How many regular decision applicants will receive a likely letter? The number varies, but for colleges who aggressively use likely letters (as most top colleges do), it's common for 60% to 95% of all admitted regular decision applicants to receive likely letters 2-10 weeks prior to the official notification date. Most of the applicants who do not receive likely letters will be rejected. Some applicants who do not receive likely letters will still be admitted; in most cases, these applications were not completed until March, so they were the last applications reviewed. If your application isn't completed until March (for whatever reason), then a decision probably won't be made until late March or early April; in these cases, the college will probably simply wait to mail you the official offer of admission on the notification date.

Chapter 29

The Academic Index & Other Formulae

"My mom read somewhere that there's an exact formula to get into Dartmouth. My counselor said that's BS. So what's the deal?"

Students, parents, and counselors are confused about formulae. There is a substantial amount of misinformation about formulae: do they exist? how do schools use them? which schools use them? Some counselors think that top colleges use a standardized formula to rate applicants, and some believe that colleges don't use any formulae. This confusion exists because colleges do not publish formulae; they keep them secret from everyone, including your college counselor.

Unfortunately, the truth is very boring and completely in line with what colleges claim: no formula is used at any top college to admit or reject people. No formula! No index. Nothing. Formulae are used to qualify recruited students for admission (mostly recruited athletes). These formulae exist so aggressive athletic directors don't recruit illiterate athletes. (It still happens, but these minimum standards make the colleges feel better.)

AI Mania. Recently, there has been a hullabaloo about the Ivy Academic Index, which is haughtily referred to as the "AI" as if it were the only academic index used in college admissions. Counselors and parents alike have furiously attempted to calculate a potential applicant's AI. First, I'll tell you what the AI is, and then I will tell you why it's not useful. Of all the insider "secrets" I'm going to tell you, the AI is the one that is least helpful. In fact, I think there is no point in knowing or worrying about the AI, but it's worth addressing because of its notoriety.

The "Ivy League" is an athletic organization (technically, there is no "Ivy League"—it's called the "Ivy Group"). That's all: an athletic organization. The "Ivy League" colleges are not formally connected in any other way (certainly not academically). Apart from recruited athletes, these colleges do not coordinate or discuss admissions during the year; they do not coordinate or discuss financial aid during the year.

The Ivy League, which is purely an athletic league, was formed to create standards in athletic recruiting. To define these standards, the colleges created an index, which is comprised of your high school rank, SAT score, and SAT II scores from three tests. By creating a minimum academic requirement for recruiting, the Ivy colleges could be sure that no college was recruiting great athletes solely for the purpose of playing sports; all recruited athletes had to meet some academic minimum.

Contrary to what you may believe, all colleges (from the best to the worst) have minimum requirements for recruited athletes. Many colleges simply follow the NCAA minimums while others add to these minimums. The Ivy League requirements are simply an adapted version of NCAA minimum requirements. Before I get into the specifics of the AI, I should point out that Ivy League colleges aren't required to follow the AI for all recruited athletes. In fact, if a college really wants to recruit an athlete who doesn't meet AI minimums, that college may still recruit that athlete if the other Ivies give their permission. One can easily see how this exception can turn into a commonly-used loophole. Also, keep in mind that AI requirements only apply to athletes recruited to Ivy League colleges. This formula is useless everywhere else. One final note before I get into the vagaries of the AI: the Ivies have occasionally changed this formula and are free to change it at any time (and obviously will not notify anyone since they do not publish this information). Therefore, there's no point in attempting to learn the specific AI formula for any given year; there's a good chance that yesterday's AI formula will not be the same as tomorrow's version.

As noted above, the AI consists of three numbers: your class rank, your SAT score, and your SAT II scores. Colleges take your class rank, adjust it according to how many students are in your graduating class, and assign you a number out of 80. If your school doesn't give you an exact rank, then the college will attempt to assign a rank using grade distribution charts. If all else fails, the college will translate your grades into a rank. In general, it's best that your high school assigns to you an exact rank if your graduating class has 100 or more students. Usually, if the college is left to assign a rank, chances are your assigned rank will be lower than your actual rank. For graduating classes of fewer than 100 students, the maximum score drops below 80 (typically between 70 and 75). Colleges do this because they assume it's more difficult to be highly ranked in a large graduating class (i.e. 500 students) than in a small class (i.e. 40 students).

If you wish to calculate your AI, assign yourself a rank score using the following scale: if you are one of the top 30 students in your graduating class, give yourself a 65. If your rank is student #31-#70, give yourself a 58; if you're #71-#100, give yourself a 53. If you're below #100, give yourself a 45. If your graduating class has fewer than 100 students, subtract 5 points from your rank score.

If you have no idea what your rank is, use your academic GPA (meaning you should not include your non-academic classes when calculating your grade average). If your GPA is higher than a 4.0 (A+average), give yourself a 75. If your GPA is a 3.6-4.0 (A/A- average), give yourself a 68. If your average is a 3.0 (B), give yourself a 63. Anything less than a B (lower than a 3.0), give yourself 50 points. If your graduating class has fewer than 100 students, subtract 5 points. If your courses are somewhat easy (few or no AP/honors courses), subtract another 5 points. Most students who are competitive applicants to top colleges will have a rank score of 55 or higher.

For your SAT scores, Ivy League colleges will take your highest math and verbal score, average them, and drop the last zero. For example, if you scored a 680 math and a 720 verbal, then the average is a 700, and you would be assigned a 70. (Therefore, for AI purposes, your SAT score will range from a 20 to an 80.)

For SAT II scores, you should take the average of your top three scores and drop the last zero. For example, if you have a 650, 700, and 750 on three SAT IIs, the average is 700. Drop the last zero, and you have a 70.

At this point, you have three scores: a class rank score, a SAT score, and a SAT II score. Add them up. You will get a score between 60 and 240 (although no one actually gets a 60). Most students will get a score between 160 and 210. The average competitive applicant to a top college will get a score of about 195, and the average admitted applicant will have a score of 200-215.

So what does all these mean? Remember that the AI is only used for the eight Ivy Group colleges, so if you're not applying to them, this formula is meaningless. If you are a recruited athlete to an Ivy, it still means nothing. If you aren't a recruited athlete to an Ivy, it also means nothing. Hence my admonition at the beginning that worrying about admission formulae is silly.

If you are a recruited athlete, your specific AI may be meaningless. Ivy Group athletic directors are not so much concerned with the AI of any specific athlete as they are concerned with the average AI of the recruited athletes for the entering class and the AI average of specific teams. Often, if a coach wants to recruit an athlete with an AI of 150, then he may also recruit an athlete with an AI of 220 to bring up the overall average. The athlete with the 220 AI may, in fact, not be very good and may never start on the team, but since athletic directors are primarily concerned with averages, they can use high-AI athletes to balance the low AIs of other recruited athletes. This is why you will sometimes see a basketball player at the end of the bench who never plays. He was recruited to help balance the AIs of some of the other players. In most cases, football, basketball and hockey are the sports with the lowest average AIs.

The AI system primarily uses and prefers rank, which means that many students are treated a bit incongruously. Between 30% and 65% of all applicants to top colleges come from high schools that do not rank. Many of these schools will provide a grade distribution, so that the college may assign a rough rank; usually, these rankings are lower than if the high school provided an exact rank (particularly if they assigned an exact weighted rank). However, many schools, particularly very small private schools, will provide no ranking information at all, so the college is forced simply to use the GPA. You may have noticed the scores given for GPAs are surprisingly lenient. Students with B averages can earn a rank score 65. What does this mean? Often, students from very small private schools (that do not give any indication of rank) who have mediocre grades often get higher rank scores than they should. If you attend a very large school, a 65 rank score would mean you were ranked in the top 10% of your class. However, you can get a rank score of 65 if your school gives no indication of rank and you have a B average. The advantage is clear: it's usually impossible to be ranked in the top 10% at a school with a B average, and yet both students would receive the same rank score of 65.

The manner in which your high school contextualizes your grades and course work is very important. I encourage you to talk to your counselor about your rank and about how your grades and courses compare to the rest of your class. Too many students apply to colleges without knowing exactly how their counselor will portray their courses. It is almost always better for high schools to weight honors and AP courses. Although some of the students at the bottom of the class may be at a slight disadvantage, the students at the top of the class are at a significant advantage. Most academic formulae and indices top out at 4.33, so any GPA above 4.33 is given the maximum points permitted. Under these circumstances, a 5.2 GPA can significantly improve a low SAT score. So take the time to understand the information your high school will use to rank or contextualize your grades. If your high school ranks in any way, find out how it ranks and what your rank is; if your school provides a grade distribution, ask for a copy. If your school does neither, then simply have a discussion with your counselor about how your work compares to your classmates' work. The sooner you do this, the better.

Some claim that the AI illustrates that Ivies generally accept or reject students primarily based on grades/rank and test scores. This assertion would mean that all the other stuff (activities, recommendations, essay) doesn't count for much. To prove this assertion, they will quote statistics that show that students with higher AIs have higher acceptance rates. However, these statistics are misleading.

No top college simply admits students by the numbers and all top colleges weigh essays and activities fairly heavily. A very poor essay or an empty activities list could sink your application. It's true that applicants with higher AIs have a higher acceptance rate, but that statistic is "self-selecting." Those students who have good grades and test scores are simply more likely to write a good essay and actively participate in school activities. Good students tend to be good all around, from French class to the French Club to the SAT II in French, whereas below-average students who don't participate much in class tend not to participate much in anything at school. In those rare cases of students with great grades and SAT scores who don't do anything outside of class, colleges typically reject them. Consider that about 10% of all students with an AI of 220 or higher are rejected—usually due to a bad essay and/or limited activities. Imagine, a 220 AI is an SAT score of 1460, three SAT IIs of 750, and a class ranking within the top five of all graduating students. How do 10% of these students get rejected? Bad essays and extracurricular activities. Try telling one of these students that essays and extracurricular activities don't count!

Another factor that severely limits the usefulness of knowing your AI score is that once a college computes an AI score for you, an admissions officer may raise or lower your AI. If your rank and test scores give you an AI of 205, an admissions officer may lower that if your courses are weak or your recommendations are mediocre. An officer may raise your AI if your have a few good AP scores (usually 2-3 AP tests with scores of 4 or higher). Therefore, the AI a college may use to consider your application may be quite different from the one you compute yourself, which is another reason not to worry too much about the AI.

And a final reason not to worry about the AI: even though all Ivies are required to use the AI system when admitting recruited athletes, they are not required to use it at any other time. Some Ivies compute an AI for all students for easy comparison, while other Ivies don't compute an AI at all (unless they are required to for recruiting purposes.) Some Ivies, like Princeton, will recalculate your grades based on their own scale (and, in Princeton's case, leave out your freshmen year), while other Ivies will more heavily weigh personal and extracurricular data. For these reasons, there's simply no reason to bother trying to understand the AI other than to understand that your grades and test scores are very important.

More Useless Examples. Are other formulae used? Sure. Almost every college uses some formula to make your academic performance (rank/grades plus test scores) quickly comparable to other students' performances. Georgetown uses a system somewhat akin to the AI system, but they give more weight to your transcript.

For Georgetown, class rank and test scores are used, and if no rank is given, then the formula isn't used at all. Other lesser competitive schools will use a system like this: multiply your GPA times 370 and add your SAT score (400-1600). As long as you have at least a 2.0 average, your total score will be an 1140 to a 3200. If your school weights and your GPA is above a 4.33, then your total score may go much higher than a 3200. This system weights SAT scores and grades (on a 4.0 scale) equally. If your school weights grades and your GPA is above a 4.33, then your grades are automatically weighed more heavily than your SAT scores (in a sense, you're automatically rewarded for taking and doing well in honors and AP classes). Many larger state schools will use this type of formula and automatically accept or reject students based on a cut-off derived from the prior year's statistics (for example, the cut-off score may be a 2010).

Almost every school uses different databases, formulae, and scoring criteria to produce this comparative data. Even the Ivies do not use the same database system to compute AI scores. You could look at the formulae for three very similar colleges and find three completely different formulae. In the end, if you're worrying about specific formulae, then you're worrying about the wrong stuff. Concentrate on good grades and good test scores. Every formula rewards good grades and good test scores, and knowing a specific formula won't help you improve either. So get the highest grades and test scores possible, and the rest will take care of itself.

Chapter 30

You Make the Call

"I tried to guess which friends would get into their top choices and
which would get rejected. I was wrong almost every time."

In this section, I'll present you with a few applicants to top colleges. Now that
you know how to put together a great application, you make the call. I'll provide
the regional reader's summary of each applicant; you pretend you're an admissions committee member casting a vote. For each pair of applicants, only one is
admitted. Answers are at the end of this chapter.

ROUND ONE. Applied to Princeton, Harvard, and Yale.
Applicant 1: Jim from Kansas City
The Numbers. Rank: 57/581 (top 10%); SAT I: 730V, 690M; SAT II: 750
Writing, 680 Math IC, 710 History, 700 Latin; AP: English Lit, 5; Latin, 4; U.S.
History, 5; Biology, 3.

The Grades (Read from left to right as 9th grade to mid-year of 12th grade.)
English: B, A, A, A
History: A, A, A, A
Latin: B, A, A, A
Science: C, A, A, A
Math: C, B, B, B

Extracurriculars
Soccer: 9-12, JV captain 9, captain 12
Debate team: 10-12, captain 12
School newspaper: 9-12, editor 12
Urban Youth Theater: 10-12 (founder; 650 hours per year)

Church Youth group: 9-12
Teach 3rd grade Sunday school, 11-12 (2 hours per week)

Essay topic: Founding and managing the Urban Youth Theater, which worked with poor urban children and helped them write plays, builds sets, and stage their plays. The theater operated all year, but the main production was at the end of the summer. The theater operated on private donations and government grants.

Applicant 2: Josh from Greenwich, CT
The Numbers. Rank: 39/470 (top 10%); SAT I: 670V, 800M; SAT II: 650 Writing, 780 Math IC, 760 Math IIC; Spanish, 650; AP: Calculus BC, 5; Physics, 5, Chemistry, 5.

The Grades (Read from left to right as 9th grade to mid-year of 12th grade.)
English: A, A, B, A
History: A, B, A, B
Spanish: A, A, B, A
Science: A, A, A, B
Math: A, A, A, A

Extracurriculars
Soccer: 9-12
Lacrosse: 9-12
Baseball: 9-12
Spanish club: 9-11
Class treasurer: 10-11
Summer jobs: 10-11 (various)

Essay topic: He broke his ankle playing club soccer the summer between 10th and 11th grade, and worked very hard to overcome his injury. He was worried that he wouldn't get to play sports his junior year, but he recovered after two months of arduous daily physical therapy.

ROUND TWO. Applied to Penn, NYU, and BC.
Applicant 1: Jenna from New York City
The Numbers. Rank: 13/117 (top 12%); SAT I: 710V, 660M; SAT II: 700 Writing, 650 Math IC, 710 Spanish; AP: English Lit, 4; Spanish, 3; U.S. History, 4.

The Grades (Read from left to right as 9th grade to mid-year of 12th grade.)
English: A, A, A, A

History: A, A, B, A
Spanish: A, A, A, A
Science: B, B, A, A
Math: B, B, A, A

Extracurriculars
Field hockey: 9-12, JV captain 9
Spanish club: 10-12
School newspaper: 9-11
Act Now! Theater Troupe: 10-11
Ski Club: 9-12
Book Club: 10-12
Cheerleader: 9-11
Honor Society: 12
Class President: 12
Camp Counselor, 11-12
Travel, Europe and Asia, 9-12

Essay topic: As the class president, she worked to get the school to consider student input more seriously; worked with administration to create more student-friendly policies.

Applicant 2: Maria from New Orleans
The Numbers. Rank: 91/740 (top 12%); SAT I: 660V, 680M; SAT II: 640 Writing, 680 Math IC, 800 Spanish; AP: Calculus AB, 3; Spanish, 5, U.S. History, 3.

The Grades (Read from left to right as 9th grade to mid-year of 12th grade.)
English: B, B, B, A
History: B, B, A, A
Spanish: A, A, A, A
Science: B, A, A, A
Math: A, A, A, A

Extracurriculars
Cheerleader: 9-12, captain 12
Softball: 9-12
Spanish club: 9-12
Volunteer for local political campaigns: 10-12 (75 hours per year)

Worked night shift at A.B.G. Chemical, an emergency oil services company: 15 hrs/week during school year; 50 hrs/week over summer (about 1200 hours per year)

Essay topic: Balancing priorities between getting good grades and contributing to the family income; the family needed the $11,000 she made each year, so she took a few easy classes; she feels a little guilty taking Spanish since she speaks Spanish fluently (it's the language spoken at home).

The Decisions.

When April 8th arrives, who's going to be accepted? Who will get the "likely letters" in late February? Here are the decisions.

ROUND ONE: Jim's SAT score of 1420 is average for the three colleges he applied to (even a little below average), but the fact that his verbal is higher than his math helps. He has three SAT II scores of 700+, including Latin, and he has decent AP scores. Josh has a higher SAT score (a 1470) but his 800 math isn't as impressive as you might think. Similarly, his SAT II math scores are great, but his non-math scores are low and exhibit a weakness. His AP tests are all math/science, which shows that he stayed away from his weaknesses.

The decision? There are three important differences between these applicants. First, Jim's weaknesses are clearly math and science, but he did not shy away from them (he took AP Biology). But Josh stayed far away from his weaknesses; he did poorly in the writing and Spanish SAT II tests (two of the easier SAT IIs offered), and all his AP courses were math and science. Second, Jim's grades are consistently improving while Josh's grades are a bit random (and the senior year grades in history and science do not bode well). Third, Jim has a significant community service activity (look at his essay) that exhibits maturity, initiative, and leadership. Josh's essay is very common, and his activities are mostly sports.

The conclusion? Jim's strong verbal skills (SAT, SAT II Writing and Latin, AP English and History) are more impressive than Josh's math and science skills. (Great math/science skills are actually somewhat commonplace, particularly among male applicants.) Jim's founding of the Urban Youth Theater gives him an extracurricular score of 1 whereas Josh has an extracurricular score of 4. Josh's grade trend makes admissions officers uneasy, and he seems to be a bit too narrowly focused on math/science and sports. The admission goes to Jim.

ROUND TWO: Jenna has good SAT and SAT II scores. Her grade trend is generally improving. She attended a small prep school in the city, so her rank is good but not great. Her extracurriculars are nothing special, and her essay probably put a few readers to sleep. Overall, Jenna is a very typical applicant. Maria is from a large urban school in New Orleans. Her SAT score (1340) is low overall but very high for her high school (her high school's average SAT score is a 820). Her SAT II Math IC is very impressive while her Spanish score may not be too impressive because she noted on her application that she is a native Spanish speaker. Her grade trend is good.

The conclusion? There is one huge difference between these two applicants that you can pick up from the information provided. Once an admissions officer sees this information, she will look at a few other things: *where does the applicant live? is she applying for financial aid? did the parents attend college? what do the parents do for a living?* The difference is that Jenna is from a wealthy family, attends an expensive prep school, and both her parents are lawyers. Maria comes from a poor family (who needs her to work), attends a large, poor public school (where less than 20% of the students attend competitive colleges), and neither of her parents attended college. The admissions office expects Jenna to be far above average, and since she's completely average, she probably won't be admitted to a top college but has a chance at NYU and BC. Maria, on the other hand, will be admitted everywhere. Her 1200/hr-per-year job puts her over the top. That job mitigates slightly lower grades and test scores. The admission goes to Maria.

What You Can Learn

- Don't put admissions readers to sleep. Essays on how you saved the world are boring.
- Grade trend is important; your grades should be improving.
- Don't run from your weaknesses. If your weakness is math, you should still take a hard math class your senior year.
- A great extracurricular activity can go a long way.
- If you have some advantages in life, you must do your best with them— more will be expected of you.

Chapter 31

The Worst Things You Can Do

"My dad put a coffee stain on my Stanford application and my mom mailed it. I'm going to call them and ask for it back."

The "Best Things You Can Do" to gain admission to the college of your choice are probably obvious by now: great grades, good test scores, unique essays, everything submitted on time. I don't need to reiterate that list. After working with thousands of students and many admissions offices, I've collected a list of the worst things you can do when applying to college. Some of these may be obvious, but many are not; all of them are things I've actually seen happen (believe it or not).

Lie. Blatant dishonesty is almost an instant disqualifier. Obviously, only a fool would lie about his grades or test scores; a college will get the official results and will notice the difference. More importantly, students are sometimes dishonest about other things such as community service hours, the nature of their positions or responsibilities in school clubs or sports, and so forth. You can't claim that you're captain of the soccer team when the team had co-captains. If you're the co-captain, then you need to state that you were co-captain. Admissions offices have regional directors who specialize in each region or state and usually know the specifics of each school. In addition, admissions officers will not hesitate to pick up the phone and call your counselor to ask for clarification. Do not give an admissions committee any reason to think that you are anything other than completely honest.

Of course, as mentioned above, some students do prevaricate and get away with it. For example, many applicants to top colleges use private counselors, and yet very few of them will admit it on their applications. See the chapter on private counselors for more.

Seem Vague. A cousin to lying is being evasive. In most cases, colleges assume the worst. Do not say you were suspended from school for a day without saying what the offense was; do not claim you had a "leadership role" without clearly stating what that role was. If you are vague or evasive, colleges will usually assume you're being vague for a reason, and that reason is not a good one. Admissions officers will often interpret unclear writing as an attempt to hide unfavorable information, so you should be clear and direct. A good way to test your writing for clarity and appropriate detail is to have someone read it who does not know you well (such as an independent counselor); if that reader understands everything, then you're probably okay. If the reader doesn't understand something, then you probably need to clarify it.

Submit an Incomplete Application or Leave Out Information. One way of accidentally being vague is to completely leave out some information; some students forget to submit their SAT scores or to write the essay. This may seem impossible, particularly to a top college, but almost 600 applicants submitted incomplete applications to Penn in a recent admissions cycle. In fact, it's not uncommon for 3%-5% of all applications to top colleges to be incomplete. An incomplete application is an automatic rejection. Yes, most colleges will notify you (usually via postcard) that your application is incomplete, but they aren't going to hunt you down for that missing information (unless you're being recruited). The bottom line: only you are responsible for the completion of the application, not your parents, or your counselor, or your teacher, or the admissions office. This includes answering every line, checking every box that needs checking, making sure all necessary signatures are provided, and requesting all necessary items be mailed to the college (test scores, recommendations, transcripts).

Be Sloppy. What happens when a student applies to fifteen colleges? The applications start to get sloppy. Perhaps there's a misspelled word, a hastily answered question, an unchecked box. Each year, Columbia receives about five applications on which the name of the college is spelled "Colombia." (Colombia is a country in South American, not a college in Manhattan.) While the admissions officers at Columbia claim that misspelling the name of the college won't sink an application, it's worth noting that as far as I know, none of those applicants are admitted.

Colleges know the telltale signs of the student who rushes an application. One of the most common ways students give a bad impression is by submitting sloppy applications. You can be sure that if your application is sloppy, the admissions office will assume that the college isn't your first choice (and probably not even one of your top three or four choices). Most top colleges are not interested in being anyone's safety choice, so sloppiness can quickly lead to rejection. A sloppy application also smacks of immaturity; college is serious, and admissions offices expect you to take it seriously. And no, using the Common Application or computer application doesn't help; sloppiness shows through any form or application designed to limit errors.

Here are a few ways to avoid the sloppy application. First, plan ahead, and start early. You should start working on your applications in September or October with the goal of getting them all out by Thanksgiving. Inevitably, some mistake will occur, and you will still be working on an application or two in December, but if your goal is to get them all out by Thanksgiving, then you will only be working on two applications in December instead of ten. One sure-fire way of submitting sloppy applications is to rush them all out the day before the deadline. If you're still working on applications in January, then there's a high probably you're making mistakes.

Second, only apply to 4-8 colleges. You only have so much time and energy. The more applications you intend to submit, the less time and energy you will have to spend on each one. Any student applying to 15 colleges is almost guaranteed to make mistakes. (In addition, if you're applying to 15 colleges, you probably have not done the necessary research.)

Third, do not trust application software to do everything for you. Some students plug everything into the software, print the applications, and assume they are ready to go. Computers make mistakes that they are unable to detect or correct. In general, I recommend against using any software application program.

Finally, you should have a trusted, objective person read your entire application before it is mailed in; make sure your reader is looking at the final copy. Bottom line: you have complete and immediate control over the neatness of your application, any sign of sloppiness will count against you.

Write a Bad Essay. Some applications are perfect…until you get to the essay. It's a mistake—a huge mistake—to assume that college admissions essays aren't read; in fact, your essay could make or break your application. A "bad" essay includes those with spelling or grammatical errors, poorly constructed sentences, or poor logic. Do not write about anything untoward, which includes everything from sex to psychological illnesses. Admissions officers want to get to know the real you, but they expect a decorous and mature essay. Your essay is not a trip to the therapist.

The admissions office of a top college will reject you if you write an essay about your first sexual experience, even if you are an otherwise highly qualified applicant. So choose a topic that reveals the real you, but don't be risqué. And finally, don't try humor. Writing a humorous essay is extremely difficult—far more difficult than writing a serious essay. You may be light-hearted, but if your jokes fall flat, then so will your entire essay. Do you want to risk that? In most cases, your parents, grandparents, friends, and even teachers are poor judges of humor. If an objective adult finds your essay humorous, then you may consider using it. (By objective, I mean an independent reviewer who can say that your essay is bad; your beloved grandparents won't tell you that you aren't funny.)

Write A Common Essay. Another version of the "bad" essay is the common essay, the essay written on a common theme. Every admissions office sees too many essays on Thoreau, *The Great Gatsby*, and John Steinbeck. You should write about yourself, not someone (or something) else. And you should write about a unique experience. Don't send an essay on the myth of water in *Beloved*. If the admissions office wants to know about that, it'll ask its own English department. Unless you have an extraordinary experience, do not write an essay about Outward Bound, Amnesty International, Habitat for Humanity, NOLS, Sierra Club, or any sports team. Top colleges get thousands of Outward Bound/Amnesty essays each year; they are trite and predictable. (See the chapter on essays for more details.)

Slack Off Your Senior Year. Believe it or not, each top college typically revokes 5-15 acceptances each year at the end of the senior year. That's right: you could be accepted to Penn or Princeton in December (early decision) only to have your acceptance revoked in June. It happens more than most people would think. Keep in mind that a college can revoke an acceptance for any reason it deems reasonable. Typically, about half of these revocations are academic, and half are for disciplinary problems. If your straight-As drop a little so you get two Bs, you probably won't have a problem. However, if you drop more than two courses or drop any one course more than two grades (an A to a D, for example), then you will probably receive a letter. Most of the letters that go out simply ask for an explanation in essay form. In most cases, students with slight grade drops who write a reasonably good essay will not have their acceptances revoked. Students who have more than two courses drop more than two grades will get a different letter (Calculus, AP Physics, and AP Spanish all drop from As to Ds, for example). Your letter will also ask for an explanation, but your explanation must be very good (a death in the family, a serious illness). If you don't have a substantial explanation, the admissions office will be inclined to revoke your acceptance. No college is interested in working with a student who has recently discovered lethargy. In many cases, the admissions office will contact your counselor and/or the teacher who recommended you to get an update. In a few cases, teachers who wrote recommendations for you in November will write to colleges again to inform them that they no longer recommend you. How do colleges find all this out? In June, just before they close the books on the year, they review all of the admitted students. They look for new letters, declining grades, or suspicious notes (such as "Principal called last week and wishes to talk. Call back before final filing.")

Students who have their acceptance revoked for disciplinary reasons need no explanation: if your school suspends you for a week for drinking and hazing, then your counselor will (or should) notify the college. If the college considers this incident serious, they will revoke your acceptance. Every year, a total of 125-175 students nationwide are involved in disciplinary problems serious enough to have their acceptances revoked from top colleges.

Bottom line: colleges are watching you even after you've been accepted. Don't let your grades drop, and don't do anything stupid. Top colleges revoke a total of about 300 acceptances each year; don't be one of them.

Chapter 32

Strategies

"My friend broke her arm just before she was going to mail her Brown application and now she wants to say she's handicapped."

There are millions of rumors floating around high schools and homes on how to get into a top college. We all know about grades, SAT scores, and the essay, but what little back-door tricks can we use? Your best friend will tell you to try everything because they all work, while the admissions office will tell you that none of them work. The truth is that some work and some don't. Admissions offices will not acknowledge that sometimes they admit students for crazy reasons. One word of warning: don't believe the rumors you hear about admissions tips. Most of them are crazy and untrue. Believe what I'm about to tell you and nothing else.

I'm going to address the most common strategies, including everything that works and some common tricks that don't work; I'm assuming that you're doing everything else in this book. None of these tips will make up for very low grades; if that's what you're looking for, then put down this book, and go back to your homework.

Excel in an Unusual Instrument or Sport. Bingo. Top colleges are loath to admit that they recruit unusual talents, but most Ivies maintain more varsity teams than public universities, and most top colleges have very good music departments. (There are other useful, obscure skills you could develop, but I think these two are the most obvious.) Each year admissions offices get lists from athletic directors and music departments of requested admittants. Each team and each department wants certain talented students to be given special consideration. In most cases, admissions departments at top colleges are fiercely independent—not to mention that if they complied with every request, they would admit far more students than the freshman class can accommodate. In the end, most of the students on the top of these lists are given special consideration.

Admissions departments do give very special consideration to emergency requests: all of the football team's tight ends are graduating, or the marching band desperately needs one more tuba player. In some cases, very good colleges, even the Ivies, admit below average students in response to an emergency request. It should be noted (again) that this doesn't mean that Penn will admit a student with a 2.2 GPA and a 920 on the SAT, but it does mean that many below-average students get admitted to top colleges because they fill an emergency request. If you have a special talent, a 1250 and B average might be enough.

So how does this help you? If you are a junior or senior and have no special talent, it doesn't. But if you are a sophomore or earlier, it could be very helpful. Should you go out and develop a unique talent? Why not? First, it might be fun; second, it makes you more interesting; third, it will benefit you in the admissions process. If you're going to play an instrument or a sport, why not choose something a little different?

What's unique? If you're thinking about taking piano, guitar, or violin lessons, why not consider the oboe, tuba or viola? Music departments, marching bands, and college orchestras are always in need of good musicians, and if you play an obscure instrument, they may be in need of you. In most cases, you will need to start playing the instrument in 7th or 8th grade for your virtuosity to be an asset; few colleges will be much interested in someone who's played the oboe for a year (unless you've got great talent). And usually, you will need to have outside recognition of your musical skill (awards, membership in the local junior orchestra, playing at summer festivals) and/or send in a tape of your playing, which a professor of music will review.

If you're thinking about playing sports, it's more helpful to excel at an unusual sport than to be average at a big-money sport (football, basketball). Obviously, only the very best get recruited for the big-money sports, so you have a much better chance at being above average in low- or no-money sports such as squash, swimming, diving, and fencing. You never know who is looking to maintain their powerhouse women's Ivy League softball team (Harvard) or fencing team (Princeton). Harvard is the perennial favorite in squash though recently Princeton grabbed the Ivy League championship. It's worth noting that sometimes varsity athletes at top colleges did not play the sport in high school, so experience isn't always necessary. This means that a little experience may go a long way; unlike playing a musical instrument, you may only need a year or two of a sport to impress a college.

As with musical instruments, if you're thinking about playing sports, it's to your advantage to excel at a less competitive sport (fencing, diving, squash, crew); you will have a greater chance of being noticed by a college. If your high school doesn't offer squash (very few do), then join a local gym that offers squash lessons and participate in club tournaments. Two or three years later, your squash skills may impress a recruiter.

Choose an Odd "Intended Major." This is another strategy that colleges are loath to admit works. Most colleges ask you what your intended major is; they know that you really have no idea, and your choice is not binding. However, admissions offices want some idea so that they don't admit a class of students that lacks balance. It would be a mistake, for example, to admit only students who are interested in majoring in English literature; the science departments might shut down for lack of interest.

So admissions departments seek to admit students roughly in proportion to the size of academic departments. In addition, colleges would also like to bring diversity to departments. For this reason, women improve their chances of being admitted if they intend to major in a hard science or engineering (particularly physics, chemistry, and mechanical or industrial engineering), whereas the soft sciences, health professions (excluding pre-med), and religion departments are often looking for more men. How many women do you think apply with English, psychology, or education as their intended major? Too many. If you're female but not science-oriented, then you might try history, philosophy, or political science, all of which tend to be dominated by men.

In addition, you may choose interdisciplinary majors; for example, if you excel at biology and history, you may state that you're interested in the history of science or the philosophy of science. But there's one significant caveat to this advice: your intended major must be corroborated by your academic achievements. Don't put "chemistry" as your intended major if you never took chemistry (or performed very poorly in it). You cannot simply choose an intended major out of thin air; it must be a logical goal given your academic experiences in high school.

Recently, Duke's President admitted in the email that Duke favors students with odd intended majors, intended career goals, and hobbies. Make sure you consider this before you check off "English major."

Give Lots of Money. And now I'm going to annoy development departments across the country—as an aside, the "development" department is responsible for raising money for the college. Once you graduate college, you will receive untold letters from them pleading for your every last dime. Some alumni, including a few particularly humorous cases at Cornell, actually tell the development office that they're dead just so the office will stop soliciting money from them.

And now back to the development office: its responsibility is to raise money for the university, and the top development offices raise hundreds of millions of dollars each year (and a few have multibillion-dollar fundraising campaigns). They track alumni donations and, of course, legatee applicants. In most cases, they provide the admissions office with a list of desirable applicants—those whose parents and/or grandparents donate or intend to donate sizable gifts (money, artwork, rare collections of colonial Spanish bullion, and so forth). While some admissions offices, such as the University of Richmond's, give special consideration to this list, most admissions offices do not. Deans of admissions tend to be fiercely independent and strive to admit students based on their over-all credentials. So while it doesn't hurt to give money, it usually doesn't help either. You will usually need to donate $100,000+prior to applying with the understanding that you (or your family) will donate $100,000+after you are accepted just to get on the development office's "most desirable" list. To be one of the development office's auto-admits, your family will need to donate several mil-lion dollars. Typically, anyone under the $15-$20 million range will still need to be academically qualified at some basic level. Bottom line: your $5,000 donation will go completely unnoticed by the admissions office.

Be Geographically Desirable. Most admissions offices deny the importance of location. In fact, Princeton's Dean Hargadon states that Princeton would never admit someone "just because" they are from an underrepresented town or state. On the face of it, this statement is true; in fact, Princeton doesn't admit anyone "just because" of any single factor. But this statement is disingenuous. All top col-leges look for geographic diversity. All students know that top colleges won't take too many students from a single high school; usually the limit is 5-8 students from the same school. If a college's top thirty applicants were all graduating from the same high school, the college would never take them all. They would reject 15-20 of those applicants and accept lesser-qualified applicants from other schools.

Similarly, colleges do not want all their admitted students from the same state. Every year, top applicants from New York, New Jersey, Connecticut, Pennsylvania, Massachusetts, and California are rejected in favor of lesser-quali-fied applicants from states that are barely represented in the applicant pool—the Dakotas, Wyoming, Idaho, Nebraska. (I should note that colleges would deny this statement because they include being from an under-represented state as a higher qualification than being from, say, New York. These college would argue that Bob from Montana may be more qualified than Jim from Long Island pre-cisely because Bob is from Montana.) Over half of a recent Harvard class was from the Northeast. You think Harvard likes that? I know they don't-they are looking for Bob from Montana and, everything else being equal, would admit Bob from Montana over Jim from Long Island.

Nearly every top college will try to admit students from at least 30 states (at minimum); anything less is a failure. However, most of the top college applicants in this country live in about a dozen states, so inevitably colleges must make deci-sions about geography versus academic success. Northeastern colleges are the most aggressive in recruiting students from outside the Northeast; therefore, it's most difficult for a student in the Northeast to be admitted to a Northeastern college. If you're in the Northeast, it is imperative that you consider colleges outside the area (and preferably outside the mid-Atlantic states too). Take a look at Wake Forest, Washington & Lee, Davidson, Tulane, Vanderbilt, the University of the South, Northwestern, U. Chicago, Kenyon, Reed, Pomona, and Rice. There are many more good colleges outside of the Northeast, and in many cases, you could be admitted to a better college outside the Northeast than you would within. For example: if you attend a good high school in the Northeast, how many students do you know who are applying to Penn? Cornell? Boston College? NYU? Chances are you know a dozen or more students who are applying to Penn. Now how many are applying to Washington and Lee? Perhaps none. Would you rather be the only student from your high school applying to a college or one of eight applying? This advice generally only applies to private colleges. Most public colleges have in-state quotas, making the out-of-state admissions rate very competitive. Nevertheless, there are some public colleges that are worth applying to even if you are out-of-state because they are extremely good; University of Virginia, the College of William and Mary, and UNC-Chapel Hill are all very difficult to get accepted to as an out-of-state applicant, but they may be better than the in-state public or private colleges to which you are applying. (If you're in the Northeast, those three public colleges are better than any public college you could apply to in-state.)

All applicants should consider colleges outside the region in which they live. This is difficult for students on the East Coast. Only about 15 of the 100 best non-specialized colleges in this country are west of the Mississippi, which means that almost every good college is in the East. Of the roughly thirty top colleges in America, only six—the Air Force Academy, Cal Tech, Stanford, Rice, U. Chicago and Northwestern—aren't on the East Coast.

In particular, you should consider inland colleges, as applicants tend to be attracted to the coasts. Few inland colleges, with the noticeable exceptions of U. Michigan and U. Colorado-Boulder, attract considerable interest from students outside the region. I know very few students from the Northeast, South, or West who would consider attending college in Ohio or Illinois, but both states have great colleges that are interested in attracting a diverse group of applicants. So if you're from New Jersey, New York, or Connecticut, and Yale and Columbia look a little intimidating, you should try U. Chicago, which will be more interested in a New Yorker than Columbia will. Some good colleges in the Midwest include U. Chicago (one of the best schools in the country), Hillsdale, Northwestern, Kenyon, Notre Dame, Case Western Reserve, Oberlin, Wheaton, and Grinnell. Now I bet that you probably didn't think there were that many good colleges in the Midwest. (Two Midwest asides: There's Cornell College in Mount Vernon, Iowa which is actually twelve years older than Cornell University in upstate New York. So the original Cornell is in Iowa! And there's God's Bible College in Cincinnati. For some reason I suspect that if God were to found a college, Cincinnati wouldn't be the first choice.)

The other side to geography is your high school: do many students from your high school apply to top colleges? If the answer is yes, then your chances of being admitted to a top college are a little more difficult. That's the great irony of attending a great high school: you want to attend a great high school so you can take tough classes (like APs) and impress colleges with your course work, but if a dozen students from your school are applying to Penn, your chances are worse. But remember that the majority of students accepted to top colleges nevertheless attend top high schools (and disproportionately attend private schools); contrarily, just because no one from your school intends to apply to a top college doesn't mean you will be admitted to Yale.

However, colleges love good applicants from bad high schools. Let me repeat that: colleges love good applicants from bad schools. So if your high school is awful, that's actually an advantage for you. You must take the most difficult classes offered, earn great grades, do well on the SAT IIs, and engage in extracurricular activities. Admissions officers recognize and value a student who excels despite the odds, which is why, for example, the Ivies take note when a student applies from a Chicago public school (a notoriously awful school system). Many top colleges will go years without seeing a single applicant from a Chicago public school. So if you are stuck in a bad public school, use it to you advantage: do the best you can and aim high.

Transfer to a Top Boarding Prep School for your Junior and Senior Year. Perhaps in seeming contradiction to what I stated above, colleges love graduates of top boarding schools. Why? Many reasons, one of which is the obvious academic rigor that top prep schools require of their students. The other reason is the level of maturity required of students at boarding schools. Such students live away from their parents (as you will in college), must organize their days without parental supervision (as you must in college), and spend every hour, academic and social, in a campus setting (as you do in college). It's understandable that colleges are attracted to these students: they are already tested and have already proven themselves capable of succeeding in a college—like atmosphere. Many students attend a top boarding school starting in 10th or 11th grade to gain this advantage; in truth, whether or not it's an advantage will depend on your specific situation. If you're a great student, chances are your current high school counselor will advise you not to transfer (because the counselor wants you to apply from her high school). You should seek the advice of an independent counselor, and discuss your situation with the principal or counselor from the boarding school you are considering.

Transfer to Podunk High. Some students (and parents) concoct crazy plans to transfer to remote high schools with the notion that applying to a top college will be easier. Once again, admissions offices deny—but this strategy works. If the high school is remote (the high plains of South Dakota), and few students apply to college, then your chances of getting into a top college are better than if you were attending a good suburban school. Of course, it would be silly to leave friends (and possibly family) merely to gain a slight edge, but if knowing the answer aids your decision, then the answer is yes. Podunk High applicants are favored over grads from good suburban schools. As always, you still need the great grades and test scores.

Have Your Favorite Senator/CEO/Pope Write a Nice Letter of Recommendation. Many students know someone famous, powerful, or notorious who might put in a good word. This idea is not recommended for two reasons. First, unless the person really knows you, the recommendation will be a very transparent attempt to apply pressure or impress the admissions committee. Admission officers are expert at recognizing these Gilded Recommendations (shiny on the outside, cheap on the inside). Second, most admissions committees (and especially deans) respond quite negatively to being pressured. Some admissions deans at top colleges have been known to write nasty letters to the applicant or writer of the recommendation informing him that such a recommendation is useless and, in fact, counter-productive. So a Gilded Recommendation may hurt you more than help you. (Please remember; it's always so tempting to get Mr. Bigshot to fax an aggressive letter of recommendation to Princeton, but I can assure you that Princeton will probably be more annoyed than impressed.) Follow the advice in the chapter on recommendations, and you will be fine. The only thing that matters when choosing a person to write your recommendation is how well he or she knows you, not what he or she does for a living.

Have Your Parent Write a Letter. If you think this idea is a good one, then I have one question for you: What planet are you from? Despite the fact that this is a patently awful idea, I know of many admissions officers who receive nice letters from parents who would like to inform the admissions committee of all of their lovely son's achievements (he's such a nice boy, he really is). It seems that some parents just can't help themselves. If your parents might be inclined to write a letter, be firm with them. Remove all paper from the house if necessary. A letter from parents often sets off a little alarm for admissions officers; they don't want to deal with unstable parents, and unstable parents may indicate an unstable child. Parents should not contact admissions offices at all unless the office contacts the parents first. At its core, the admission process is a dialogue between the applicant (the student) and the dean of admissions. Others only get involved when necessary.

Call Incessantly. You should call an admissions office while you're considering the college, investigating your options, and thinking about your choices. But once you've applied to the college, you should not call unless you're invited to do so. You should not call; your parents should not call; your parent's friends (who are alumni) should not call. Incessantly calling is an irritant. Admissions offices are not equipped to deal with numerous phone calls once the applications start rolling in; I know it may be tempting to pick up the phone and put in a good word for yourself or ask about the status of your application, but patience is a virtue. If you wish to know the status of your application, you should check the college's web site (many post the status online), call the college's status hotline (many have a specific automated phone line dedicated to providing status information, usually accessible with your social security number), or ask your high school counselor to call. The only person permitted to call an admissions office to check on the status of an application is you, your high school counselor, vice principal, or principal. (As an aside, some special recruits—athletes, minorities, musicians—will have special contacts within the college they can call to inquire about their applications. This contact is okay, but you must be sure that your contact doesn't mind a phone call.)

Take Classes At the College. Many colleges offer classes over the summer or special classes/programs during the academic year for high school students. It seems obvious that such classes would help one's chances of getting admitted, but they don't help much. Taking such a class does show your interest in the college, but so does visiting the college and requesting an interview. It also depends on where you're applying and to which programs you're applying. Less selective colleges and highly specialized programs do tend to favor students who have taken classes at the college. For example, if you apply as an intended English major to Harvard, no summer classes will aid your chances of being admitted. However, if you intend on being a veterinarian, then perhaps summer classes at Tufts will help. If your intended major is specialized, colleges like to know that you actually know something about that specialization. If you want to be a veterinarian, your application should show more than simply your love of animals; you should have some veterinary experience before you claim that you want to be one. So taking a veterinary summer program for high school students will corroborate your intended major.

In most cases, though, participating in an open-admission program at a top college will not particularly help your application. Of all the things that you can do with four weeks and $4,000, summer programs at colleges are low on the list (but much better than summer camps). If you're going to take a summer program,

I suggest taking one in a foreign country. Many universities offer programs for high school students in Europe and the Caribbean.

Apply Online, with Software, or In-person. There are many different ways to apply to college: the college's own paper application, a web site, software that prints or e-mails the application, the Common Application, and so forth. While almost everything is easier than using the college's own paper application, no college will admit you because you applied the easy way. In fact, despite what colleges claim, top colleges prefer that you use their own paper application for an obvious reason: applicants who take the time and effort to complete the college's own paper application are usually more interested in the college than applicants who use other, easier, applications, such as the Common Application. Students who use software or the Common Application often use the admissions process like a lottery, applying to 15-20 colleges assuming that the more colleges they apply to, the more likely they are be get lucky and get admitted to one. If you wish to impress top colleges, then apply using their own paper applications. I know it's a pain, but it will show that you spent the time and energy to research and apply to that particular college. And studies show that top colleges do, in fact, accept more applicants who applied using the college's own paper application than those who used common or software-generated applications.

The one caveat to the above advice is that some colleges only use the Common Application, such as Boston College. Although BC also uses a proprietary secondary application, they require all students to file an initial application using the Common Application. Obviously, in this case you must use the Common Application.

The same advice holds true for filing online: most top colleges view applicants more favorably if they apply using the old-fashioned paper application (though they usually won't admit it). There are a few colleges, particularly large public universities such U. Michigan and the U. California system that actually prefer electronic applications. These colleges, none of which are top colleges, prefer electronic Internet applications because they process applications like McDonald's makes hamburgers: they have a predetermined system that they apply consistently to every normal applicant. In these few cases, you may use the Internet application, but be forewarned: applying online can lead to innumerable headaches from lost, corrupted, or misdirected applications so keep copies, printouts, and notes of everything! If you apply electronically, you should receive confirmation from the college; if you don't, then contact the college to find out if they received everything. In most cases, such colleges are not "top" picks, so applying to your safety using the web shouldn't be cause for much worry.

As noted in a previous chapter, the College Board offers a program called ExPAN that allows you to search through colleges, send a letter of inquiry and apply using the Common Application via computer. It's quick. It's easy. It's the wrong way to conduct a college search. If "quick" and "easy" are priorities to you, then college may not be right for you (a bachelor degree is neither quick nor easy). You are about to spend four years and $100,000+on one of the most important parts of your life; take your time, take the slow and hard route, and do it right. You should look through college guides and view books, contact colleges yourself (not through some automated computer program), and apply using their own applications. The assembly-line approach will lead to poor decisions and poor applications.

Some applicants drive to the college to drop off their application in person. This makes sense if you live near the college; otherwise, it neither hurts nor helps. In addition, colleges have somewhat complex systems for receiving and processing applications that assume that the application will arrive via mail, so dropping it off in person may actually slow the processing of your application.

Send a Portfolio of Artwork, a Video of Sport Performances or other unusual items. Many special departments require portfolios (art, music), and if you're a special admit, then you may be required to include unusual items (i.e. if you're being recruited). If you are not applying to a special program or applying as a special admit, then you should not include unusual items unless they are truly spectacular. (Often, you can gauge if something is spectacular by observing other students at your high school; if you know other students who can send in similar unusual items, then they probably aren't spectacular.)

You should not send unusual items with your application unless you're required. Admissions offices do not want to wade through audiotapes and videotapes, portfolios and floppy disks full of evidence of talent or skill. Most top colleges are reasonably assured that you are talented, and do not wish to evaluate your talent for themselves—the process is time-consuming and not particularly helpful.

If you truly have a spectacular talent or skill, then include evidence of it. But you must get the approval of a college admissions professional first; he will be able to evaluate for you if your unusual item warrants inclusion.

Chapter 33

Last Minutes Tips for Seniors

"I bought flowers for all my teachers.
Spent like $300. I hope it was worth it."

If you're a senior and only have a few months to apply to college, here are some last-minute tips for you.

1. Kiss your counselor's butt! Your counselor will write a recommendation for you; perhaps he has a poor opinion of you, and perhaps you can turn that opinion around with a few weeks of hard work. Talk to your counselor often, appear very interested in college, ask questions, and take his or her advice.

2. Kiss your teachers' butts! Same as above. A few weeks of hard work may significantly improve a teacher's opinion of you.

3. Show great interest in the colleges. Most colleges believe student interest and motivation is almost as important as grades, test scores, and extracurricular activities. In fact, some colleges (Connecticut College, Emory) will reject students simply because they didn't seem that interested, even though they were otherwise very qualified. Colleges assume most students can do the work—prove to them that you really want to do the work! Apply early decision or early action, visit the college twice, visit classes, stay overnight, do a tour, do an interview, visit a professor or two, talk to a coach or two, write thank-you notes to everyone involved (tour guides, professors, deans, everyone!).

4. Write a very unique essay. Go out on a limb. Hire someone to help you. A great essay can push you over.

5. Apply to a college far away from you, declare a strange major, be different (in a good way).

6. Apply as early as you can, and make the application very neat.

7. Talk to professors and coaches at the college so that you can get a professor or coach to recommend you.

Chapter 34

College Directories

"My friend had that Barrons' book and handed it to
me but it slipped and fell on my foot. I had to go to the doctor.
I'm not making that up—that book weighs about thirty pounds."

Backroom deals. Many years ago when I was a new manager at Princeton Review, I was assigned to represent the company at a convention of admissions officers. The hotel was filled with a thousand admissions officers from colleges all over the country. Around 8am on the first day of the convention, an admissions officer from a small, private college cornered me in the hallway leading to the main convention floor and asked, "How much does it cost to be in your book?"

I was obviously confused. "To be listed in your college guides," he continued. "I can get a check to you by tomorrow. I just need to know how much. We need to be in that *best colleges* book." I was very perplexed. What was he talking about? I didn't think I was at the convention to collect payments. I was a new employee, but I didn't think Princeton Review asked for payments to be listed in college guides. And yet I felt bad for this college admissions officer; he was so eager to give me money. I smiled and told him that I'd get back to him, and then I went to discover the truth of the matter.

There are myriad college directories on the market—Barron's, Kaplan, Princeton Review, Peterson's...the list goes on. Most of them look like and are as useful as telephone books. They give the name, address and phone number of the college (like a telephone book), and sometimes they give you a little more. Which college guide is best?

Most major college guides have at least one of three things in common: they are compiled by a database; they take money from the colleges they review; they are affiliated with a specific college. So what does this process mean to you?

Computers say the craziest things. First, books that are compiled by a database are known for their mistakes—computers cannot catch a mistake. For example, both Kaplan's and Princeton Review's college guides have contained some of the most outrageous mistakes you could think of (listing colleges as "most competitive" when in fact they aren't competitive at all; listing colleges as "all black" when, in fact, they are 90%+white and Asian; printing erroneous admissions statistics). As you can probably tell, these sorts of mistakes can cause you to make bad college decisions. When a computer is responsible for writing the book, mistakes large and small aren't discovered and corrected. Unfortunately, you pay the price for these blunders.

These "computer-written" college directories often contain outrageous mistakes, and they almost always contain myriad minor mistakes. For example, one states that the company that writes the SAT is the "Education Testing Service" (it's not), and another claims that SAT stands for "Scholastic Assessment Test" (it doesn't). These errors may seem small, but they certainly make one wonder about the quality of the information contained therein.

Money talks. Second, nearly all major college directory companies from Peterson's to the Princeton Review accept money from colleges; in fact, they solicit money from colleges, and in many cases, the more a college pays, the bigger and better the write-up. Often, the "review" you read about the college is, in fact, written by the college. This pay-for-play scheme explains why you won't find some colleges listed in a directory; for example, Peterson's recent guide contains no in-depth listing for Georgetown University because Georgetown didn't pay. The lesson here is simple: most college guides are not independent reviewers and do not publish objective reports. Most guides are just like the telephone directory for businesses: if you pay, you're published. You can't trust any guide that takes money from colleges.

The Objective College Directory by the Staff of Bob's College. Third, there are a few college guides that do not request payment in order to be listed and are not compiled by a mindless computer; however, most of these guides are affiliated with a specific college, which doesn't exactly make for an objective publication! It's difficult to trust a college guide that is published by a college (or one of its organizations).

As up-to-date as a Roman toga. The one other little secret of the college directory world is that most of the non-statistical information is not updated each year. So when you buy the latest edition of a college guide, you may notice that the surveys and narrative reviews are exactly the same as they were in the previous year's guide. Many college guides only update their survey and narrative descriptions/reviews once every 2-4 years. So that amusing little survey you're looking at may be from 3-year-old information!

So it's hard to trust college directories because most are written by mindless computers, take money from colleges, and/or are affiliated with a specific college.

Such guides tend to be riddled with mistakes and rarely contain objective information. So what should you do?

Until a truly objective, error-free guide is published, your only option is to purchase a few guides. If you constantly check a college's information in 2-3 guides, you will be able to catch erroneous information. Which 2-3 guides should you buy? It doesn't matter.

You should buy a college guide as soon as possible so you can be sure that you have the minimum number of courses required to even apply to a top college. All public high schools require fewer classes to graduate than colleges require to apply. So if you graduate from a public school with the minimum number of required classes, you will not have the basic required classes to apply to a top college. I know many students who have effectively disqualified themselves from applying to a top college by their sophomore year in high school simply because they were not aware of the minimum requirements for applying to a top college.

When you look up a college in a guide, notice that median and mean SAT scores and grades are typically reported. If a college reports an average SAT score of 1300, that means that half of the students admitted had a score lower than 1300. (In most cases, those students had something else that was above average to balance out their below-average SATs). In fact, Ivy League colleges admit students with scores below 1200! While they are typically recruited students (minorities, athletes), the point is that the grades, SAT scores, and other numbers reported to the college guides are averages; you don't necessarily need to hit every number to be admitted. Here are a few reasons why the numbers in college guides should not necessarily discourage you from applying.

Self-reported, self-massaged, self-aggrandizing. College directories reflect another dark secret of the admissions world: colleges may exclude any student they wish when reporting SAT scores. (Remember, colleges are largely unregulated.) Many colleges exclude foreign students, minorities, recruited athletes, art students, legatees, or any other group who is lowering the average SAT score. Some colleges report the average score of admitted students instead of matriculated students. Why is this problematic? Do you think Villanova would admit an applicant with 1500 on the SAT and a 4.0 GPA in ten AP classes? Of course. Do you think that student actually attends Villanova? No, she goes to Penn (who would also admit an applicant with a 1500 and a 4.0). Villanova may choose to report the average SAT score and GPA of "admitted" students, which would include that 1500 and 4.0, or Villanova may choose to report the SAT score and GPA of matriculated (enrolled) students, which would not include that 1500 and 4.0. Obviously most schools report admitted students (as long as they don't get in trouble) because those numbers are much higher; and just as obvious is that those numbers don't reflect the students who actually attend the college. In effect, a single applicant's 1500 SAT score and 4.0 GPA may be reported by several colleges under "SAT" and "GPA" in those college directories! (Think about it: the top student in your high school probably applies to ten colleges but only enrolls at one college. The other nine colleges may also report her high SAT scores and grades as "average SAT scores and GPA" simply because she applied.) Just keep in mind that many colleges report SAT scores and average GPAs that are actually much higher than the average SAT score and GPA of students who actually attend the college.

Many colleges now report ranges. For example, a college may report that the SAT scores for the 25th-75th percentile of admitted students was 1200-1300. But even this means that about 25% of students admitted score below a 1200. Similarly, a college may report that 80% of admitted students were in the top 10% of their graduating class. This statistic sounds a little intimidating. It means that 20% of admitted students were not in the top 10% of their admitted class. So if everything else is average (grades, SAT scores, etc.), then you need to be in the top 10% of your class. But if you're above-average in one category, you may be able to be below-average in another category and still be admitted. The bottom line: don't get discouraged by the numbers in college guides.

A college guide should always be a starting point, not a deciding point. If you spend thirty hours investigating a college (view book, web site, talk to friends, campus visit), not more than ten minutes should be spent using college guides for the college.

Chapter 35

Test Prep Courses & Books

"I took a prep course because everyone else did.
I figured I should at least show up so if I get a 900
I won't feel as bad because, you know, I tried."

You must prepare for the SAT. Colleges and many high schools dislike expensive test prep programs for one reason: they work. Because prep programs raise SAT scores, many colleges and high schools think these courses provide an unfair advantage. Independent studies from Harvard and Penn to Roper Starch and other auditing firms consistently show that commercial SAT prep programs raise scores by 100 or more points. Since many colleges put so much weight on test scores, 100 points can really help.

There are many ways to prepare. I've helped over 10,000 students prepare for the PSAT and SAT, and I've written SAT prep courses for commercial companies, so I'm going to let you in on a few secrets.

Books and Software. Most students buy some sort of SAT prep book or software (by "software" I'm including Internet-based preparation). Using software or the Internet to prepare for the SAT is a waste of time and money; the SAT is a paper-and-pencil test, so you should practice with "paper-and-pencil" test-taking techniques. If you practice online, you will develop techniques that simply don't translate to a paper-based test. If you prepare for the SAT using software or online, you will leave 30-60 points on the table. Let me be clear: test prep companies heavily market software and online prep because they are highly profitable, and many students prepare using software because it's more entertaining than a book. Regardless of how entertaining a software program is, it will not raise your score as much as a book will. If a book will raise your SAT score 60 points, software will raise it by 30 points. Which do you want?

SAT prep software and books have one significant problem: they are boring. Most teenagers need to be motivated in order to prepare for the SAT. If you're a highly motivated student and can prepare yourself for very boring tests, then you should purchase a SAT prep book. SAT prep books are about $800 less than most courses and just as effective if you're highly motivated. If you're anything less than highly motivated, then you need a prep seminar/course or private tutoring. I estimate that about 95% of all students need a seminar/course or private tutoring; for those students, SAT prep books and software mostly go unused.

Which SAT prep book is best? The answer may surprise you, but most SAT techniques are the same. The difference isn't the techniques; it's the presentation. Most of the techniques in Kaplan's and The Princeton Review's test prep books are the same as the techniques in The College Board's *10 Real SATs*. Of course, getting SAT prep advice from ETS is like getting tax tips from the IRS: the information is okay, but they're not exactly going to give you the best tips. There are other companies that publish test prep books, but none of them are worth mentioning. Many of them actually teach you how to solve problems that aren't even on the SAT! So stick with Kaplan, Princeton Review, and the College Board.

Usually, I would recommend The Princeton Review's *Cracking the SAT*, but the most recent edition contains so many errors that I can no longer recommend it. Some of the errors actually render certain parts of the book useless. The book hasn't changed much in ten years and the older editions actually contain fewer errors—so the book has actually grown worse with age. My advice is to buy either Kaplan's or Princeton's book along with the College Board's book. The bottom line: don't use software or online prep to prepare—you will cheat yourself out of 30-60 points! Buy a book from Kaplan/Princeton Review and the College Board if you are highly motivated. You will need to spend about six hours per week for 2-3 weeks to prepare using a book.

Courses. There are many PSAT and SAT prep courses and seminars, ranging from 3-hour school programs to 50-hour courses. Some are expensive; others are cheap. Which are best?

The College Board released a study a few years ago that showed what most people know: short, cheap prep courses offered by high schools are useless. On average, a student improves from one SAT to the next by about 20 points by doing nothing. A cheap ($50-$140) prep course offered by your high school will improve your score by about 40 points. You're better off saving your money and simply buying a book. (As an aside, most high schools claim that SAT prep courses don't work because their own prep courses don't work. They ignore the fact that high school teachers are not SAT professionals and cannot teach SAT courses.)

The standard commercial SAT prep course is 5-8 weeks in length and about 30 hours of teaching. Many of these courses will add another 20 (or so) hours of testing to that, bringing the total number of hours to about 50. These courses typically cost $800 to $1000 and are offered 5-8 weeks prior to each major administration of the SAT. They tend to be significant commitments of time. Independent studies show that these courses raise most scores by 90-140 points. The major players in the 5-8 week course business are Kaplan and Princeton Review; each prepare tens-of-thousands of students each year.

Kaplan is a bottom-line driven division of the publicly-traded Washington Post Company. So the same company that owns Kaplan also owns many newspapers, Score! (which primarily tutors young children), *Newsweek* magazine, and several other ventures. As a public company, their primary responsibility is to their shareholders. Princeton Review is a public company with franchises. Some of the Princeton Review locations are owned by the management company (i.e. Chicago and Atlanta), while other locations are owned by independent franchisees (i.e. Florida, Connecticut, parts of New York). Princeton Review franchises are owned/divided by county, so many states such as New York, California and Ohio are owned and operated by multiple franchisees. Princeton Review franchisees have a lot of freedom in what programs they offer, how they market, their pricing and their policies (which is why you can have two very different experiences at two different Princeton Review offices).

Kaplan tends to be much more highly centralized, whereas you will find a wide variety of courses, prices and policies with the Princeton Review depending on which franchise you contact. On the whole, Kaplan tends to be more organized and integrated. They behave like a division of a large conglomerate (which they are). The Princeton Review is a smaller, more localized organization; this can be both good and bad. This local administration can be good because some franchises better adapt to their local markets; it can be bad because the quality of the program can vary widely from franchise to franchise.

Both Kaplan and Princeton hire the same type of teacher: usually a 20- to 30-year-old with some college experience but no teaching experience, heavily trained and paid $10-$15 per hour. Both companies boast of the extensive training they require of their teachers; of course, both programs must extensively train their teachers because they hire mostly cheap, young, inexperienced people who wish to make a little extra money at night and on weekends. Your Kaplan or Princeton SAT teacher may only be a few years older that you!

It is a myth that these companies are "education" companies. They are simply businesses and do what they do in order to make money. Kaplan is notoriously filled with MBA-types, not educators. Although Princeton Review tends to have more of an education-oriented reputation, you should not assume that all Princeton Review teachers and administrators are college graduates. In fact, their top SAT franchisee never graduated from college, their top NJ/NY/CT trainer (the person who trains their SAT teachers) never graduated from college, and another top trainer/teacher barely broke 1200 on the SAT. So their claims of hiring only "top college graduates" and "top scorers" are simply not true.

How can you be assured a prep program will work? References are okay, but many premium tutoring programs do not offer references because their clients do not wish to be used for marketing purposes, while some larger course companies pay students to act as references. The best way to be assured of a program's quality is to look for a good guarantee. In general, a seminar or course prep program should guarantee100 or more points, and private tutoring should guarantee 150 or more points. In most cases, the guarantee will require that the student attend the seminar/classes and complete the work. You will typically be required to provide copies of the actual scores and perhaps need to return the materials in order to qualify for the guarantee. Regardless of the details, you should look for a good guarantee.

Chapter 36

Frequently Asked Questions

"The application fee is $65. Will it help if I write the check for $150?"

1. Why do private colleges cost so much? Colleges cost so much because they spend as if there was no limit to their revenue, and they ignore costs because of massive government underwriting of loans. Any idiot can get $40,000+in government-subsidized loans. Why must the government subsidize loans? Who else will loan an unemployed 17-year-old $15,000? No one in her right mind would saddle a 21-year-old with $30,000 in debt and seriously expect it to be repaid. Given this, it should not prove surprising that student loans are often unpaid. It's irresponsible for a college and the government to saddle a 21-year-old with $30,000 of debt in the first place.

So somewhere between massive over-spending and easy access to more money through government loans and grants is the fiscal irresponsibility that causes tuitions to increase annually and to increase far more than inflation.

2. My grades and/or test scores are well-below the college's average. What should I do to maximize my chances of being admitted? Your recommendations must be great. Your recommendations and activity list should exhibit some major commitment and achievement outside of school. You should highlight this achievement. Your essay must be outstanding. Your grade trend should be improving (9th through 12th grade) as your courses increase in difficulty. And you must be able to convince the admissions office that you would significantly contribute to the college's community. Most students who are admitted with below-average grades and test scores are either recruited or have extraordinary talents recognized on a regional or national level. If you're in the below-average category, your real chance of getting admitted lies in offering the college something significant outside of academics (i.e. you're a world-class violinist). If you only offer your academic side, and your academic side is below average, then you will probably be rejected.

3. My grades and test scores are above average. Why would a college reject me? You may be rejected if anything on your application is particularly awful (your essay, interview, recommendations) or if you show no signs of life outside of the classroom. You may also be rejected if your essay or recommendations bring up any taboo subjects in a negative way—for example, if you come across as racist, misogynistic, or crude. You may also be rejected if you have a serious disciplinary problem. Colleges have no interest in admitting students who they believe will be problematic. If you do have something obvious on your record, such as a major infraction of the honor code, you must address it. In these cases, you should work with your parents and counselor to formulate the best approach, but if a college will see something negative, then you must assuage their concerns.

4. My grades and test scores are completely average. What can I do to stand out? First, your grade trend should be improving and your course work should be continually increasing in difficulty. You should do as many academic activities as possible to show that although your academics aren't great, you are committed to them. (Do academic summer camps, night classes, weekend community college courses, and so forth.) Take some significant leadership roles within your school and highlight them on your application. And finally, be sure to illustrate in your essay how you enjoy school and learning. Academically mediocre students are often rejected because the admissions office gets the impression that they don't really enjoy school.

5. I attend a magnet school. Doesn't that help me, and can't my grades be lower? The short answer is no. If you attend a magnet school, you will still need an average grade of B or higher in academic courses, and you may only have one (maybe two) Cs on your transcript. Regardless of how difficult your high school is, you may not have many grades of B- or lower. There are a great number of schools, both public and private, that offer courses as or more difficult than those courses offered at magnet or honors schools. If you attend a school with an IB program, then colleges will rely heavily on your IB test scores. Being in an IB program is great, but you still need to score 5 or higher on your tests in order to get credit for them. If you can't manage a grade of B or higher (or IB scores of 5 or higher), then you should transfer to an easier program.

6. I'm a "gifted" student. Do colleges treat me differently? If you have a large number of AP scores of 4 or 5, IB test scores of 5 or higher, or an IB diploma, then most colleges will treat you differently. Colleges usually allow gifted students to complete their undergraduate studies early. A few top colleges, including Yale, allow gifted students in some subjects to complete their bachelor degree work in three years and complete their master degree work in a fourth year. They graduate with their class as they normally would, but they receive a master instead of a bachelor degree. At Harvard, students with an IB diploma enter as a sophomore.

Usually, I don't recommend this route. If you can complete all the work required for a B.A. and an M.A. in just four years, then you're probably working too hard. The college experience is only 50% academic; the other half is social. If you have a lot of time on your hands go to the opera, start a rock band or write a novel. Many students who push themselves too hard end up regretting it later.

7. Why do TAs exists? Where did they come from? Teaching assistants (TAs) are the migrant workers of the university. They are graduate students, usually 22-28 years old, who teach undergraduate classes in exchange for reduced tuition or small payments (typically called a stipend, not a salary). Most TAs teach 2-6 classes per year and are paid $9,000 to $14,000 per year (in total). Most large colleges such as New York University, Yale, and Harvard, replace professors with TAs simply because TAs are much cheaper (a professor will make about $95,000 per year—about $80,000 more than a TA). By using fewer professors, colleges can run their undergraduate classes more profitably. Many larger universities, such as NYU, employ more than 1,000 teaching assistants to teach classes in place of professors. TAs are most prevalent at large public universities. When TAs were "invented" about thirty years ago, they did not teach classes—they only corrected papers and took attendance. But colleges realized that they could save millions of dollars by hiring TAs instead of professors. Unfortunately, colleges do not pass this savings on to you. The cost of attending college has significantly surpassed inflation annually for the past thirty years despite the tremendous growth in the use of TAs. By my estimation, NYU saves about $55 million per year by using TAs, and yet they have significantly raised their tuition every year for decades.

8. I didn't get admitted, and my dad wants to write an angry letter. Should he? Often, when a student ranked #20 at a high school is admitted and a student ranked #4 from the same school is rejected, the parents of the higher ranked student want to call the college and inquire as to the details of their child's rejection. More often, your father simply wants to yell at someone. Your father should write an angry letter only if he wants an angry letter in return. You should write a letter that says, "Thank you for considering me—I'm sure that assessing all those applications was a difficult process." Writing a nice letter is the mature thing to do. If your father wants to write an angry letter, tell him to write one to your local public university to complain about the quality of public education. If your father (or mother) wishes to inquire about the details of why you were rejected, you should know that admissions offices won't provide such details (for fear of law suits). They will be vague. Finally, if admissions offices did respond to your father with details, they would probably say things your father doesn't want to hear, such as "Your kid is boring and very commonplace," or "We really wanted to admit him but he seems like such a nerd." In most cases, you don't want to know the truth.

9. I don't want to give out my social security number. Technically and legally, no one should use your social security number except the Social Security Administration and your employer (and others related to your employment). Lawyers will tell you that you should not give out your social security number to anyone but employers. However, most colleges use your social security number (SSN) for identification purposes. This is illegal, but no one is doing anything about it. So if a college requires a social security number, then either give them your SSN or don't attend that college. If all else fails, you can apply for and use a personal Tax I.D. number (which is used in place of a SSN).

10. Why don't top colleges award financial aid based on merit? A few top colleges offer merit-based financial aid, particularly to minorities. But generally, top colleges do not need to offer merit-based awards because they already attract the top applicants. Merit-based awards are used by colleges to lure top students. The bulk of merit-based financial aid awarded at colleges comes from mid-level colleges that are aggressively trying to improve the quality of applicants (U. Miami and U. Richmond come to mind). So if you're looking for some money for your 3.9 GPA and 1440 SAT scores, don't look to the top colleges—aim for the mid-level colleges.

11. I hear Ivies don't give athletic scholarships—is that true? Technically, this is true. The Ivy Group agreement prohibits any Ivy Group college from offering an applicant money based on the applicant's athletic skill; all financial awards must be "need based." However, this is mostly good public relations. There are federal and institutional methodologies for determining how much financial aid an applicant "needs," but colleges may use any methodology they choose. For example, Princeton recently altered its formula in a significant way that will result in massive increases in the amount of aid they award. They permit applicants to exclude their parents' real estate equity in determining net worth.

The different methodologies that Ivies use usually result in a $5,000 to $14,000 variance in the amount of financial aid you will receive over four years. In addition, all colleges have various scholarships and grants that aren't necessarily need-based but also aren't technically considered "financial aid." So how much will you get? It depends on how desirable you are. Although Ivies are technically bound to use the same financial aid formula for all admitted students, it's been my experience that they always find a way to offer a large amount of "aid" to highly desirable students. Colleges always have reasonable-sounding explanations for this, but the bottom line is that every college will find a way to offer money to highly desirable applicants.

It should be noted that if an Ivy gives a financial aid award that seems to be a breach of the Ivy contract, a coach from another Ivy can challenge the award. So Ivies can be very aggressive unless someone complains. (Similarly, the AI is a "standard," but an Ivy can admit a student below the standard if the other colleges approve the decision.) If you are highly desirable and you inform an Ivy of your financial aid award from a non-Ivy, the Ivy will match the offer. So if Swarthmore, Williams, Amherst, or Bowdoin offers you $X to attend their college, an Ivy will try to offer you $X+1 if it finds you highly desirable.

As an aside, you should know that the Ivies cannot communicate with each other regarding financial aid, so one college won't know what another college has offered you. As a result, colleges are very competitive with financial aid (and why so many were irked to discover Princeton's latest maneuver which will allow Princeton to offer more financial aid to its applicants).

A recent example puts this into perspective. In August 2000, the Ivy Group heavily sanctioned Brown University for financial aid violations. In consistent and blatant violation of the Ivy Group agreement, Brown had been promising and arranging financial aid from outside foundations for particularly desirable applicants. These applicants included recruited athletes for Brown's football, women's volleyball, men's basketball and soccer teams. This special financial aid was specifically offered to highly desirable athletes; other students could not apply for it. The Ivy Group stripped Brown's football team of ten recruits over the next two years, limited Brown's contact with prospective athletes, and banned the director of the Brown Sports Foundation from having any contact with any athletes or potential athletes. The ultimate slap in the face, however, was the Ivy Group's decision to ban Brown's football team from competing in the Ivy League championship the following year. Brown, of course, was a bit taken aback by the severity of the Ivy Group's decision. Brown could have used Shakespeare's line in addressing the Group's decision—*the lady doth protest too much, methinks.*

12. What about all those college rankings? College rankings, such as those reported in *U.S. News*, are entirely useless. Take a look at what they use to rank colleges: admissions rates, graduation rates, and reputation. As noted earlier, admissions and graduation rates are reported by colleges and easily manipulated. Student-to-faculty ratios are grossly manipulated by colleges. And reputation? This is about as useful as those "Best Party College" surveys. What does the dean of one college know about the quality of teaching at a college he's never even visited? Another sign of the dubiousness of the "reputation" survey is that fewer than 2,700 people were surveyed in regards to about 1,300 colleges. That's about two people per college—not exactly a good sample of people.

U.S. News also seems weigh "alumni giving" because, they claim, it corresponds to alumni satisfaction. This would make sense if it were true, but anyone remotely acquainted with alumni giving knows that the amount of money raised corresponds to the effectiveness of the campaign—it's about good marketing by the development and alumni offices not satisfaction. And good marketing (hence, alumni giving) is significantly determined by the wealth of a college's alumni (i.e. do your parents have money) and the popularity of a college's sports teams. So if you come from a notoriously "upper-class" college with a decent sports program, and the development office puts together a good marketing program, then (in most cases) the "alumni giving" will be high. What does that have to do with satisfaction? Nothing.

I could go on and on about the uselessness of college rankings. They are insipid, grossly inaccurate, and preposterously assuming. Most of the information is either self-reported by colleges (hence unreliable) or gathered from small-sample "surveys" and "polls." No one trusts self-reported information from an unregulated source. Surveys and polls concluded that Thomas Dewey easily won the 1948 Presidential election. (He didn't.) The idea that self-reported information and surveys can produce a definitive conclusion about anything is remarkably unsophisticated.

Finally, review the statistics that *U.S. News* publishes in its college ranking survey: student/faculty ratio, selectivity, SAT scores, alumni giving. Which statistic actually reflects the quality of the teaching (which is, in the final analysis, what you're paying for)? Where is the number that shows how many good professors are in front of small classes? There isn't one. No one has devised a decent way to measure the quality of a college's teaching. Ranking is counter-productive as it feeds off the fear and anxiety that is already all too prevalent in high schools. Who's number one? Who's number two? Who cares? Take your time. Research each college and forget about what some magazine publisher thinks is important. His primary job is to sell magazines, not help you make a good decision about which college to attend.

13. Why is college so much more difficult to get into today? In 1963, Columbia College was the undergraduate college of 2,300 men. Today, Columbia has about 1,900 men—so it has 400 fewer men today than it had 30 years ago. So today, Columbia has more male applicants for fewer freshmen openings for men. In total, Columbia has about 3,900 students today (men and women). So Columbia has only grown by 1,600 students in the past thirty years while the total number of applicants to American colleges has grown ten-fold.

And in the past, 98% of Ivy League students were American. However, of those 3,900 current Columbia students, about 400 are from foreign countries, which means that for U.S. students, Columbia has only grown from 2,250 to 3,500 in the past four decades (and the number of U.S. men at Columbia has shrunk from 2,300 to 1,700). So while the population of the country and the world is booming, the number of seats at top colleges is not booming (and, in some cases, is actually shrinking).

So getting into a college is not more difficult; getting into a *top* college is because most top colleges have not substantially increased the size of their undergraduate colleges. Many more students are attending college in the United States, but most of the growth comes from the increasing size of mediocre public colleges, not top private colleges. (And as shown above, the number of men accepted to many top colleges has actually shrunk over the past decades.) And finally, the tremendous growth of international students applying to American colleges has caused colleges to become increasingly selective; some American colleges such as NYU, Columbia, and Harvard have a very large number of international students.

14. I hear that ETS envelopes for SAT registration are often rejected by the Post Office. Is this true? A post office official recently told me that envelopes such as those provided by ETS for SAT registration are often rejected by the post office's automated sorting machines because the outside-front of the envelope contains too much writing, particularly below and around the address area. That extra writing on the envelope can cause the machine to become confused and mark the envelope "return to sender." The post office official suggested mailing the registration form in your own plain white envelope. If you mail your registration a week before it's due and the post office's machines reject it, you probably won't find out until it's too late. So either use a plain white envelope or register online.

15. I was told by an admissions officer that early decision doesn't help because the last candidate could be as strong as the first candidate, so they don't take lesser-qualified candidates during early decision. Is that true? Not true. First, the "last candidates" that top colleges get are usually disorganized, not motivated, and not that interested in the college. Second, the admissions rate for early decision applicants is often five- to ten-times as high as the admissions rate for non-recruited regular decision applicants. (Penn early decision applicants are admitted at about a 45% rate while regular non-recruited applicants are admitted at a rate of less than 10%.) Although early decision applicants tend to be of a slightly higher quality than regular decision applicants, colleges also strongly favor early decision candidates. (The only reason colleges offer early decision is they strongly favor admitting applicants early. For this reason, all colleges are interested in admitting as many qualified early decision applicants as they can.) See the chapters on the admissions process for more details.

16. I seem to have the grades and test scores the college wants, but I was rejected. Can I do anything to have a chance of getting admitted? Yes. Take a year off after graduating high school and do something outrageous: work cleaning fish on a boat off of Alaska, travel throughout the Far East, write a book, attend classes in Egypt. Chances are if you have the numbers (grades, rank, test scores) but were rejected, you probably had nothing unique on your application. Do something extraordinary, and apply again the following year.

17. Top colleges claim they admit applicants regardless of financial need. Is this true? During the early and regular admissions process, admissions officers do consider your financial situation. Ironically, the poorer you are, the better. Admissions officers require more of wealthy students than of poor students. So most top colleges do consider your financial situation, and it's to your benefit to need substantial financial assistance. The only time this isn't true is for early action/decision applicants who are deferred in December and reviewed again in April/May/June. Often, colleges will not accept applicants in May/June who need substantial financial aid because they probably will not receive the aid necessary for them to attend college. Since most financial aid is awarded on a first-come, first-served basis starting January 1, students applying for aid in June aren't likely to receive very much. With that in mind, most of the students admitted in May/June do not require much financial aid.

18. Colleges talk about a group of required courses called a "core curriculum" or "distribution requirements." I don't want to be required to take a bunch of uninteresting courses. What should I do? Don't worry. Regardless of how draconian they seem, most core curriculums are a joke. Harvard's retooled core was the talk of academia in the early 1980s, but by the late 80s it had degenerated in the same way that most cores do: there were 100+courses from which to choose and many were mind-numbingly easy to pass. Conversely, a good core curriculum is actually a part of a good education. One certainly cannot consider oneself educated if one only takes courses in a single area. Very few colleges require serious student participation in several disciplines—Columbia, U. Chicago, St. John's in Annapolis. Aside from these, you need not fear a core curriculum.

19. I'm homeschooled. How is the admissions process different for me? Most colleges are beginning to come to grips with homeschooled applicants. The statistics on homeschooled teenagers defies the dated stereotype of homeschoolers being poor, backwoods fundamentalists. On average, the parents of homeschoolers make about $15,000 more per year than the national average income of parents with children, and homeschooled children score significantly higher on standardized tests than their peers in public or private schools. The first, second, and third place winners at the 73rd Scripps Howard National Spelling Bee were homeschooled. Colleges are taking note: homeschooled applicants tend to be above-average students.

A few top colleges accept homeschooled applicants on homeschooling terms: no diploma (not even a GED), no formal transcripts and no standardized tests required. Colleges that treat homeschoolers favorably include Stanford, Clark,

Colorado College, Kenyon, Occidental, Southern Methodist, Vanderbilt, Wesleyan and Wheaton. In most cases, no formal transcript, diploma or test scores are required in order to be admitted. At many of these schools, home-schoolers are actually admitted at a higher rate than traditionally schooled children. Students typically submit a homemade transcript, a description of their studies, examples of their writing, an essay on why they chose homeschooling, and a portfolio (if helpful).

A few colleges, notably Columbia and Notre Dame, require homeschooled children to submit more than traditionally schooled children. In most cases, this entails submitting 5 or 6 SAT II scores and occasionally earning a GED. But admissions offices are always changing their guidelines for admitting home-schooled children and admissions standards are trending toward greater willingness to evaluate homeschooled applicants on their own terms (which usually means no GED or standardized tests).

If you are homeschooled, the best way to improve your application to a top college is to offer the college several above average standardized test scores. Though many top colleges require no test scores from homeschooled applicants, they always view great test scores favorably. If you can submit great SAT scores and 5-8 good SAT II and/or AP scores, then your applications will be very strong. Keep in mind two things: (1) on average, homeschooled teenagers score much higher on standardized tests than traditionally schooled children, so you shouldn't fear these tests, and (2) submitting any test scores (including SAT or ACT scores) is optional for homeschooled applicants at most colleges, so you should take these tests, send the scores only to yourself, and submit them to the colleges if they are above average.

In the end, homeschooling will slightly limit your options because a few schools do not treat homeschoolers fairly. In all cases, colleges have three primary concerns when reading an application from a homeschooled student. First, does the student have a balance between math/science and writing/literature? You will need to demonstrate that you have been exposed to high school-level literature and science. Second, does the applicant communicate well? You will need to submit writing samples that show you're a great writer. Third, does the applicant have any strange social problems? Occasionally, students are homeschooled because they don't fit in at traditional schools. While most colleges respect the independence and freedom that homeschooling offers, they are aware that a few children are homeschooled because they cannot successfully coexist with other students.

You may also want to consider Patrick Henry College in Purcellville, Virginia. This new college is designed specifically with the homeschooled, independent student in mind.

Chapter 37

Internet Sites

"I applied to USC online. I think I accidentally submitted
my application four times. I think all four of me got rejected."

Here is a list of a few potentially useful Internet sites. Remember that the Internet
is a place to start your college search, not end it. You should do most of the
admissions process the old fashioned way: talk to admissions officers in person,
visit the college, and apply with the paper application.

I did not list every web site I could think of—I only listed the sites that are
popular or useful. While most of these sites are established, please keep in mind
that web sites occasionally disappear without warning.

General Resources for college admissions, teens and parents
College Board (www.collegeboard.com) From the fine people who bring you
the SAT, SAT II, AP tests, and assorted other standardized atrocities, this web site
allows you check on test dates and locations, find out financial aid information,
general information about colleges, release and report test scores, and register for
tests (with a credit card). Most of the good things on this site require payment, so
bring a credit card.

CollegeValues (www.collegevalues.org) An interesting site dedicated to values
and character on college campuses. Provides information and links to values-
related information for various colleges. Highly recommended.

CollegeNet (www.collegenet.com) Apply to college and find money online.
This site is slow and poorly designed.

College Quest (www.collegequest.com) This site is published by Peterson's
(the same people who publish those college phone directories). This site has a lot
of everything—college research, facts and figures. Keep in mind that Peterson's
takes money from colleges in order to publish reviews, so this isn't an objective
source of information.

CollegeView (www.collegeview.com) Similar to College Quest (above). I'm not really sure why anyone would be interested in using this site.

Kaplan (www.kaplan.com) They've got test prep, CPA courses, and for-profit law schools. In the near future, you will be able to order pizzas from this web site. (Just kidding.) Kaplan seems to change their web site significantly every six months, so I think they know it's not very good. Nothing to recommend this site.

Morganroth Forbes (www.mind2mind.org) Low-frills site offers premium tutoring services, test prep and college admissions seminars, and the CASIS (a survey which helps students through the college and career process).

Nerve (www.nerve.com) If you think I was inventing that story about Princeton, it's here that you can find Princeton's notorious Prof. Peter Singer waxing eloquent on the wonders of sex with animals.

Parent Soup (www.parentsoup.com) An iVillage site for parents who think something is wrong with their kids. This site will give you pseudo-psychological labels for all your fears. Main topic categories include "Potty, Puberty, Birth control, Rivals." (I am not making this up.)

Review (www.review.com) This site is operated by the Princeton Review (no connection to Princeton University). This site tends to be slow and require cookies at all phases. If you wish to purchase something from Princeton Review, visit a bookstore or call 800-2REVIEW.

Spank (www.spankmag.com) E-mag for teens (motto: "5 years of kicking ass"). Amusing, somewhat insightful—not too useful, but at least you won't fall asleep. Contains such thrilling articles as "Prostitution at 16" and "Sex, Drugs and Knives." Guidance counselors sometime recommend this site to prove they are hip.

US News (www.usnews.com) This site is probably the most comprehensive. College facts and figures, innumerable articles and, of course, that facetious little college ranking list they put out. Some of the articles are good. It was recommended until it started charging for college searches—go to Review.com for free college searches.

Learning Disabilities

LD Online (www.ldonline.com) "The interactive guide to learning disabilities for parents, teachers, and children." That says it all. Includes free newsletter, artwork by LD teens, and information about taking the ACT and SAT.

Homework

Grade Saver (www.gradesaver.com) Free ClassicNotes on all major books! Why go to the bookstore and spend $7 on book notes when you can get them free at grade-saver? (Not only free, but searchable!) They will also edit your essays.

Sparknotes (www.sparknotes.com) Only teens living in caves in Tora Bora don't know about this site—TONS of useful stuff. Sparknotes is primarily known for its FREE notes on many subjects…everything but the kitchen sink. (If you search for "kitchen sink," you will get Chapter XIX of *Uncle Tom's Cabin.*) Very highly recommended.

Apply to College

I don't recommend using any of these resources, but they do allow you to work on a college's application before receiving it in the mail. These resources are also helpful for the "You in 12th Grade" exercise in this book.

My CollegeLink (www.collegelink.com) Scholarships, applications, articles by college students.

Common Application (www.commonapp.org) If you've read this book, then you know all about the common application.

Financial Aid

Financial aid—the process, the deadlines, the amounts available, the requirements—is constantly changing. Be sure that your information is the most recent available. If you get forms from your counselor, make sure that they are the forms for this year (not last year). If you buy a financial aid book, make sure it was published this year. If you use a web site, make sure it is updated monthly. Here are two good web sites.

FinAid (www.finaid.org) This site will tell you everything you need to know about financial aid. Includes information on loans, scholarships, grants, applications, ROTC, and also has useful calculators. 100% free. Very highly recommended.

Fastweb (www.fastweb.com) Free scholarship search site. Claims to have over $1 billion in scholarships.

Chapter 38

The Best, The Worst & The Rest

"I just need a list, you know, a top ten or something. It doesn't have to be funny. It's just got to tell me where to apply. I wouldn't know what to do I had to make up my own mind."

I do not particularly care for college lists or rankings. They tend to be reductive and counterproductive. Despite that, I understand that you may want a place to start, a few colleges to think about, something to hold on to. With that limited goal in mind, here are a few lists—a few objective and a few subjective—to help you sort things out.

The Best. My years of experience and research lead me to believe that the following colleges are the "best," meaning that they offer a better education than most other colleges. These colleges (mostly) promote a "real" education with actual professors who facilitate a dialogue with our culture and history. Notice how these colleges vary in selectivity; you do not need to attend a top college to get a great education. The best are: Yale, Amherst, Williams, Washington & Lee, Georgetown, University of Chicago, Boston University, St. John's College (MD), College of William and Mary, New College (FL), Pomona. Conspicuously absent: Columbia. In the first edition of this book, Columbia was at the top of this list. But over past two years, some of Columbia's professors have become increasing and aggressively anti-Semitic (e.g. Professors Said and De Genova, just to name two). The administration has done little to address this disturbing trend—in fact, many of Columbia's bigots get promotions after they say or write something atrocious. Given that the university seems to care little for this assault on decency, I cannot recommend Columbia.

Most Overrated. Everyone hears about them; everyone talks about them; everyone thinks they're great. But a little objective investigating reveals that a few well-known colleges don't exactly live up to their reputations. In all these cases, these schools offer less than their peers. If you can get into Stanford, then you can get into Yale, Chicago, or Georgetown, all of which tend to offer a better education. I can't imagine anything about Harvard that isn't overrated: their undergraduate classes are not very good, the students are obsessive, and Cambridge isn't as safe or student-friendly as you might think. The most overrated colleges are: Harvard, Princeton, Cornell, Penn, U. Michigan, Stanford, Duke, Emory.

Most Underrated. There are a few colleges that you don't hear much about, but they quietly do a great job. The kids are satisfied; the professors are happy; the campus feels great, and you leave more educated that you were when you arrived. You should consider these colleges—they aren't as hard to get into as they should be! The most underrated colleges are: Washington & Lee, College of William and Mary, New College (FL), Northwestern, St. John's (MD), Haverford, University of Chicago, USMA (West Point), and Vanderbilt.

Up-and-coming. If you traveled back to colonial times, you would find that no one thought much of Penn (serious students attended Harvard or Yale). In the 1950s, New York University was not a very good college; it more resembled a community college rather than a four-year college. Today, NYU is nearing the top-college level (less than 30% of applicants admitted). The moral of the story: many top colleges were once not incredibly competitive. Here are four colleges that may be tomorrow's top colleges.

Drexel (PA). A business college, Drexel's acceptance rate has fallen from about 80% to less than 60% in the past few years; a ton of money has been spent wiring the campus; a medical school was recently acquired; the endowment has boomed. Drexel may soon be competing with Boston University and NYU for students. Current average admitted student: 3.3 GPA and 1220 SAT.

Elon (SC). Similar to Drexel, Elon's acceptance rate has dropped while the school works harder to attract top students. The student body has grown and tons of money has been spent improving the college. It seems that each year a new $10+million building is finished. Recently, a fabulous new science building and a new stadium have been completed. Elon may soon compete with Wake Forest and Davidson as the South's premier medium-sized liberal arts college. Current average admitted student: 3.5 GPA and 1130 on the SAT.

New College (FL). The small college on Sarasota Bay that has no grades and no required courses just took a big step: it ended its affiliation with the University of South Florida and became Florida's 11th public college. New College has long been ranked one of *Money* magazine's "best buys" in the country (and held the #1 position for several years) and often attracts the best students from Florida. What makes it so attractive (aside from its waterfront location)? It combines many of the best student in Florida and the most dedicated teachers in the country with very small classes (sometimes 3-8 students!). And an Oxford-style tutorial system allows for maximum flexibility and personal attention. Because the college is committed to remaining small, as the number of applications increases, the acceptance rate will plummet. Current average admitted student: 3.9 GPA and 1340 on the SAT.

Colorado College. Often considered the Unknown Amherst of the West, Colorado is a small liberal arts college that uses a unique "one course at a time" system. Few outside of the west know about Colorado College, but word is starting to get out. Expect the acceptance rate to drop each year as more people learn that you can get an Amherst education at a Boston College acceptance rate. Current average admitted student: 3.7 GPA and 1270 on the SAT.

Hi-frat content. Each of these colleges has a hi-frat content: usually over 50% of the men on campus belong to fraternities. Avoid these colleges if you don't love frats. The hi-frat colleges are: Washington & Lee, Dartmouth, M.I.T., University of the South, Davidson, Randolph-Macon, Rhodes, DePauw, Dickinson, Wabash, Centre.

Hi-Sorority Content. Same as above. Hi-sorority colleges are: Washington & Lee, Wake Forest, Vanderbilt, University of Richmond, DePauw, California State-Fresno, Rhodes, Hillsdale, Randolph-Macon, Centre.

Campus Community. Here are colleges that boast a strong campus community as measured by the number of students who live on campus. (Usually, a weak community is signaled by a mass student exodus in the junior year.) The college at which 95% or more of all undergraduates live on campus are: Harvard, Amherst, United States Air Force Academy, United States Military Academy (West Point), United States Naval Academy (Annapolis), Haverford, Wheaton, Williams, Princeton, Connecticut College, Kenyon, Thomas More College, Massachusetts Institute of Technology, Trinity (CT), Hamilton, Colby, Virginia Military Institute, The Citadel, St. Lawrence University, Vassar.

Big Debt. Here are the colleges that will stick you with a big bill. At these colleges, 50% or more of all students graduate with $20,000+in debt. If you're interested in these colleges, be sure you're ready to get a job when you graduate. The

Big Debt colleges are: Brown, Penn, New School (NY), Pepperdine, M.I.T., Wesleyan, Middlebury (VT), Oglethorpe (GA), Pitzer (CA), Bennington (VT), Virginia Commonwealth, U. Vermont, Tulane, Case Western, U. Rochester, Worchester Polytech, Marquette, U. North Dakota, U. Denver, Vanderbilt, Dickinson.

Small Debt. If you're looking for a small, private liberal arts college that won't saddle you with $25,000 in debt upon graduation, then consider these—typically about 50% of graduating students have around $12,000 in debt and the other 50% have no debt. The Small Debt colleges are: Hampden-Sydney (VA), DePauw (IN), Furman (SC), Grinnell (IA), Amherst (MA), Colgate (NY), Drew (NJ), Centre (KY), Mount Holyoke (MA), Virginia Military Institute.

Great Deals. If you live in a state with a good public college, you will be able to get a great education for about $5,000 per year in tuition. You should always apply to the state school and to whatever private schools in which you're interested, then wait until the spring and compare financial aid packages. You may decide that you want to graduate without $25,000 in debt. States with good public college are: Virginia (U. Virginia, William and Mary, Mary Washington, James Madison), North Carolina (Chapel Hill), Florida (New College, U. Florida), Texas (UT Austin), California (UCLA, Berkeley), Wisconsin (Madison), Michigan (U. Michigan), Pennsylvania (Penn State), Connecticut (U, Conn—Storrs).

High Crime. Colleges don't like to talk about crime, and before federal regulations enacted a few years ago, they weren't required to talk about it. Now, through the miracle of federal law, colleges must report on-campus crime. Here are the colleges with the highest crime, as indicated by having the highest number of arrests for alcohol, drugs, weapons, murders and manslaughter: Michigan State, UC Berkeley, U. Wisconsin at Madison, Western Michigan, UNC Charlotte, UNC Greensboro, Indiana U-Purdue, Morgan State, U. Maryland-Baltimore.

High Salaries. Professors are like anyone else: they are attracted to high salaries. One can reasonably assume that the colleges who are willing to pay the most are able to get the best professors. So which colleges pay the most? The colleges who have the highest average salary for full-time undergraduate professors (all over $100,000 per year): Harvard, Stanford, Princeton, Yale, U. Chicago, Cal Tech, NYU, U. Penn, Columbia, M.I.T., Northwestern, UC Berkeley, Duke, Emory, Rutgers at Newark UCLA, Georgetown, Rice, Babson, Georgia Institute of Technology, Washington U., Boston College, U. Virginia, Notre Dame, U. Michigan at Ann Arbor.

The New Ivies. According to the *Wall Street Journal*, these colleges are the "New Ivies." These colleges were once thought of as safeties and are now first-choice schools. They are: Northwestern, Duke University, Georgetown University, Johns Hopkins University, New York University, University of Notre Dame, Vassar College, Swarthmore College, Williams College and Pomona College.

Glossary

"If the book has an index, then I don't read the book. Don't tell
Harvard that—I got in early but they might still take back my acceptance
if they discover that I didn't read a lot in high school.
Glossaries, though, are of no help."

ACT. Primary competitor to the SAT. Perhaps a "fairer" test but less coachable. Primarily taken by applicants in the mid-west.

Advanced Placement (AP). Standardized subject tests offered by the College Board; scored on a 1-5 scale (5 is best), and students may earn college credit for a high score. While not required by any college, top colleges generally expect to see at least 3-4 AP courses on your transcript. Many students apply to top colleges with 6-10 AP courses on their transcripts.

Academic Index (AI). Specifically, a formula used by the Ivies to index rank/grades and test scores, primarily used as a standard in the recruitment of athletes. Generally, any formula used to quickly compare applicants' academic numbers.

All-American. A high school athlete who is one of the best in the country and is usually recruited.

All-county/all-state. A high school athlete who is one of the best in the county or state.

Alma mater. What you call your college after you graduate. Latin for "soul mother." (Your country is your father, and your college is your mother.)

AP Scholar. A student who scores a 3 or higher on 3 or more AP exams.

College Board. Also known at the CEEB, they own the SAT and myriad other standardized afflictions (SAT II, AP). They pretend to care about students but are, in fact, wildly profitable. After bashing test-prep for decades, they recently started a for-profit test-prep division. They can be found at www.collegeboard.com. People are often confused with the difference between "College Board" and "ETS." ETS is the company that actually produces the SAT, whereas College Board owns the test and simply pays ETS to make it. Still confused? You'll be fine if you just assume these two companies are the same.

CSS/Fin Aid PROFILE. Financial aid form/report produced and processed by the College Board. Most top colleges and many others require this form from those who are seeking financial aid.

Common Application. Once intended for underprivileged applicants, now used by everyone, this form is a standardized application accepted by over 200 colleges. You can obtain a copy online or in your counselor's office. See the section on the common application.

Consortium. A group of colleges that combines their resources (often, expensive physical resources). Often, smaller colleges will agree to share libraries or science labs. In some cases, students can take classes at other colleges (called "cross registration"). Consortiums are a great way to get all the resources of a large college while getting the personal attention of a small college. For example, Penn, Swarthmore, Haverford, and Bryn Mawr are members of the Quaker Consortium, which permits cross-registration at all four colleges.

Commuter college. Any college at which less than half of the students live on campus. If over 50% of the students do not live on campus, then the college will have a "commuter" atmosphere (large parking lots, little on-campus camaraderie, poorly attended campus events). Commuter colleges tend to be large, mediocre public universities.

Deciles. A division of tenths used to rank students; the top decile is the top 10%, and the second decile is a student who ranks in the second 10% of his class (better than 80% of the class but lower than the top 10%).

Deferral. An early decision or early action student about whom an admission decision will be made during the regular decision period. If you're deferred in December, the college will typically notify you in April/May of a decision.

Demonstrated need. Take the total annual cost of attending college and subtract the "Expected Family Contribution" (or ERC) and you will have your demonstrated need, which is the amount you will need to attend college. (If college will cost $40,000 per year and you can pay $15,000 per year, then your demonstrated need is $25,000 per year.)

Early action. Sometimes called "early notification," a process by which you can apply and be notified early of a college's decision, which is non-binding. In the fall of 2003, Yale joins Harvard and Brown as the only early action Ivies. Some colleges offer both early action and early decision.

Early decision. A process by which you can apply and be notified early of a college's decision, which is binding. You must also withdraw all of your other applications. All Ivies offer early decision except Yale, Harvard and Brown.

ETS. Educational Testing Service is a huge testing company that makes about 500 tests including the SAT. About as friendly as the KGB. No 800 (toll-free) number, charges for everything, and will assume you've cheated if your SAT scores improve by over 300 points.

Federal methodology (FM). A formula of calculating your EFC using the FAFSA. (Many colleges do not use this methodology.)

Financial aid package. The combination of loans, grants, scholarships, and work-study that a college offers you to meet you demonstrated need.

FAFSA. The Free Application for Federal Student Aid is the most common financial aid form, produced by the federal government. As its name suggests, it is free.

GPA. Your Grade Point Average—basically, the average of all your grades in high schools. Formulae vary widely, so check with your school to see what your GPA is and how it's reported to colleges. Note that top colleges typically only consider your academic GPA, which means you should omit all non-academic courses when calculating your GPA.

Institutional methodology. The IM is a college's own financial aid formula, which typically uses information from the FAFSA, CSS, or the college's own financial aid forms. Some top colleges use an IM instead of a FM because an IM can be more generous (which means the college can be more aggressive).

International student. In most cases, you're an international student if you're not a U.S. citizen and don't live in the U.S. Most international applications are not considered on a need-blind basis because they are ineligible for federal financial aid. However, many colleges have endowments specifically to attract international students (such as Wesleyan's endowment for Irish students), so you may still be able to get significant financial aid.

IB. The International Baccalaureate program consists of college-level exams similar to AP tests and a diploma offered by more than 300 U.S. high schools and many foreign high schools. The tests are scored on a 1-7 scale (7 is best).

Legatee. Typically, the child of a graduate of the college. Each college's definition of who is a legatee may vary, so check with the school.

Magnet school. A selective, focused public school usually intended to be "college preparatory." Some magnet schools are highly regarded, while others are mediocre. Students often make the mistake of thinking that they can get Bs at a magnet school and still be admitted to a top college.

Minority. For admissions purposes, a minority is someone who is black, Hispanic, or indigenous. For reporting purposes, colleges typically include those of Asian heritage and sometimes international students (a few colleges actually count a black international student as two minority students).

National Merit. A marketing program primarily based on PSAT scores. About 7,000 students each year will receive, on average, a few thousand dollars for college. Most top colleges do not give merit money to National Merit scholars. At top colleges, commended or semifinalist merits scholars are average and most top colleges will only be interested if you are a merit scholar.

Need-blind admissions. Most early and regular applicants at top colleges are admitted "need-blind," which means colleges don't consider how much aid an applicant might need. As noted, many colleges actually give preference to poorer, disadvantaged students. Often, "need-blind" ends when it comes to admitting students late (April/May/June) because at that point, colleges have little aid remaining to award. Lesser competitive colleges often consider whether an applicant can pay; some colleges simply do not have the financial resources to admit all students "need-blind." Ironically, though all top colleges review early action/decision applicants need-blind, these early applicants are usually the wealthiest and therefore the least likely to need financial aid.

PG year. Post-graduate year attended after graduating high school; usually completed at a prep school in order to compete in sports or improve grades.

PSAT. "The Pre-SAT" serves no discernable useful purpose, other than to market the SAT.

Preferential aid package. A process by which colleges award better financial aid packages to more desirable applicants. Most "mid-level" colleges do this in order to attract top applicants.

Quartile/quintile. A division of fourths or fifths used to rank students; the top quartile is the top 25%, and the second quintile is a student who ranks in the second 20% of his class (better than 60% of the class but lower than the top 20%).

Rank. Your position in your graduating class. Most ranks are expressed as a fraction; for example, your rank may be 5/400, which would mean you graduated 5th in a class of 400.

Recentering. A College Board policy enacted in 1995 by which all SAT scores magically improved by about 100 points. The mean SAT score had dropped to about 900, and College Board, under scrutiny regarding the validity of the test, increased the mean score to about 1000. Colleges followed suit and increased their average SAT by about 100 points. So a 1350 scored in 1997 is equivalent to about a 1250 scored in 1993.

Residential college. Has two meanings: (1) a college at which more that 50% of the students live on campus, usually a college at which more than 75% of the students live on campus; (2) a residential organization within a larger college, often of 200-600 students. Yale is the father of the "residential college" system, whereby students are assigned to a smaller college within Yale (such as Berkeley) and typically live in that college during their fours years at Yale. Helps make the college experience more personal and diminishes the need for fraternities.

Rolling admissions. A process by which colleges evaluate applications as they arrive and admit students until the freshmen class is full. Usually, a "rolling admissions" college will have a decision for you within 4-6 weeks of receiving your completed application. If a college is rolling admissions, you should apply as soon as possible (usually in September of your senior year).

SAT I and II. The SAT I is the old SAT, and the SAT IIs are the old Achievement Tests (or CBATs). Most colleges require the SAT I, and most top colleges require three SAT IIs.

Score choice. Your ability to withhold SAT II scores from colleges is called "score choice." You may choose to have SAT II scores of tests taken on or before June 2002 go unreported. This is okay to do while you are a junior but not recommended if you take SAT IIs as a senior because using score choice slows down the process. If you choose score choice, your scores are not automatically reported to any college, and you must go through another process of "releasing" your scores before they can be reported. As with everything with ETS, score choice costs extra. Score Choice is not an option for tests taken after June 2002.

Squeeze play. A situation in which an offer of admission has been made unusually early (i.e. early February), and the applicant uses the offer of admission from one school to force other schools to make an early decision. Early offers of admission, often accompanied by generous financial aid awards, are usually only given to recruited applicants.

Student Aid Report (SAR). The report you receive after submitting the FAFSA that lists your EFC. Colleges use this report to determine how much aid you need.

Unweighted/weighted. Unweighted means that every class is graded on the same scale, and these grades are reported as such. No extra points are given for honors or AP classes. A weighted GPA is one in which the school awards extra points to grades earned in difficult classes (honors, enriched, AP). In many cases, schools award an extra .5 for an honors class and an extra 1 to an AP class (so a 3.7 in an AP class may be recorded on the transcript as a 4.7). Good students who take 3+weighted AP classes often have GPAs above 4.0.

Valedictorian/salutatorian. In theory, these are the first and second ranked students in a graduating class. Some high schools finagle the system and graduate twenty "valedictorians" so whether or not being a valedictorian is estimable depends on the school.

View book. A college's sales brochure. Thick. Glossy. Chock full of seemingly hip "students" who look as if they stepped out of a GAP advertisement. Every view book has essentially the same message: you too can be hip, well dressed, having fun, and not living with your parents if you attend this college.

Wait list. A list of applicants who were not admitted in the regular decision cycle but who may be admitted (typically in May/June) if the college's yield is low.

Westinghouse. A competition for high school students. The finalist award is given to a few students each year who have completed outstanding scientific research; this is perhaps the most notable award a high school student can earn and is highly regarded by all colleges.

Who's Who. A for-profit operation that publishes books listing the "top" students across the country. The listing is meaningless and not considered relevant by top colleges.

Work-study. A federally-financed program whereby financial aid students work at campus jobs; the wages are calculated as part of your financial aid. Typical work-study jobs include working at the library, answering the phone in the student center, or assisting with campus events. Work-study jobs are low-paying.

Yield. The percent of admitted applicants at a college who decide to enroll. For example, if a college's yield is 50%, then the college must admit 4000 applicants in order to have 2000 enroll. Most applicants on the wait list are used to make up the difference if the yield is low.

**If you enjoyed *College Admissions Trade Secrets,*
check out this iUniverse title:**

David Currier with Jay Frost
Be Brief. Be Bright. Be Gone.

A comprehensive, fast-paced guide that will help jump-start your career in pharmaceutical sales.

"Be brief, be bright, be gone" is the philosophy that helped launch author David Currier to a successful career as a pharmaceutical sales representative and sales trainer.

Simply stated, this philosophy suggests that aspiring pharmaceutical sales representatives should:

- Be brief-Keep your sales presentations short and to the point.
- Be bright-Understand your product and its clinical context.
- Be gone-Respect your customer's time.

"I wish I had read this book when I got started. It would have shortened my learning curve considerably and will do just that for anyone starting out today. This is easily the best book I have seen on the subject."
- Ellen F. Simes, Springfield, Massachusetts
Pharmaceutical sales trainer, former pharmaceutical sales representative and registered pharmacist

**Available through your local bookstore
or at www.iuniverse.com.**

0-595-19897-X

Printed in the United States
1288300004B/88-90